The Girls and Boys of Belchertown

The Girls and Boys of Belchertown

*A Social History of the Belchertown State School
for the Feeble-Minded*

Robert Hornick

University of Massachusetts Press
Amherst and Boston

Copyright © 2012 by Robert Hornick
All rights reserved
Printed in the United States of America

LC 2012016941
ISBN 978-1-55849-944-7 (paper); 943-0 (library cloth)

Designed by Sally Nichols
Set in Quadraat OT
Printed and bound by Thomson-Shore, Inc.

Library of Congress Cataloging-in-Publication Data

Hornick, Robert N.
The girls and boys of Belchertown : a social history of the Belchertown State School
for the feeble-minded / Robert Hornick.
    pages cm
Includes bibliographical references and index.
ISBN 978-1-55849-944-7 (pbk. : alk. paper) — ISBN 978-1-55849-943-0 (library cloth :
alk. paper) 1. Belchertown State School—History—20th century. 2. Children with mental
disabilities—Education—Massachusetts—History—20th century. 3. People with mental
disabilities—Institutional care—Massachusetts—History—20th century. I. Title.
LC4633.B45H67 2012
371.9209744—dc23
2012016941

British Library Cataloguing in Publication data are available.

In memory of my parents,

Newton Hornick (1913–1983) and Julia Rigan Hornick (1915–1982)

Contents

Preface ix

A Note on Terminology xiii

1. Beginnings 1

2. "Idiots for Life"—The Language of State Care 10

3. The Officer and the Dentist 23

4. Working at the State School 48

5. Family and Friends 69

6. The Tragedy of Belchertown 84

7. Endings 104

8. Ghosts and Graveyards 128

Notes 145

Index 187

Illustrations follow page 68

A complete bibliography is available online at

http://scholarworks.umass.edu/umpress/

Preface

There were no signposts, only memories. It was a Saturday or Sunday afternoon in late spring. I was attending an Amherst College reunion with my wife and young son. We had a couple of free hours. On a whim, I decided we would try to find what was left of Belchertown State School, where I had worked briefly as a volunteer during my sophomore or junior year. The three of us climbed into our blue Volvo and headed out Route 9, Belchertown Road, through wooded countryside, past what had been a small graveyard where a friend and I once rubbed wax paper impressions of an old marker, past the little roadhouse where as seniors with access to a roommate's car we sometimes escaped for dinner. After twenty minutes or so of driving we arrived at the intersection with Route 202. I knew to turn right onto North Main Street and drive into Belchertown proper, past the town's long, lovely common, and then right again at the far end, down the hill. We must have gotten close—I could sense the proximity—but we never found the school, and I was too stubborn to ask directions. It would be another decade (by then I had begun to research this book) before I found the abandoned site, its foreboding buildings boarded shut and overgrown with weeds.

My time at the state school was, as I have said, brief—consisting of part of an afternoon every week or other week for a couple of semesters, taking boys from one of the cottages to run outside, play ball, and walk in the woods. The setting was idyllic; on fall days, the crisp air and colored leaves stirred the soul as only autumn in New England can. We would park in a lot near the administration building and walk to the cottage. I remember noise—lots of it—as we opened the door and waited in the front hall for the boys to be gathered. We helped them put on coats, and then they rushed outdoors to the ball fields. The group was diverse in its abilities—though,

I now realize, all were what they then called "higher functioning types." Several were physically deformed. Most craved attention; some wanted to hold hands. Memories of one boy, whose name I have forgotten, haunt me. He liked to walk in the woods behind the state school fields, up the hill to a spot overlooking a small lake. There we would stop and talk—he, with much feeling, about the beautiful landscape around us. I wondered why this sensitive and articulate young man was at Belchertown. Little did I know and, sadly, I lacked sufficient curiosity to pursue it. What became of my young friend? I do not know.

Such memories, long dormant but lately roused, led me to write this book.

There are many to thank for their help with this book, several of whom I would like to mention by name. First and foremost, I am indebted to Doris Dickinson, longtime resident of Belchertown, author of several engaging local histories, and for many years archivist of the Belchertown Historical Association. When I began this project I did not know Doris and did not know that she herself had been collecting material on the state school for some time. Doris befriended me early in the project, generously made available to me all of her research both old and new, introduced me to others (such as former state school employees) with their own stories to tell, and always encouraged me to keep going. Thank you, Doris. If a book such as this can be said to have a muse, you were it.

I also thank Owen Maloney, director of the Clapp Memorial Library in Belchertown at the time I was doing my research, who put the full resources of the library at my disposal—including his cozy second-floor office. Owen and his staff extended every courtesy to me on my frequent visits. You will not find a more courteous, friendly, helpful group of people in any library anywhere in the world. Thanks as well to the librarians, assistant librarians, and staff at Amherst College, Belchertown Historical Association, Boston Public Library, Forbes Library in Northampton, Jones Library in Amherst, Massachusetts State Library in Boston, Mount Holyoke College, Springfield Public Library, and the University of Massachusetts Amherst, who allowed me to use their facilities and responded promptly and courteously to my many questions and requests; Don LaBrecque of the Massachusetts Department of Developmental Resources (formerly the Department of Mental Retardation), who shared his intimate knowledge of Belchertown State School and responded helpfully to several inquiries; Paul Friedland, my former law partner and friend, who read my manuscript and gave many helpful comments; James W. Trent Jr., who also read and commented on the manuscript and encouraged me to publish it; and the former employees and volunteers at Belchertown State School who shared experiences and anecdotes with me. At University of Massachusetts Press, Clark Dougan and the editorial staff helped make this a better book.

Thanks also to George B. ("Brownie") Leach, my Amherst classmate and friend, who recruited me to volunteer at Belchertown in the early 1960s.

Last but not least, I thank my family: my son, Will, who reviewed the manuscript, including the notes, and whose undergraduate thesis on American volunteer ambulance drivers in World War I was an inspirational example to me of what, in the words of his adviser, "historical work is meant to do (and so often falls short of) which is to recapture not just the letter but the spirit of an enterprise"; my brother, Joe, who read the manuscript and gave helpful comments; and my lovely wife, the opera singer Gabrielle, who always said I could do it.

A Note on Terminology

Throughout history, there has been a tendency to describe people by their disabilities. Some have decried this tendency because it masks the essential humanity of those so described, making it easier for the rest of us to ignore them and to dismiss them as less than fully human—or worse. But the tendency persists, and it is part of the fabric of our language. Particular terms may change, but the identification-by-disability does not. Individuals whom we today call "intellectually disabled" were, when Belchertown State School was founded, called "feeble-minded" and, later, "mentally retarded." The earlier terms are now rightly disfavored for having become pejorative, insulting, even abusive; the latest iteration not yet so.

This lexical thicket presents special problems for one trying to tell the history of an institution for intellectually disabled persons which closed before the currently accepted term—intellectual disability—gained favor. In 1922, when it was established, Belchertown State School was officially called a school for the feeble-minded. Throughout its history it was administered, variously, by the Insanity Board, the Department of Mental Diseases, and the Department of Mental Retardation.

Most people—parents, friends, administrators, employees, reporters, reformers, the disabled themselves—used these terms without irony or ill will when talking about the residents of Belchertown State School, because that is how people—good people and bad people—talked then. For the most part, I have chosen to stay in character with the times I write about, using the terminology that was in common usage then: feeble-minded, retarded, and the like. On the one hand, it seems to me anachronistic to do otherwise; it is part of trying to make that period come more fully to life. Filtering history through contemporary moral and linguistic conventions doesn't ameliorate past sins. On the other hand, I don't want to demean or insult the residents whose history I seek to narrate; they have suffered enough. I hope my choices will not offend them.

My title is a case in point. Most of those admitted to Belchertown State School were, at the time of their admissions, children, youths—mere boys and girls. Like other boys and girls on the outside, they eventually grew into men and women. Unlike men and women on the outside, they continued to be called children—boys and girls—and, for the most part, they were mistreated as such. My title acknowledges this grotesque fact, but it also introduces a dissonant note: by reversing genders, I mean to hint that something is not right: a school that isn't a school, boys and girls who aren't children. If I have told my story well, the reader should, in the end, want to celebrate with me the muted triumph of those souls buried in the state school graveyard—all former residents—who suffered unspeakable sorrows and humiliations, but the naming of whom (thanks to the efforts of Albert Warner) enshrined forever the memory of their *adult* humanity.

The Girls and Boys of Belchertown

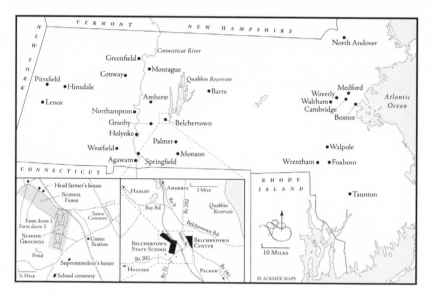

Massachusetts, showing the town of Belchertown and the Belchertown State School.

—BLACKMER MAPS.

CHAPTER 1
Beginnings

Word came on the wire too late in the day for that week's *Belchertown Sentinel* to report it; the edition of February 18, 1916, had already gone to press. But someone rang the school bell—and most of the town's two thousand residents guessed why. Dozens took to the streets in celebration. A procession formed to greet the hero of the hour, D. D. Hazen, back from Boston on the evening train. The happy crowd waved flaming torches and cheered. A makeshift band of bass drum and cymbals dinned. Whether Hazen was hoisted onto shoulders and carried through the streets is not known. We do know the celebrants wound their way to Roswell Allen's place, and Roswell gave a speech. Then they repaired to the Park View Hotel for refreshments.[1] The editors of the *Sentinel*, though they couldn't stop the press, did stamp on page 1, in bold caps, the gist of the day's good news:

JUST DECIDED!
THE HOME FOR THE FEEBLE MINDED
TO LOCATE IN
BELCHERTOWN

Nestled in the foothills of western Massachusetts, ten miles east of the Connecticut River, with commanding views of the Holyoke Range, Belchertown was best known in nineteenth-century New England for its manufacture of fine carriages.[2] Orders came from as far away as Persia and Australia. No less a personage than Queen Victoria was said to have owned a Belchertown buggy. By mid-century, at the peak of its fame, the town boasted eight factories with an annual production of 1,100 wagons, buggies, carriages, and sleighs worth $100,000. H. T. Filer alone employed fifty men making three hundred carriages and fifty sleighs per year worth $35,000.[3] Best known was T. & S. D. Cowles, whose shop stood near what would become the standpipe of the future state school's water system. To possess a vehicle of their make was, it was said, "the height of a young man's ambition."[4]

After the Civil War, when the carriage trade moved west and the local shops closed, enterprising descendants of Belchertown's merchant class invested in hotels. "The place is becoming justly famous as a summer resort," a local chronicler wrote in 1888, adding that "its quiet beauty, pure air and the beautiful drives in the vicinity have attracted many, of refined tastes, who prefer to spend the summer here rather than amid the bustle and rush of the so-called fashionable resorts." The Highland, at the south end of the common, boasted 250 feet of piazzas, balconies 9 to 20 feet wide, and a rooftop observatory with unobstructed, breathtaking views of meadow and mountain. Inside there were gas lights, steam heat, electric bells, and hot and cold running water, as well as "bathrooms and closets . . . liberally provided on the different floors." Mr. Butler, the proprietor, promised his guests "the purest water and the best food."[5]

Alas, the bustle and rush of the so-called fashionable resorts proved the more alluring. One by one, Belchertown's hotels failed or burned down. They were not rebuilt. A cigar factory, erected in 1886, provided some employment. A number of dairy farms prospered into the second decade of the twentieth century, and Belchertown butter was much coveted throughout Massachusetts. Even so, the town's economy was in steep decline by the start of the First World War.

It was the genius of Hazen and his colleagues on the Board of Trade to see opportunity in the state's appropriation of $50,000 to buy land for a new "school for the feeble-minded in the western part of the commonwealth." The board, of which Hazen was president, had been set up in 1914 to develop the town's "latent possibilities."[6] Besides Hazen, the officers were Roswell Allen, a local real estate broker and scion of one of Belchertown's oldest families, as first vice president; E. A. Fuller, purveyor of general merchandise, as second vice president; Wilbur Nichols, a former math professor at Yale, as secretary; and Milton Baggs, president of the Belchertown Water Commission, as treasurer.

Daniel Dwight Hazen was a perfect choice for president of the Board of Trade. The enterprising son of Daniel L. and Clara (née Dwight) Hazen, Dan opened his first business, a small grocery store "fitted out in a room of his father's home," in 1893 at age nineteen.[7] He quickly outgrew the space and moved to the Snow block in the center of town—only to be wiped out in a huge fire a few days later, without insurance. Hazen Sr. then bought the Longley building, where Dan developed, initially under his father's name and later his own, Belchertown's first department store. It comprised two floors and 10,000 square feet of floor space. You could buy anything, "from a rat trap to life insurance." The younger Hazen also parlayed a passing acquaintance with Henry Ford into Belchertown's first auto dealership.[8]

Hazen and his colleagues certainly believed in the "latent possibilities" of Belchertown, and they had reason. It was only 88 miles from Boston and 75 miles from the New London tidewater. It was served by two railroads and fourteen passenger trains daily. A new auto road connected it to the nearby cities of Holyoke and Springfield. There were free factory sites, free schools, a public library, churches, electric light and power, and no town debt. One hotel—the Park View, with thirty rooms—was still in business. "With electric lights in the streets, macadam roads to Springfield . . . and the water system completed," a local newspaper reported in 1914, the town would be "ready to take its place among the most prosperous in the State."[9] Somehow, though, opportunities kept slipping away. Apparently there was a local legend that the town had once turned down the possibility of locating Amherst College there, and it was feared that the state school prospect would suffer the same fate. So important was it, therefore, to procure a good result that Hazen himself was appointed chairman of the committee set up to pursue the opportunity.

The site that Hazen and the board assembled for their bid started a half-mile west of the town common. It was composed of five farms, measuring in aggregate—so it was claimed—approximately eight hundred acres.[10] The owner of one of the farms, David Jepson, whose acreage adjacent to the rail line was needed for the school's power station and rail spur (to bring in supplies and coal), was reluctant to sell and had to be arm-twisted. Weeks after the appropriation was made and the other four parcels were purchased, the town elders confronted him in Colby's Barbershop; they laid out on a table, in gold coins, the state's offered price and threatened Jepson with eminent domain if he didn't sell. He sold.[11]

The Central Vermont Railroad agreed to run a spur line to the school site free of charge. The area was well drained and there was, it was thought, an abundant supply of water within the grounds. There were, finally, old houses and barns on the land that could be converted into usable buildings at modest cost. It was a credible package that compared favorably with those of Belchertown's principal competition—the small town of Conway and the cities of Westfield and Holyoke.[12]

In the end, though, it was probably the remoteness of Belchertown more than railroad spurs, barns, and water supply that was attractive to the State Board of Insanity. Early twentieth-century Americans feared the feeble-minded (as those with intellectual disabilities were then called). Enlightened opinion, spurred by the new "science" of eugenics, held that the condition was inheritable and that the racial stock could be easily and fatally compromised if vigilance was not practiced. It was imperative to track down the defectives at an early age, before their reproductive capacities matured, and remove them to remote locations where they could be confined apart from the general population and cared for until God saw fit to call them to the Last Judgment. Henry Goddard, a researcher at the New Jersey Training School and author of a best-selling book about the hapless degeneracy of six generations of the Kallikak family, spoke for the majority of those concerned for the public welfare when he wrote in 1915, "We need to hunt them out in every possible place and take care of them, and to see to it that they do not propagate and make the problem worse, and that those who are alive today do not entail loss of life and property and moral contagion in the community by the things they do because they are weak-minded."[13]

One of the Springfield papers, explaining to its readership the anticipated benefits of the state school, noted, "There is a growing recognition of the hereditary nature of much mental defect and the necessity of segregating cases likely to transmit the defect."[14] Besides, it was the only humane thing to do. The feeble-minded could not care for themselves. To leave them alone was to condemn them to a life of poverty and prostitution. It was therefore in their own best interest as well as the best interest of society at large that they be gathered and kept in peaceful, bucolic settings, out of harm's way and under the watchful care of sympathetic guardians.

Of course, it was one thing to send the feeble-minded away, quite another to solicit their relocation to your hometown. You could say all you wanted to say about the projected benefits to the local economy: more visitors, money, jobs. The fact was that you would be settling a substantial retarded population within striking distance of your wives and children. Not everyone, therefore, supported the efforts of Hazen and the Board of

Trade—at least not right away. The editors of the *Sentinel* were sensitive to the dilemma:

> Probably not all favor the idea of such an institution being here. It could hardly be expected that they would. Many would prefer an institution of a different nature, yet if we are correctly informed, there was some opposition to having Amherst College located here.
>
> As the land in question is some distance from the center, it is doubtful if any serious inconvenience would be experienced by anyone. An institution of like nature is located in Palmer and those living there say that one would hardly know that a Home of this kind was located within its bounds.[15]

Linking Amherst College and a school for the feeble-minded (don't make the same mistake twice!) was perhaps a stretch. But the point was taken and the town rallied. When Hazen climbed down from his Boston train four months later with the state's decision to buy eight hundred acres in Belchertown safely in hand, there was no local opposition and much jubilation.

The Insanity Board's vote on February 17, 1916, to buy the Belchertown acreage was followed in June by a further legislative appropriation, not to exceed $150,000, for buildings and improvements, including two dormitories with a total of 155 beds, as well as service buildings and infrastructure work.[16] It turned out, though, that the tender was not yet secure. Water supply was a major concern of the state. One of the farms' pastures included a set of springs whose water was said to have been examined by an engineer and pronounced "perfectly pure and of unlimited supply."[17] The Department of Health, which investigated the competing sites, reported in favor of Belchertown largely because of the supposed abundance of its water.[18] It was only later, in the spring of 1917, that test wells were finally drilled at the site, with negative results. The subsoil was composed wholly of hardpan and rock—materials impervious to water. No water-bearing strata were penetrated.[19]

The uproar in Boston was considerable, threatening the project. Fortunately, over the summer, a consulting engineer (the well-regarded James Tighe of Holyoke) successfully drove several test wells east of the village in nearby Jabish Brook Valley. He found "a great deposit of water bearing sand and gravel having a depth of many feet." Any of the wells, if pumped to capacity, would yield 100,000 gallons per day "without a perceptible lowering of the water level." Moreover, the samples from the wells were all excellent: colorless, odorless, free from pollution, and "exceptionally soft." Four wells connected to a common header with a large-capacity pump could yield 500,000 gallons during any twenty-four-hour period— more than the school would need.[20] The Commission on Mental Diseases, which had replaced the Board of Insanity a few months before, was satisfied. The wells, though, were about one mile from the proposed buildings; it would be necessary to acquire the well site, run a straight-line pipe to the school, and build a storage reservoir that would also serve as a standpipe to maintain good water pressure. The additional cost—$50,000—had not been appropriated. The commission also noted that the existing appropriation did not include any money for a power station, which would be needed to heat and light the school. Finally, the commission was having second thoughts about the size of the site. They were now anticipating as many as 1,500 "inmates" for the school. The rule of thumb was that you should have one acre of ground per person, and therefore more land might be needed.[21]

The project was stalled. Frustrated, the town held a public meeting to decide what to do. The several farms whose land now comprised the site had long been known in the area for their rich soil, excellent pastures, and abundant crops. R. E. Fairchild, a local resident, once told a reporter that the biggest corn he'd ever seen anywhere—stalks eighteen feet tall—came from one of the farms.[22] The town voted to petition the state's governor to use the land temporarily to raise crops. One local paper reported that on two of the farms were barns "filled with barnyard manure ready to be used."[23]

The prospect of two cellars full of fresh manure there for the taking carried the day. The Commission on Mental Diseases asked the Wrentham State School near Boston to start a small farm colony at the new Belchertown site. In July 1917, two Wrentham employees, Mr. and Mrs. John Hawes, moved to Belchertown with eleven of the school's "boys" (likely grown men) in tow. They cleared the land, planted crops, and picked fruit, that summer shipping large crops of hay and apples to the parent institution.[24] The land proved productive and the soil well suited for institutional farming. Visitors to the colony the following summer reported that a large number of acres were under cultivation and that the crops were "doing nicely," adding, "From six to eight acres are planted to potatoes, and there are between sixteen and eighteen acres of beans. There are also about six acres of small truck, including beets, kohlrabi, carrots, turnips, cabbages, pumpkins and squash."[25]

Warden and Matron Hawes said that they hoped to develop a "cordial relationship . . . between themselves and the townspeople." The Board of Trade pitched the colony as a kind of experimental farm to showcase new techniques. "Local farmers would be welcome at all times at the institution," they said, "to inspect it and to get ideas."[26] The Belchertown State School was not yet a refuge for the feeble-minded and had not yet employed a single Belchertown resident. But at least productive use was being made of the land, and the first tentative collaboration between future school and town was being forged. Of the "boys" who accompanied the Haweses from Wrentham to Belchertown, we know nothing.

As the beet and kohlrabi seedlings pushed their way up through the fertile soil of the future Belchertown State School, a proposal to appropriate $50,000 more for the school's water supply finally reached the state legislature. The debate was intense. Representative Frederick E. Pierce of Greenfield called the project "a great fraud," complaining that the waterworks would now cost $65,000 altogether (the $15,000 appropriated in June 1916 plus the additional $50,000 being sought), "in spite of the claim that a chief reason for taking the land was a good water supply." Representative Harrison H. Atwood of Boston, noting that $200,000 had been appropriated already, railed against the project in general, which he said would cost $1.5 million to complete. Representative Fred P. Greenwood of Everett, seeking the high ground, stated that "the more important question is whether the state shall suffer the feeble-minded to propagate and increase their evils." The bill finally passed the House of Representatives in May 1918 by a substantial majority of 97–41.[27] The Senate approved a short while later.

The water appropriation now in hand and the prospect of substantial additional funding for bricks and mortar suddenly looking good, the Commission on Mental Diseases decided to engage contractors and begin development of the site, without waiting for more land. It hired the architectural firm of Kendall, Taylor & Co., which had designed the Wrentham State School in 1906 as well as several state hospitals for the psychopathic and insane, to do a layout design and prepare blueprints. When the state's Legislative Committee on Public Institutions visited Belchertown in January 1919 and showed Hazen the blueprints, he was delighted. "The dream is taking form," he declared.[28]

The design was for an extensive, totally self-sufficient campus-style network of integrated buildings and landscape. More than one visitor would later liken it to a New England college—a town within a town. Besides dormitories, classroom buildings, and staff housing, there would be a power plant, kitchens, a laundry, carpentry and print shops, a shoe repair shop, a hospital and dental clinic, and an auditorium, as well as gardens, playing fields, walkways, and trees. The onsite farm, with cattle, poultry, and over two hundred acres under cultivation, would produce most of the school's food. The school would even have, in addition to its own water system, its own sewage system, telephone system, and fire department. For invalids, each dormitory had a cement porch opening out of a hall, onto which beds could be moved to give the bedridden fresh air. Inclines ran from the porch to the ground to make access easier for wheelchairs.[29]

The Committee on Public Institutions approved plans for construction at the state school site, and the legislature appropriated an additional $350,000 to supplement the $150,000 appropriated in 1916 and the $50,000 appropriated in 1918.[30] Bids for the construction work were solicited in the fall of 1919, and the contract was awarded to M. J. O'Connor of Northampton. He and a crew of 125 men from nearly towns improved the roads, built the core campus, and dug 1,500 feet of concrete tunnels to connect the buildings.[31]

The Belchertown State School opened on November 15, 1922, under the direction of Dr. George E. McPherson, the school's first superintendent. A staff of eighty-seven employees—30 percent from Belchertown itself—and two physicians was hired to teach and care for the new residents and to maintain the facility.[32] In the first week, 75 boys transferred from the Wrentham State School.[33] More boys would arrive from Wrentham, as well as from the Massachusetts School for the Feeble-Minded in Waltham, the following week, bringing the total opening enrollment as of the end of November to 187. The first group of girls (some 250) came in January.[34] Of varying ages "from six up," the first boys reportedly arrived "with well-shined shoes on their feet, warm overcoats on their backs and an extra suit of clothes in their baggage." H. M. Watkins, senior assistant physician, pronounced them "contented and well fed." Some were heard singing in the day hall "a chorus of song."[35]

"Here then in our midst," the Sentinel rhapsodized,

> is an institution whose very existence is made possible by an advanced civilization. Here will be gathered through the years those who by their very circumstances ask for special opportunities and privileges. And here also will come those who have a

sympathetic understanding of the needs of the unfortunate and
will give their years in an effort to help them.

Because of these conditions there should be, and we feel that
there is, a growing dignity in the words, "Belchertown State School"
and a growing friendship between the supervisors of the institution and the townspeople.[36]

Friendship did grow between institution and village. For most of its history, until it closed in 1992, Belchertown State School would be the largest employer in town. The school's population, too, would grow steadily,
peaking at more than sixteen hundred residents in its busiest years. There
would be unremembered acts of kindness and love to ease the burden of
some and give hope to a few. Dignity, though, would elude the school's
grasp. The Great Depression, a world war, and indifference would ravage
its budgets. Inattention or fatigue would seize the day. Conditions would
deteriorate unspeakably, and the worst excesses of the nineteenth-century
almshouse would be repeated in the dress of an institution of learning.

The average age of the school's population would also creep upward—
to something over thirty years old—as fewer and fewer of those admitted
were allowed to leave. More than two hundred would die in residence and
be buried in a potter's field at the southeast corner of the property, their
graves numbered and nameless until 1998, when Albert Warner, himself
a long-time resident, would rescue their identities in a final, humble act
of grace. A carousel, hand-carved in Brooklyn, New York, at the time the
school was founded, would feature prominently in the last act.

CHAPTER 2

"Idiots for Life"—The Language of State Care

From the beginning, the state institution at Belchertown was called a "school." This was not mere euphemism. Although by 1922 quarantine had replaced education as the principal motivation for state care, the possibility of teaching the feeble-minded, which had inspired nineteenth-century reformers, was still a motivating factor.

State schooling for feeble-minded persons in the United States began in Massachusetts in 1848 with an appropriation to Samuel Gridley Howe of $2,500 per annum for three years "for the purpose of training and teaching ten idiotic children, to be selected . . . from those at public charge, or from the families of indigent persons in different parts of the Commonwealth."[1] Howe, director of the Perkins Institution in Boston, a semiprivate training facility for the blind, had for two years chaired a commission that was charged "to inquire into the condition of the idiots of the Commonwealth, to ascertain their number, and whether anything can be done on their behalf."[2] The appropriation for Howe was a response to the commission's findings and recommendations.

Howe and his fellow commissioners understood the term "idiots" to encompass three categories of persons: the absolute idiot, the imbecile, and the simpleton. The absolute idiot was a person who "has hearing, but seems not to hear; sight, but seems not to see; who never learns to talk; who cannot put on his own clothes, or feed himself with a spoon, or learn to do the simplest thing." The imbecile was one who, though incapable of caring for himself, could "do pretty well under the direction of others." The simpleton "thinks he is a man" but "hangs on the skirts of society, the victim of some, the butt of others, until at last he comes upon the public for support" and then "degenerates into idiocy as he advances in age."[3]

Based on a sample taken from sixty-three towns "in which very minute inquiry was made," Howe (for all intents and purposes, the commission was Howe) determined that there were "between twelve and fifteen hundred" idiots in Massachusetts.[4] Their condition was grim:

> The whole of them are at the charge of the community in one way or another, because they cannot help themselves. . . . They are not only neglected, but . . . through ignorance, they are so often badly treated and cruelly wronged, that, for want of proper means of training, some of them sink from mere weakness of mind, into entire idiocy; so that, though born with a spark of intellect which might be nurtured into a flame, it is gradually extinguished, and they go down darkling to the grave, like the beasts that perish.[5]

Howe urged that "measures be at once taken" to "rescue this unfortunate class from the dreadful degradation in which they now grovel." He was, however, curiously circumspect about the details of the degradation from which rescue was sought. More than once he asserted in his report that residents of the state's almshouses were, in general, "kindly" treated and that there was "little or no *intentional* cruelty" (my emphasis). He makes no mention of the "cages, closets, cellars, stalls, pens" in which Dorothea Dix famously reported finding insane and idiotic men and women "chained, naked, beaten with rods, and lashed into obedience."[6]

Certainly Howe was well informed about such details; he had read these very words to the state legislature five years earlier on Dorothea Dix's behalf.[7] But Howe's agenda in 1848 was not the same as Dix's. Whereas Dix crusaded to improve conditions in the almshouses and the quality of custodial care provided there, Howe sought to replace them. It was the premise of custodial care, not the quality, that Howe took aim against. His ultimate goal was not to make the feeble-minded more comfortable; it was to develop their minds and help them achieve greater self-sufficiency. The principal measure he recommended, foreshadowed in his earlier phrase "for want of proper means of training," was to establish state-funded schools for feeble-minded persons.

> The benefits to be derived from the establishment of a school for this class of persons, upon humane and scientific principles, would be very great. Not only would all idiots, who should be

> received into it, be improved in their bodily and mental condition, but all the others, in the State and the country, would be indirectly benefited. The school, if conducted by persons of skill and ability, would be a model for others. Valuable information would be disseminated through the country; it would be demonstrated that no idiot need be confined or restrained by force; that the young can be trained to industry, order, and self-respect; that they can be redeemed from odious and filthy habits, and that there is not one of any age, who may not be made more of a man, and less of a brute, by patience and kindness, directed by energy and skill.[8]

Even today, a century and a half after they were written, these words have a capacity to move and inspire. They are remarkable not only for their compassion but for the insight they display regarding the possibility of amelioration "by patience and kindness, directed by energy and skill." Certainly Howe had the authority of experience to back him. His successes training the blind had won him world renown; his advocacy on behalf of educational reform (with Charles Sumner and Horace Mann), the insane (with Dorothea Dix), and the emancipation of slaves (with his wife, Julia Ward) had gained him moral stature that few could match. He had also treated at his institute, "with considerable success," three blind children who were feeble-minded. "If so much could be done for idiots who were blind," he reasoned, then "still more could be done for idiots who were not blind."[9]

Still, the notion that the feeble-minded could be taught was a most radical idea; it presumed, contrary to the weight of religious and scientific evidence to that time, that idiots had intellect. Martin Luther warned that they not only lacked intelligence but were soulless and should be drowned.[10] The term "changeling," referring to a child possessed of the Devil instead of a soul, captures the idea well. True, Christian doctrine had evolved since the Reformation. The Puritan preachers of the Massachusetts Bay Colony may indeed have believed that idiocy was a marvelous manifestation of God's diversity and a God-given opportunity to practice mercy.[11] Other nineteenth-century reformers, Dorothea Dix foremost among them in Massachusetts, had argued in favor of moral, humane care. But education? *Schools?*

Howe insisted that idiots, even the lowest of them, manifested "sense and understanding." They possessed intelligence. Their intelligence differed from that of other men, but only "in *degree*, not in *kind*":

Take the case No. 349. . . . William —— has the form and name of a human being, but not much else. He is at the age of early manhood, when some have gained victories in fields of war or science; but William has not yet learned enough to go alone, to feed himself, or know his own name. An intelligent dog knows more than he. . . . He lies most of the day upon a mat on the floor, rolling his lack-lustre eyes, and tossing his limbs. . . .

Surely, it will be said, this man is an idiot; and yet he is not devoid of sense and understanding.

He knows no arbitrary language; words are to him of less import than to a horse; and yet he has a natural language that tells you he has consciousness, memory, hope, fear, and even judgment and discrimination, feeble though it be. This language, too, tells imperfectly the story of his experience; it tells what kind of treatment he has received; it tells of kindness and cruelty, of gentle and harsh tones, of curses and blows.

When he is first approached abruptly, he shows signs of fear, which you cannot mistake; he shrinks from your raised hand, and manifests signs of resistance and defense; but if you draw near to him gently, he does not shrink away; if you speak kindly to him, he smiles; if you caress him he is pleased; and if you continue your gentle attentions, you may make him yield obedience to your wishes, as far as he can understand them. He has a yet higher faculty, the sense of music; the poor creature loves sweet sounds, and, in his most uneasy moments, all his contortions of body and all his wild cries are soothed into calm, and hushed into silence, by any music.[12]

Howe's recent favorable experience teaching three blind children at Perkins who were feeble-minded must have reassured him in his conviction that the feeble-minded could be taught. But it was the work of European pioneers, especially the French physician Édouard Séguin, that provided shape and authority to his conviction.[13]

Séguin began teaching feeble-minded children in Paris in 1837, at the age of twenty-five. His success was recognized by Jean Étienne Esquirol, then France's leading authority on mental disease and one of the first scientists in the world to distinguish idiocy from insanity. Esquirol's endorsement was the more remarkable because he had long held the view that the feeble-minded were not teachable; his admission that Séguin had, apparently, done the impossible was therefore consequential. It led directly to Séguin's being invited to teach more feeble-minded children at the Hospice des Incurables (Salpétrière) and the Bicêtre in Paris and launched him—still a young man—into the forefront of his specialty. In 1844, a commission of the Academy of Sciences, upon investigating his work, declared that he had "solved the problem of idiot education."[14]

The methods that Séguin employed to teach the feeble-minded, which he called physiological education, were the subject of a treatise he published in 1846. *Traitement moral: hygiène et éducation des idiots et des autres infants arriérés* quickly became a classic in the field. It emphasized physical education and touch. The initial goal was to strengthen wasted muscles and develop coordination, so that the pupil was physically able to endure the rigors of training. But the exercises were carefully designed to be pleasurable as well as therapeutic. Séguin believed that learning proceeded from enjoyment and companionship, not repetition for its own sake. The second stage of training was to stimulate the senses: first touch, then sight, hearing, taste, and finally smell. For example, pupils were exposed to a great variety of tactile experiences: to handling objects of different textures, temperatures, sizes, and weights; to rhythm and music; to the sounds of falling objects and moving objects as well as the sounds of joy, pain, and fear; to different colors, visual forms, and sizes; to drawing; and much more. Finally, Séguin sought to awaken what he believed to be the dormant will of his feeble-minded pupils by establishing an authoritarian relationship between teacher and pupil in a congenial learning environment.[15]

In 1846–47, George Sumner, youngest brother of Howe's close friend Charles Sumner, visited Séguin's school at the Bicêtre and wrote enthusiastically to Howe about Séguin's results:

> During the past six months I have watched, with eager interest, the progress which many young idiots have made . . . under the direction of M. Seguin. . . . I have seen, with no less gratification than astonishment, nearly one hundred fellow-beings who, but a short time since, were shut out from all communion with mankind, who were objects of loathing and disgust, —many of whom rejected articles of clothing, others of whom, unable to stand erect, crouched themselves in corners and gave signs of life only by piteous howls, —others, in whom the faculty of speech had never been developed, —and many, whose voracious and indiscriminate gluttony satisfied itself with whatever they could lay

> hands upon, with the garbage thrown to swine, or with their own
> excrements; —these unfortunate beings—the rejected of human-
> ity, I have seen properly clad, standing erect, walking, speaking,
> eating in an orderly manner at a common table, working quietly as
> carpenters and farmers; gaining, by their own labor, the means of
> existence; storing their awakened intelligence by reading one to
> another: exercising towards their teachers and among themselves
> the generous feelings of man's nature, and singing in unison songs
> of thanksgiving.[16]

Howe challenged the state legislature: "We claim for idiots a place in
the human family. We maintain that they have the germs of the human
faculties and sentiments, which in most cases may be developed."[17] The
legislature was much moved and voted Howe his money. Howe used the
appropriation to establish an experimental school for the feeble-minded
at his institute in South Boston. The school was incorporated in 1850 as
the Massachusetts School for Idiotic and Feeble-Minded Youth. Séguin,
who by then had emigrated to America, taught there briefly.[18] The school
was judged a success, and the legislature's Joint Committee on Public
Charitable Institutions successfully recommended that it be made permanent. Funds for a permanent facility were appropriated in 1855, and the
school moved to a separate site in South Boston. It changed its name to
the Massachusetts School for the Feeble-Minded and relocated to a larger
campus in the suburban town of Waltham in 1890. Some years later it was
renamed the Walter E. Fernald State School, in honor of one of its long-
serving superintendents (about whom more later).[19]

At the time Howe established his experimental school, government
responsibility for care of the feeble-minded, insofar as it existed, resided
more at the municipal and county levels than at the state. This remained
so for a number of years. But as with the care of other populations deemed
to be deviant—the incarcerated, the deaf and blind (or otherwise physically disabled), the poor, the epileptics, the inebriates, and the insane
(with whom the feeble-minded were often grouped by custom and law)—
the state gradually assumed more responsibility and by the end of the
nineteenth century was largely responsible for the care of these citizens.
Howe's eloquence contributed to this shift.

The Massachusetts legislature had not asked Howe to investigate the etiology of idiocy, only its numbers and conditions. Howe nevertheless

produced a supplement to his report, detailing the causes of idiocy, "the knowledge of which," he proffered, "may tend to lessen the number of idiots in the next generation."[20] As Howe conceived it (in this, he was both a creature of his times and a visionary), idiocy was neither an accident nor inherent in the condition of man. It was a social disease, the product of certain kinds of immoral behavior—sometimes immoral behavior of the afflicted themselves, but most often the immoral behavior of their parents:

> The moral to be drawn from the existence of the individual idiot is this,—he or his parents, have so far violated the natural laws, so far marred the beautiful organism of the body, that it is an unfit instrument for the manifestation of the powers of the soul. The moral to be drawn [from the number of idiots] is, that a very large class of persons ignore the conditions upon which alone health and reason are given to men, and consequently they sin in various ways . . . and thus bring down the awful consequences of their own ignorance and sin upon the heads of their unoffending children.[21]

Chief among parental sins that "predisposed" persons to idiocy were "scrofulous temperament, and poor flabby organization," intemperance, intermarriage of relatives, attempts to procure abortion, and self-abuse. (Self-abuse—that is, masturbation—could also be a direct cause of idiocy in those who practiced it.)[22]

Howe demonstrated with tables covering 574 of the idiots studied that one or more of such parental sins were prevalent in most of the cases. "By far the most prolific" was scrofula (in the popular, not the pathological, sense), which Howe discussed under the heading "The low Condition of the Physical Organization of one or both Parents." Scrofulous parents were identifiable by their stooped posture, "red and sore eyelids, turgid lips, spongy gums, swelling in the glands," and "liability to eruptions and diseases of the skin." Internally, they suffered "morbid tendencies" as well, "of which cancer is the worst." Many were inveterate drunkards. Indeed, "careful inquiry" revealed that "not one quarter" could be considered temperate persons.

Howe assures his readers that great care was taken to ascertain the "physical peculiarities" of the blood relatives of the idiots his commission had studied and that the "affections above named" were found in "the great number of cases." Several examples are discussed in detail. The dots are then connected: "By temperance, cleanliness, and careful observance of all the natural laws, they [the parents] might have corrected the vicious humours of their bodies, lived pleasant lives, and been blessed with children to comfort their old age; but they chose to outrage nature in every way, and she sent them their punishment in the shape of their idiotic children."[23]

Truly, therefore, it was a case of the sins of the fathers having been visited upon the sons. But precisely because the sons were not to blame, it was all the more imperative that mercy and understanding be extended to them, and that the conditions of their degradation be ameliorated.

Howe's goal in establishing his school was not only to improve, for their own sakes, the bodily and mental conditions of his charges. He hoped and believed that many, perhaps most, could be trained to reintegrate into the community as productive participants rather than wards. He never intended or imagined that state-funded schools would become, like the almshouses they were meant to replace, holding pens—warehouses for the indefinite custodial incarceration of those he sought to teach. Unfortunately, the education of feeble-minded persons proved to be a more daunting task in the event than it had been in the design. To make things worse, the schools were soon confronted with three unanticipated and seemingly insurmountable obstacles to reintegration.

First, although the original intent was to admit only "improvable idiots"—those with intellects deemed sufficient to learn what was needed to return to and survive in the outside world—a certain number of profoundly retarded individuals gained entry and had to be accommodated. For them, no matter what the quality of education, the prospect of returning to and surviving in the outside world was dim.

Second, a number of feeble-minded persons (or persons thought to be feeble-minded) who were admitted to the schools suffered physical disabilities as well—epilepsy, for example, but more profound disabilities too. Like the profoundly retarded, their prospects for reentering and surviving in the outside world were diminished.

Third, and most daunting of all, even in the case of "improvable idiots" who did learn enough to make it in the outside world—at least, if they could get a little help and find jobs—the community at large resisted their reentry. It proved more efficient, for example, to hire new immigrants to perform the menial tasks that the feeble-minded were capable of doing, and thus there weren't enough jobs for the graduates of the schools. Further, the poor (from whose ranks the attendees of state schools were overwhelmingly drawn) lacked the resources to care for the feeble-minded after graduation (especially so in the case of graduates who could not find jobs). Since the almshouses (and jails), which had previously housed this element of the population, were no longer an acceptable alternative, the schools themselves began to take on a long-term custodial role to supplement their training function. Even Howe came to accept this reality, as foreshadowed by remarks he made at a sister institution in 1857, less than a decade after his own school was opened: "Do all that we may, we cannot make out of the *real idiot* a reasoning and *self-guiding* man. We can arrest the downward tendency to brutishness which his infirmity entails. We can teach him even some elementary truths; and, what is more important still, we can draw out and strengthen his moral and social faculties, so as to make them lessen the activity of his animal nature; but, after all, he must ever be in a child-like dependence upon others for guidance and support."

"They can indeed be made less burdensome," he concluded, "but not materially productive. They are idiots for life."[24]

The implications of merging school and asylum soon became manifest. First, the institutions themselves started to grow larger, to accommodate a permanent—and growing—resident population. Warnings by Séguin (among others) that quality education and care were incompatible with bigness were ignored. Second, the institutions became more self-sufficient. This was necessary for financial reasons (the state could not afford the full cost of long-term care; therefore the schools had to produce more of their own food and supplies, and the able residents had to help care for the less able ones) but also for practical reasons: the popular view was that the resident population needed to be kept busy so as to stay out of trouble. Thus, for example, the schools began to develop their own farms and farm colonies to grow food for the residents and to provide work. (As one physician explained at a meeting of the Massachusetts Medical Society, "You cannot work these boys too hard. If they work them as hard as they can, they will not practice the vices to which [the previous speaker] alludes.")[25] Third, the educational programs began to shift from an academic to a vocational orientation. This maximized the chances that graduates could find work outside the institution, but, just as important, it also created a cadre of in-house workers to assist the paid staff and improve the institution's productivity at little or no cost. Fourth, medical professionals rather than educators began to occupy the most senior administrative positions at the schools. This, too, reflected the new reality: that state schools existed more to provide care than education. It was also a tacit admission that the medical needs of profoundly disabled residents of a large institution were substantial and that feeble-mindedness was being viewed less as a learning disability than as a disease.

In short, institutions for feeble-minded persons, like Howe's facility, came to resemble asylums more than schools, and their inhabitants came to be seen and described as inmates or patients more than pupils.[26]

But if circumstances (not least the inability of state school graduates to find jobs to support themselves in the outside world) conspired to ensure from the outset that the state schools for feeble-minded persons would perform a custodial as well as an educational function, the principal impetus for long-term custodial care was more "scientific"—and more sinister. Careful observers in the last quarter of the nineteenth century had begun to notice what they thought was a "continuity of disabilities over generations."[27] This was not Howe's sins-of-the-fathers correlation. The ideas of Darwin (and, by the beginning of the twentieth century, Gregor Mendel) were now in the air. This was heredity: idiocy was an inheritable disease, not a punishment. Moreover, reformers began to insist on a connection between feeble-mindedness, degeneracy, and crime. The degenerate (meaning, for example, sexually promiscuous) and criminal classes drew disproportionately from the ranks of the feeble-minded. The feeble-minded, therefore, were not merely an inconvenience or a burden; they were a menace.

To make matters worse, their numbers—both absolute and relative to the rest of the population—seemed to be increasing precipitously. In 1881, Frederick Wines caused an uproar when he reported that the rate of feeble-mindedness in the United States was 0.15 percent of the population—two and a half times the rate reported only ten years earlier, in the 1870 census.[28] Subsequent census data suggested immigrants accounted for a disproportionate share of the increase (thereby fueling the anti-immigration sentiment that was beginning to sweep the country).[29]

These ominous signs eventually impelled the enlightened and educated classes of the country to demand protection from the feeble-minded in the form of permanent segregation and control. In Massachusetts, their principal spokesperson turned out to be none other than Dr. W. E. Fernald, the long-time superintendent of Howe's Massachusetts School for the Feeble-Minded, in whose honor the school would eventually be renamed. In 1912, Fernald addressed the Massachusetts Medical Society on the subject. "There is a large number of feeble-minded persons in our community," he warned. "The great majority . . . come from a stock which transmits feeble-mindedness from generation to generation in accordance with the laws of heredity." They are "parasitic," "predatory" people incapable of self-support. They cause "unutterable sorrow at home and are a menace and danger to the community"—one of the "great social and economic burdens of modern times." The remedy—the "only way" to reduce their numbers—was "to prevent their birth."[30]

Of course this would require "greatly increased institutional provision," the cost of which could be substantial—not, however, as great as the present cost of caring for them—"to say nothing of their progeny, in future generations." The expense, moreover, would be "counterbalanced" in a few years "by the reduction in the population of almshouses, prisons and other expensive institutions," provided that the feeble-minded were identified and segregated at an early age. To that end, Fernald recommended that "every case . . . should be recorded" by the public schools, the parents notified, and the child—voluntarily if possible, forcibly if necessary—placed in an institution until he or she was beyond childbearing age. "The most important point," Fernald reemphasized, was that "feeble-mindedness is highly hereditary, and that each feeble-minded person is a potential source of an endless progeny of defect. No feeble-minded person should be allowed to marry, or to become a parent. The feeble-minded should be guarded or segregated during the child-bearing period. . . . Certain families should become extinct. Parenthood is not for all."[31]

As it happened, contemporary science also afforded (so it was thought) a means by which to identify and segregate the feeble-minded population at an early age, before substantial mischief could be done: the IQ test.

Since the early nineteenth century, reformers and medical practitioners had sought an objective means of measuring mental capacity. For many years the leading candidate was phrenology—the careful examination of cranial size, structure, and topography.[32] Samuel Gridley Howe, it may be fairly said, was utterly obsessed by the technique—and convinced of its efficacy. Table I of *On the Causes of Idiocy* (1858), a supplement to his 1848 *Report upon Idiocy*, is filled with detailed cranial measurements of 338 persons examined. The supplement's first appendix is an extended discussion titled "The Influence of the Size of the Brain upon Idiocy." Phrenology proved to be an imperfect indicator, however, and other techniques were investigated as the century progressed.[33] In the meantime, observation continued to be the principal means of identification.

The breakthrough came at century's end, with the work of the French psychologists Alfred Binet and his student Théodore Simon. Binet had been asked by the French government to develop a method for identifying children in the Paris public schools who were not capable intellectually of keeping up with the curriculum. The goal of the government was to set up, for the first time, special classes for these individuals, not to institutionalize them. Binet and Simon studied thousands of children of different ages, gave them tasks of various degrees of difficulty to perform, and tabulated their responses. Based on this data, they determined which tasks a majority of students could or could not perform at a given age, thereby establishing a norm of performance for children at any given age. Binet and Simon published a first draft of their scale in 1905 (it was subsequently revised in 1908 and 1911).[34]

The Binet-Simon intelligence scale, largely ignored in France, took America by storm. Henry Goddard (of "we need to hunt them out in every possible place" fame) adopted it for use at his school for the feeble-minded in New Jersey in 1908 and ceaselessly promoted its benefits in public lectures around the country. By 1912 it had become a standard feature in public schools across the United States. In 1916, Lewis Terman, head of the psychology department at Stanford University, revised the Binet-Simon scale (his revision was known as the Stanford-Binet Test), introduced the term IQ (intelligence quotient), and established a new system of classification based on IQ:

> 140 and above, near genius or genius
>
> 120–140, very superior intelligence
>
> 110–120, superior intelligence
>
> 90–110, normal or average intelligence
>
> 80–90, dullness
>
> 50–70, morons
>
> 25–50, imbeciles
>
> below 25, idiots[35]

The Binet-Simon and Stanford-Binet tests revealed (or were thought to reveal) previously unrecognized gradations of deviance between "average" and profoundly disabled, including a larger than expected "borderline" group that had formerly been overlooked or viewed as merely "slow" or "backward" but that could now be seen for what it was: below average, and therefore abnormal. Fernald had warned of the dangers that this "brighter class" represented; now, the means for reliably identifying them before they could do mischief was at hand:

> The brighter class of the feeble-minded, with their weak will-power and deficient judgment, are easily influenced for evil, and are prone to become vagrants, drunkards and thieves. The modern scientific study of the deficient and delinquent classes as a whole has demonstrated that a large proportion of our criminals, inebriates and prostitutes are really congenital imbeciles, who have been allowed to grow up without any attempt being made to improve or discipline them. Society suffers the penalty of this neglect in an increase of pauperism and vice, and finally, at a great[ly] increased cost, is compelled to take charge of adult imbeciles in almshouses and hospitals; and of imbecile criminals in jails and prisons, generally for the remainder of their natural lives. As a matter of mere economy, it is now believed that it is better and cheaper for the community to assume the permanent care of this class before they have carried out a long career of expensive crime.[36]

This, then, was the final, twisted legacy of the great humanitarian and nineteenth-century reformer, Samuel Gridley Howe: schools for the feeble-minded as venues of quarantine rather than pedagogy. This, too, was the zeitgeist that gave birth to the Belchertown State School.

CHAPTER 3

The Officer and the Dentist

The Belchertown State School was designed according to the "cottage plan"—the dominant structural and operational model of the day for such facilities.[1] Earlier institutions had utilized a single large, centralized structure for housing residents and staff and doing training. In the cottage plan, prevalent since the late nineteenth century, numerous smaller buildings (dormitories, employee cottages, schoolhouse, kitchen, hospital, industrial building, farm, and so forth) were neatly arranged in a campuslike setting of trees and gardens. The plan facilitated differentiation of the resident population by gender, level of ability, and medical condition. So-called higher functioning residents could be segregated from, and employed in the care of, lower functioning ones. The most profoundly disabled could be treated as permanently sick and cared for in the hospital or infirmary. The productive work of the institution (such as farming, sewing, and laundering) could be separated from formal academic or vocational training and performed in special facilities geared to such purposes.

The cottage plan required a lot of land, and the tract assembled for the Belchertown State School was therefore large—800 acres according to the original deeds of sale, somewhat less, 622 acres, when finally reckoned. Further purchases were made over the years, bringing the total acreage to 843 in 1940.[2] The original design called for forty-two buildings housing 1,800 residents and 400 employees, including seventeen dormitories, eleven employee cottages, an assembly hall, two large industrial buildings, two gymnasiums, a schoolhouse, a hospital, an administration building, and a power station.[3] When the school opened in 1922, however, only a third of this planned construction had begun and very little was finished.

A core campus was completed in 1924, consisting of six dormitories (two for males, four for females), four employee cottages, a laundry (which doubled as classrooms and assembly hall), a storehouse (with temporary office space and a commissary where all meals were prepared), and the power station. Most of the other planned buildings were completed between 1925 and 1932. Although there would be additional construction later in the school's history (as well as demolition), the physical facility that existed in 1932, a decade after the school opened, was largely the same as when it closed sixty years later.

The completed main campus included eleven dormitories: for males, Buildings K (145 beds), L (105 beds), M (112 beds), and G (160 beds); for females, Buildings A (145 beds), B (105 beds), C (70 beds), D (105 beds), E (110 beds), and F (110 beds). Buildings K and L were completed in 1922, A through D in 1923–24, M in 1927, E in 1929, F in 1931, and G in 1960. The school added an eleventh dormitory—an infirmary—in 1952 to house 224 of its most physically disabled residents. Two nurseries (male and female) were built between 1930 and 1932 to accommodate children six years of age or younger. Each had 50 beds. A third nursery, called the Tadgell Nursery, was added in 1960.

Nine employee cottages were built between 1922 and 1932; they were described as "attractive and homelike with . . . stucco walls and green trimmings."[4] Each accommodated at least twenty employees. In addition, the school built private housing for several of its resident officers. The superintendent's house, a two-story affair completed in 1925, sat high on a hill at the southeast corner of the property. It boasted lovely views, gardens, and a private tennis court.

A large storehouse, alongside the railroad spur on the extreme northwest corner of the property, was the first building at the state school (other than the farmhouse used by the farm colony before the school opened). Intended as storage space, it also housed the school's administrative offices and kitchen for several years. A permanent administration building, to the left just inside the main gate, was built in 1927 and substantially enlarged in 1968.

Several other nonresidential buildings filled out the campus. A sixty-bed hospital was opened in 1931. It included an operating room, X-ray department, dental department, and laboratory. The laundry building, completed in 1923, was built large in anticipation of a school population exceeding 2,000 residents and 300 staff. Because the space exceeded the

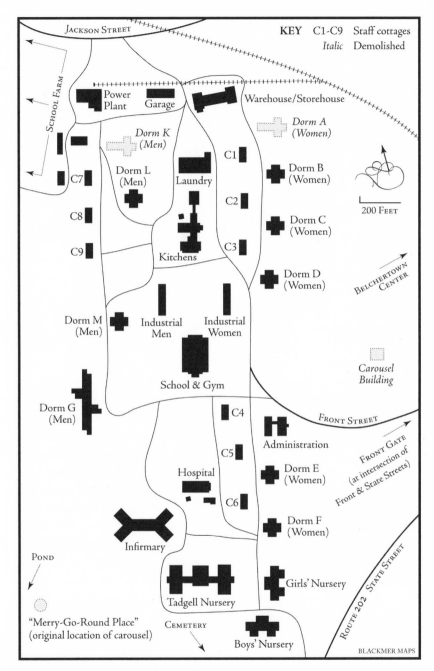

Plan of the Belchertown State School campus. ——BLACKMER MAPS

school's initial laundry needs, the building was also fitted out with temporary classrooms and a temporary assembly hall. The laundry ended up doubling as a schoolhouse for almost a decade because funding for a permanent schoolhouse, assembly hall, and gymnasium was not appropriated until the early 1930s. The service building was completed in 1924; it housed the school's permanent kitchen, several offices, two staff dining rooms (one for officers and one for employees), and a canning room. Food was cooked daily in the service building for all of the school's residents, then transferred to the dormitories.

The permanent schoolhouse was not completed until 1932. It included eight grade-school classrooms, a music room, two domestic science rooms, a manual training room, a print shop, an assembly hall (including a large stage, dressing rooms, storage rooms and up-to-date stage equipment) that seated 1,200, a good-sized gymnasium with locker room and showers, a library and head teacher's office, a canteen (in which products of the school's industrial departments were sold to the public, and incidentals like ice cream and candy were sold to residents and staff), and a large club room for employees, with two bowling alleys and two pool tables.[5]

To house its many industrial activities, the school built two industrial buildings, one for women (1930) and one for men (1932). The women's industrial building included a beauty parlor and a sewing department in which clothing for both male and female residents was cut and sewn. There was also space for manufacturing lace and knitted goods. The men's building had space to repair and refinish school furniture, manufacture household products such as brooms, brushes, games, toys, and mattresses, and repair shoes. As of 1935, the men and boys working in the shoe repair shop were mending 250–300 pairs of shoes per week. There was also a barbershop in the building.

Finally, a remarkable feature of the state school campus was its system of tunnels, many of them dug twenty-five feet below ground, which connected most of the buildings to one another. Much of the excavation work was done by resident labor.[6] Intended to facilitate maintenance of the school's steam pipes and sewers rather than for moving about in inclement weather, the tunnels were nevertheless sometimes used by the rigorously segregated male and female residents for illicit communications and contacts. Men and women would pass furtive love notes to one another in the tunnels and, some recalled, even have romantic encounters there.[7]

The school also owned and operated a large farm adjacent to the main campus on the north and west. As we saw in chapter 1, the farm began as a "colony" of the Wrentham State School in 1917, five years before the Belchertown school officially opened. The eleven boys and two supervisors who moved from Wrentham to Belchertown that summer occupied an abandoned farmhouse (the former Witt residence) and cultivated hay and apples for the home school. During the next few years they added crops, put to pasture a herd of young livestock, and enlarged the Witt house into a farm dormitory for forty boys plus staff. By the end of 1922, when the farm colony was transferred to the books of the newly opened state school, there were thirty-five boys and men working on the farm, four supervisors, and twelve acres under cultivation.[8]

The farm grew rapidly—to 130 acres in its first decade and 225 acres by World War II.[9] The finished physical plant included two farm dormitories, two horse barns, two dairy barns, a cow hospital, a dairy, a greenhouse, a poultry plant, and a piggery. (The pigs were fed in part with garbage gathered from the dining commons at Amherst College.)[10] The farm was its own self-contained community within the larger, self-contained community of the school, producing all of the school's milk and potatoes, most of its other winter vegetables and eggs, and substantial quantities of chicken, pork, and beef.[11] The production figures for 1940 illustrate the extent of the operation in its mature years, as well as something of the school's diet. That year the farm produced 460,000 quarts of milk and 29,580 dozen eggs, along with 47,250 pounds of pork and 14,000 of poultry. Fruits included apples (1,100 bushels), grapes (15,000 lbs.), and peaches and plums (65 bushels each); tomatoes led the list of vegetables (105,00 lbs.), followed by squash (66,000 lbs.), carrots (60,000 lbs.), sweet corn (45,000 lbs), beets (40,000 lbs), and lesser amounts of onions, cabbage, string beans, turnips, pumpkins, celery, and peas. A total of almost a thousand tons of silage corn, green feed, and hay were gathered.[12]

Women sometimes worked on the farm as well as men, but only male residents (always called "farm boys") and staff lived there, in one of the two farm dormitories (Farm 1 was the renovated Witt farmhouse, with thirty-five beds, and Farm 2 was the renovated former town poor farm, with fifty beds)—the farm boys in open wards, twenty-five to a floor, the staff in private rooms that included steam heat. The farm dormitories also had separate dining rooms for the farm boys and staff as well as separate recreation rooms.[13]

Farm staff and farm boys worked closely together. When they were not working, the boys might listen to the radio, watch movies, or play baseball; the staff would talk and play cards.[14] The shared work and shared accommodation (albeit on different floors) helped establish a bond between them that was qualitatively different from staff–resident relationships elsewhere at the school. It was not a relationship of equals, but there was respect that ran in both directions and that secured for the farm residents a modicum of humanity too often missing (as we will see) at the school.

The school was administered by a small group of resident officers—chief among them the superintendent. The first superintendent, Dr. George McPherson, who served for more than twenty years, profoundly influenced the subsequent history of the school. Together with the school's even longer serving first dentist, Arthur Westwell (a man whose talents ranged far beyond gums and teeth), he guided construction of the main campus, established the formal routines of admission and daily life, and shaped public perceptions of study, work, and play at the school in a way that would persist long after his retirement.

George E. McPherson, the officer of this chapter's title, was born in Cambridge, Massachusetts, in 1876. He obtained a medical degree from the University of Maryland in 1904. His passion was psychiatric medicine; after medical school, he worked at Foxboro State Hospital, Medford State Hospital, and the Psychopathic Hospital in Boston. During World War I, he was a divisional psychiatrist at military camps in the eastern and southeastern United States, attaining the rank of major. He became an assistant to the Massachusetts Commissioner of Mental Diseases in 1919, and served in that position until he received the Belchertown appointment in 1922.[15]

By all accounts, McPherson was stern, aloof, and somewhat dictatorial. A former employee, interviewed long after McPherson's death, remembered him as "an ex-colonel" who "ran the institution like the army."[16] The military metaphor seems apt. He had lots of rules and rarely bent them. He was, for example, unalterably opposed to smoking and drinking; both were banned, and employees caught doing either were summarily dismissed. His punctuality was also legendary—exceeded, it was said, only by his scorn for the tardy. "I can remember," wrote a friend, "how he would arrange on a Sunday for a set or two of tennis at 2:15 the following Wednesday afternoon. I soon learned that he would come driving over to the courts at exactly 2:14."[17] McPherson was an avid gardener as well (large flats of snapdragons, salpiglossis, and calendulas were kept at the ready near his garage—to be used as gifts for friends). Perhaps this accounts for the special pride he took in the school farm, always touting it in press interviews and in his annual superintendent's report. Production figures were routinely highlighted; prize-producing cows were celebrated for their output of butterfat. Every summer he would tour the farm's orchards, always picking and enjoying a fresh peach.[18]

Arthur Westwell was born in North Andover, Massachusetts, in 1892. He graduated from Phillips Exeter Academy, served as a sergeant in the U.S. Army Medical Corps from 1917 to 1919 and obtained a dental degree (DMD) from Tufts College in 1923. He also worked at the Massachusetts School for the Feeble-Minded from 1916 to 1923, before transferring to Belchertown and serving as the resident dentist from 1923 to 1949. Besides caring for teeth, Westwell supervised the school's recreational activities, directed most of its theatrical productions, and produced the annual Fourth of July festivities.

If McPherson was the steady hand who developed and disciplined the institution, Westwell was the free spirit who gave it personality. Importantly, from the beginning, both men desired to integrate rather than isolate school and town. As a result (not to overstate it, but more so than at similar institutions elsewhere), the school developed ties to the community that went beyond their shared name. Decades later, when the tragedy of Belchertown State School was exposed, the shame of it would be felt personally by the town's residents. They too, they would come to believe, had been complicit, and their need to expunge that shame would contribute in no small way to the reformation and, ultimately, closure of the school.

That town and school would coexist comfortably for generations through depression, world war, and cultural upheaval was not an inevitable outcome. Things could have gone differently, despite the wishes of McPherson and Westwell. As it happened, the cordial relationship between school and town was tested early, as were the diplomatic skills of the "ex-colonel." In 1926, the town gave the Commonwealth of Massachusetts, which was looking for more land for the state school, a six-month option to buy the town poor farm for $8,000. (The poor farm was running a deficit of $1,300 per year—a substantial drain on the annual budget.) The option had been kept a secret, however, and in April 1927, when the state sought to exercise it, a surprised town voted not to sell—raising the specter of a lawsuit and the possibility of a permanent rift between school and town.

The ostensible issue was price: was the town selling too cheaply? But there were allegations, too, of nefarious dealings between school and town—as well as resentment that the town had lost much of its tax base to the state school when the five farms comprising its principal acreage were turned over to it. Further, opponents of the sale argued that the town would "have to have a lock-up anyway" for its paupers, and that such facility would cost $2,000 to build—a quarter of the purchase price.[19]

Into the breach stepped Superintendent McPherson. Admitting the option was "awkwardly handled," he nevertheless insisted there was "nothing crooked" about it. The poor farm was running a deficit, the town had previously voted to sell, and the state school was the only willing buyer. Regarding the tax complaint, he noted that although the school's buildings were not taxable, the land was, and that upward adjustments to the assessed value would be made every five years to take account of improvements. He also reminded the town that the state school currently employed thirty-two town residents, accounting for $39,000 of the school's annual payroll, and that it had recently paid $25,000 to local labor for construction projects. Finally, he observed wryly that the state was criticizing him not for paying too little but for paying too much for the poor farm, given that a third of its land was marsh or rock and therefore unfit.[20]

The matter came to a head at the town's annual appropriation meeting in February 1928. The meeting was well attended. A motion was tabled to amend the purchase price of the poor farm to $12,000. McPherson reminded the citizens that the town had already agreed to $8,000 and that the state had appropriated that amount, and no more, for the purchase. A man named Frank Gold then rose to address the meeting. He said he knew of two people who would pay more than $8,000 for the poor farm; indeed, he himself was willing to pay more. The issue was thus joined. A former state senator challenged Gold to make an offer: "How much will the gentleman give? If he wants business, let's have business." Gold dissembled, opposition waned, and the town voted by a "sizeable majority" to approve the sale to the state school for $8,000.[21] The school—and its first superintendent—had survived their first school–town crisis. Henceforth the town would defer to McPherson in all matters pertaining to the state school. McPherson, in turn, would establish routines of admission, training, work, and play that would persist long after his retirement and death.

How did residents come to be admitted to Belchertown State School? As we've seen, the first several hundred admissions were transfers from other state institutions for the feeble-minded at Waltham and Wrentham—most of them persons with family or other ties to the western part of the state.

Additional transfers from other institutions were occasionally made there-after, but the bulk of new admissions came directly from their communities. Often candidates were identified by the local public schools from among their delinquent or learning-disabled populations. (The term "learning-disabled" was not then in use; rather, candidates were described in terms of their negative effect on peers: they were "children who were impeding the instruction of more educable children.")[22] The state school set up an outpatient clinic to help in the "weeding out" process. In 1931, for example, the clinic examined 385 children in the Pittsfield schools; 122 were labeled "feeble-minded," 183 "borderline," and 18 "normal." Of these, 197 were recommended for special classes and 41 for admission to the state school.[23]

Candidates were admitted in one of three ways: thirty-day observation (rare), custodial commitment by a probate court judge, or voluntary application by relative or guardian.[24] Initially, no one under six years of age could be admitted. Once nursery facilities were constructed in the early 1930s, however, the admission age was reduced to two years old. At first, many new admissions were voluntary. But the ratio shifted quickly in favor of custodial commitments; by the 1930s, three of every four were custodial. According to McPherson, voluntary admissions came mostly from the "well-bred"—that is, affluent—classes.[25]

The school regularly tracked what it called the "mental status" (mental age) of first admissions (the term for non-transferees), reporting this information each year in its annual report. Under the nomenclature of the day (derived from the Stanford-Binet test), there were three categories of feeble-minded persons: idiots (mental age less than 3 years), imbeciles (mental age from 3 to 7 years) and morons (mental age from 8 to 12 years). The next two levels of intelligence, in ascending order, were "borderline" and "dull normal."[26] Although the percentage of first admissions in the respective categories varied from year to year, the variance was relatively narrow. Between 1925 and 1940, approximately 10–15 percent of new admissions each year were labeled idiots, 25–35 percent were labeled imbeciles, and most of the rest were labeled morons. A very few were labeled "not mentally defective" (typically this meant borderline or dull normal) or otherwise went unclassified.

What is important to realize here is that a large segment of the school population, though "slow" by any standard measure of ability, was not uneducable. Today, many of them would be classified as "special needs" children; they would, as far as possible, be integrated into normal public school classrooms (perhaps assisted by an aide or given preferential treatment when taking exams) or placed in special education classes. But in both cases they would live with their families and participate in the general life of the community. Not so in 1922. Then, these children (particularly the indigent among them) were committed to the state schools, where they would then perform, uncompensated, the bulk of the labor necessary to sustain the institution. Moreover, the school made no secret of its need for new admissions of sufficient intelligence and physical health to perform this labor. In his very first annual report in 1923, McPherson wrote: "We have at present 273 boys. At least 135 are unable to work out of doors, leaving 138, including 40 at the farm, to work in the various departments (bakery, store, shops and out of doors). We are expected to do much of the excavating, filling, etc., about the grounds with patient labor but have not sufficient accommodations for more workers which we must have."[27]

New admissions were separated into two groups: those deemed educable and those not. The non-educable, whose mental age was said to range between two and four years old, were enrolled in sense-training classes. There the focus was on teaching the residents basic sensory skills: to recognize items by size, shape, and color, for example, to differentiate between odors and tastes, and to locate the origin of a sound in a room.[28] The educable residents were enrolled in kindergarten or grade school (grades one through six). To give a sense of the numbers, in 1926, 175 of 750 residents were enrolled in such classes. In 1935, about 80 percent of new admissions were enrolled in kindergarten or the first grade. Very few reached the fifth and sixth grades. All classes were segregated by gender. Girls attended in the mornings and boys in the afternoon; the other half-day was devoted to occupational training.

Enrollment at the state school grew steadily during McPherson's tenure, doubling between 1925 and 1940 from 768 to 1,525. The day-to-day resident population, though, was somewhat less (725 in 1925; 1,313 in 1940), due to occasional family visits, parole, and, after 1937, family care (discussed later in this chapter). A few residents escaped. Women outnumbered men; the ratio was approximately four to three. Of the 1,525 enrollees at the end of 1940, 36 were out on visits, 120 were on parole, 51 were in family care, and 20 were on escape, leaving 1,294 in residence. One-third of those enrolled were voluntary admissions and two-thirds were court-ordered commitments.

Between 1928 and 1940, approximately 30 percent of new admissions each year were younger than twelve years old, 60 percent were between the ages of twelve and twenty-four, and 10 percent were twenty-five or older. The average age of the school's population increased over time, as the resident population aged and few were discharged. In 1935, the average physical age was thirty years, the average mental age seven and a half.[29] As of 1940, only 7 percent of the residents were under ten years old, and 40 percent were over twenty-five. One of every eight was forty or older. The poet Robert Francis, who worked briefly as an attendant in Building M, one of the boys' dormitories, in 1931, chillingly recalled the first time he saw adult residents at the school and realized that the "boys" he was caring for were there for life: "A procession of feeble-minded men from another building passed by. One fellow wagged his head hideously, waving hello to us. It came as a swift revelation. Were the imbeciles in M Building going to stay here until they grew up? Stay until they grew old and died, all the while that [someone] screamed 'shut up' at them and some supervisor came each day to criticize a detail of the housework?"[30]

It is difficult to say whether the average mental age of the total state school population increased or decreased during McPherson's tenure, because the school did not always measure, or at least did not report on, the mental status of its transferees—a significant percentage of the total. But such information was included in all annual reports between 1934 and 1940, and it indicates that the average mental age of the total population during that six-year period declined significantly even as the physical age increased. In particular, the percentage of total residents classified as idiots or imbeciles increased (from 12 to 16 percent and 33 to 39 percent, respectively) whereas the percentage of residents classified as morons or persons not mentally defective declined from 56 percent to 46 percent. The scope and significance of this shift in mental age is perhaps easier to see if one looks at actual numbers rather than percentages: whereas the aggregate resident population in 1934 and 1940 was about the same (approximately 1,300), the number of idiots and imbeciles increased by 131, from 569 to 700, while the number of morons and persons not mentally defective decreased by 120, from 714 to 594. In effect, in an institution that relied heavily on its resident population to provide much of the needed day-to-day labor and care, the population most in need of help grew substantially while the population best able to provide that help declined substantially.[31]

One statistic that was not published regularly but was surely significant was the number of residents who were physically as well as mentally disabled. In 1929 McPherson told a local church group that 150 of 900 persons then enrolled at the state school were "of the idiot type" (having a mental age not exceeding three years), and that "most" of this group were "crippled."[32] Even assuming "most" meant something less than three-quarters, and discounting for the vagaries of "crippled," McPherson's comment suggests that a sizeable percentage of residents had severe physical disabilities—possibly more than 10 percent.

For new admissions on the so-called educable track, the curriculum was a combination of academic and vocational training. We saw earlier that students were segregated by gender, with girls attending academic classes in the mornings and boys in the afternoon, and that the other half-day was spent in vocational training. The academic side of the curriculum, as McPherson explained in a 1926 interview, stressed reading skills: "Ability to read is the most important factor in the lives of most of these children. Reading is the means of the pupil's entertainment by himself. After the pupil has graduated from the school if we can be certain that he will find wholesome entertainment in reading we will have accomplished another wonderful achievement in our work here."[33]

Producing proficient readers capable of wholesome self-entertainment may have been the original inspiration in the classroom, but if so this goal was compromised early on. By 1935 the school had converted all of its reading rooms to sleeping quarters, to make space for more admissions.[34] The reading rooms were never restored. Moreover, from the outset, emphasis was much more on vocational training than academics, despite the 50/50 division of time between classroom and workshop—understandably so, given the special difficulty of finding gainful employment for those fortunate enough to graduate from the institution as well as the labor needs of the institution itself. For all practical purposes, the school was a self-sufficient community, meeting most of its own needs for food, clothing, and shelter. This required much more labor than the paid staff alone could provide. Most of the labor, therefore, was performed, unpaid, by the residents themselves, under the supervision of the staff. Besides the farm, the school operated its own cannery, stores, kitchen, and laundry—all of which were partly staffed by resident labor.

McPherson acknowledged this vocational emphasis in the same 1926 interview: "If we can teach a child to do a given task in a manner that is acceptable, and have him do it pleasantly and finish the task, we believe we have made a good prospective employee." Males were trained to assist tradesmen or become farm hands, females to do housekeeping. Thus, for example, some men learned to repair shoes and chairs, or manufacture brooms and brushes, or weave rugs, cloth, and draperies. Others were taught to care for iceboxes (to keep meat fresh), to carve meat, or to conduct a store. Women were taught embroidery, hooking rugs, and waiting on tables. Boys and girls, men and women—all learned to make their own beds, sweep and polish floors, and operate dishwashing machines.[35]

How were residents taught? In other interviews McPherson called the method of instruction employed at the school "habit training" or "reiteration": doing the same task "over and over again for a period of years longer than is necessary in normal children," until the pupil develops "sure ways of performance."[36] As long as any progress was being made, the resident was required to attend class. Even if the pupil could absorb "no great amount of learning," he or she "gained sufficient to make life more interesting and acquired deftness of action in industrial lines." Girls eventually made "good domestics"; boys, who were willing "to do work that higher priced labor will not do," made "excellent helpers in the various trades."[37] Again, McPherson's emphasis was on vocational training.

The vocational orientation of the curriculum was on display annually beginning in 1926, when the school held the first of what would become (throughout the McPherson era) yearly two-day exhibits, open to the public, of its educational, industrial, laundry, farm, and canning activities. At each year's exhibit, the stage of the assembly hall was filled with displays of, and information about, farm produce harvested at the school farm or canned in the past year. In 1926, only three years after the school was opened, thirty-two products were being harvested, including 175,000 pounds of potatoes, 250 tons of silage corn, and 13,000 pounds of apples, and thirty-three products were being canned, including 10,000 quarts of tomatoes and 14,000 quarts of salted spinach.[38]

The school's industrial output was also highlighted at these annual exhibits. Many of the items needed by the school and its residents for their daily lives were manufactured by resident laborers working in the school's industrial department, including rugs, table runners, pin cushions, neck scarves, caps, mittens, bedspreads, and toys.[39] Rugs, for example, were made from burlap pulled to pieces and dyed on the premises.[40] Whenever possible, damaged goods were repaired rather than discarded. One of the displays in 1927 noted that residents mended 2,000 pieces per week. Every scrap was apparently salvaged and recycled. Even thread ends were saved and used as stuffing for dolls; old inner tubes were cleaned and used as covering for the stuffed dolls and animals.[41] In the mid-1930s a *Sentinel* reporter wrote: "One cannot view the State School Exhibit without visualizing the pupils who created it. One can see them in the fields tending the crops, in the bakery preparing food, in the workshop making garments, mending shoes, mending mattresses and brushes, mending and doing laundry work—yes, everything useful and many things beautiful—all with the thought of bringing to pass a more abundant life for those whose good fortune it is, or ill (or a combination of both) to be at the State School."[42]

Clearly, this was a working world, not an academy. The life revealed through the prism of the school exhibit had not much room, or time, for proficient readers capable of wholesome self-entertainment. Yet those responsible for supervising the work of the school's residents insisted that this labor was not drudgery, that it was an integral part of the school's training mission even though the institution also benefited from it, and that much of the labor was undertaken in the spirit of play rather than work. Arthur Westwell once illustrated this "work as play" approach with characteristic anecdote:

> We never talk about work to the pupils. It's always play. For example, last summer [1926] we had a two acre plot of ground that was to be reclaimed. It was filled with large and small stones. The war is still a big factor in their lives and the children still talk about Kaiser Bill.
>
> "How many want to play Kaiser Bill?" I asked one morning. Everybody shouted "Me, me" and raised their hands. We went out into this field, and 70 children formed into a ring-around-a-rosie circle. In the circle I planted a white pole with a black hat placed on the top of it. "There's Kaiser Bill. Let's see who can knock him down first."
>
> Instantly every child was searching the ground for stones to throw at the kaiser. No one hit it. Gradually the circle grew smaller as the stones on the ground disappeared. They crowded nearer and nearer to the pole, and finally the white pole fell.
>
> "Don't we bury him, now?" they asked.
>
> "Oh yes," I said, "we can't leave him without a grave. Let's make a stone grave for Kaiser Bill," I suggested, and soon 70 pairs of hands were picking up stones and piling them into a neat pile, never for a moment suspecting that what they had just done was real work. We placed poles in three more corners of the field and repeated the game.
>
> "Kill Kaiser Bill," they said, and with a zest they cleared the

entire field in less than a morning's work. This was play to them;
it would have taken our hired men two or three days to do the same
job.[43]

In addition to supervising recreational activities, Westwell directed
numerous plays and musicals that were performed by the school's residents. How the school dentist came to be chief impresario for a company
of feeble-minded actors and musicians is lost to history. But chief impresario he was, producing frequent musical and theatrical entertainments
for a quarter century. These entertainments, often open to the public as
well as the school's staff and resident population, played to sellout crowds
and earned Westwell widespread affection and admiration.

Westwell staged a variety of shows—one every two months during the
early years. In 1924, for example, he directed a three-act Christmas drama
depicting the birth of Jesus, with readings from the Bible, carols, and songs
in Hebrew and Latin. The school chorus performed Handel's "Hallelujah
Chorus."[44] Other performances that he directed included The Magic Ring,
The Student Prince, That Old Sweetheart of Mine, At 12 Midnight, The Toreadors,
Food, and The Pinafore Sails for China, to mention just a few.[45] Residents volunteered eagerly for parts; granting permission to participate (as a reward for
good behavior) or withholding permission (as punishment for bad behavior) apparently became a useful disciplinary tool.[46]

The average mental age of those who participated in plays and musicals
was, according to Westwell, eight to eight and a half years; in other words,
shows were cast from the school's most intelligent population group. Still,
learning a part could be daunting. For example, referring to one student
who had been cast as a butler in The Student Prince, Westwell explained that
the student had only two things to do: bow and then walk off stage. Still,
"it took us 12 rehearsals before we finally taught [the student] to do both
actions together. He would bow and stay on the stage or he would make an
exit without bowing." In the same 1927 interview, Westwell described his
general rehearsal scheme for all staged entertainments: "The first rehearsal
we always say is good; the second no good. Then we alternate with good
and bad rehearsals, up to about four nights before the performance. The
last few rehearsals we say are good."

Westwell believed that musical performance was particularly well suited
for the feeble-minded. "Music," he said, "plays an important part in the
lives of these children. We find they are exceptionally fond of music, and
they do especially well in things musical. This is also true of the very low

grade pupil. We have children here who cannot talk, but who can carry a tune. Apparently, Nature's gift of love of music does not seem to be withheld from our children as is their gift of acquiring knowledge."

Westwell's principal theatrical entertainment, begun in 1924 and presented annually thereafter, was the school minstrel show, which became legendary in the town, playing to standing-room-only crowds. (Now a largely forgotten form of American entertainment because of their blatantly racist overtones, minstrel shows were once hugely popular in the United States. This author remembers minstrels being staged annually at his summer camp on Lake Erie in the mid-1950s.)[47] There were choruses, solos, dancing, and special acts—all parts performed by school residents "appearing in true negro make-ups of startling combinations of colors."[48] The number of participants varied from year to year, ranging from 36 to 140.[49] In 1929, the show ended with a rousing rendition of "Old Amherst" in honor of Amherst Rotarians and their wives, who were specially invited to the show. "It was," wrote the *Sentinel*'s reviewer, "the same old story over again. The guests were at first amused, but they went away amazed at what they had seen and heard."[50]

In 1928, Westwell began taking the show "on the road" with special performances for patients at the Northampton and Monson state hospitals.[51] Other stops, such as the veterans' hospital in nearby Northampton and Mount Saint Vincent orphanage in Holyoke, were added in later years.[52] Apparently the visit to Northampton State Hospital was especially coveted by the participants, as they were given free run of the hospital's cafeteria. One year a participant reportedly consumed "22 flapjacks on a full stomach," an event later approvingly recounted by Dr. McPherson, who said it lent "a touch of normalcy to it all."[53]

During World War II, the practice of inviting outside guests was discontinued and attendance—now limited to school personnel, their family, and friends—fell.[54] The school also discontinued the colorful red programs showing blackface performers that had become a standard feature of the event—due, it was said, to paper shortages. Outside guests and colorful programs were resumed after the war.[55]

Another of Westwell's grand productions was the state school's annual Fourth of July parade. Even before Westwell's arrival at Belchertown, McPherson determined that the Fourth should be a special occasion at the school. Beginning in 1922, before the school officially opened, he arranged a special program of sports for the resident men and boys already working the school's farm. In the morning, despite inclement weather, there were races of various kinds: hundred-yard dash, potato race, obstacle race, three-legged race, sack race, and wheelbarrow race, plus other track and field events including running broad jump and tug o' war.[56] In the evening, the men and boys were allowed to attend a band concert on the town common. They were supposed to watch fireworks as well, but the display was rained out.

To the sporting events, after his arrival at the school, Westwell added a parade—which soon became the featured attraction of the day. The first, in 1924, was typical of what would follow: "The procession wound its way about the grounds, by the office and supply building, where were seated judges, guests and employees, and then went to the farm. On its return, the column again passed the reviewing line." The "column" comprised a seven-piece band, six girls in white carrying flags, and lots of floats pulled by the school's farm (and other mechanized) vehicles. First prize was awarded to the Dutch village float, consisting of a Dutch windmill, Dutch maiden with bucket, and white fence surrounded by a field of green. "The predominating colors [of the float] were blue and white." The parade, held in the morning, was followed by sporting events and games, a pie-eating contest and a picnic lunch. There were live concerts and fireworks at night.[57]

By 1928, "the Fourth at the State School" had become an annual tradition. "The program of events is much the same from year to year, but the parade is bound to be distinctive," the Sentinel wrote the next year. Besides the floats, "quite a menagerie passes in review now, elephants, lions, alligators with gaping mouths, monkeys, donkeys, rabbits—all 'manned' inside with State School pupils. . . . The line passes the stand three times, while the winners show up again for the banner awards."[58]

Although old floats were reused, new ones were added regularly, including "Liberty Bell" (the first-prize winner in 1926), "Valley Forge," "Zulu Land," "Treasure Island," "Gay Madrid," "In Old Virginia," and "A Temple Garden."[59] One of the more popular fixtures was a Ford motorcar, whose demise in 1938 became the centerpiece of its own float in that year. The Sentinel reported: "Of course the last outfit in the parade nearly brought tears. Here a wrecking car was pulling that old faithful Ford that had been a bucking bronco and every other old thing for the amusement of the Fourth of July parade fans for so long. In the old bus was a mournful black sign with an inscription to the effect that when called for this year, poor Lizzie couldn't make the grade. The date of birth and death were duly given."[60]

During World War II, the school began to scale back on the event. In 1942, presumably to save on gas, the floats were drawn by "horse, cattle, etc." rather than tractors and farm trucks. Recorded music was substituted for live evening concerts. The official explanation was that there was a "shortage of help" and "a need for keeping farm equipment on the job."[61] After the war, some of the old features, such as live band concerts, were restored until Westwell left in 1949. Thereafter, Fourth of July celebrations were scaled back for good.

On the occasion of Westwell's twenty-fifth anniversary at the school, the Reverend Thomas Hanrahan, chaplain of Mount St. Vincent's in Holyoke, delivered a brief testimonial. "For the past 25 years," he said, "every child in his institution was the same to Dr. Westwell. He did all he could for them, giving of himself generously of his great talent and time, his only ambition being to bring happiness into the lives of the children, to help them get a little lift and a bit of confidence in themselves."[62]

To give the feeble-minded a "little lift" and a "bit of confidence in themselves" seems about the right claim to make for Westwell's productions. They likely didn't transform lives, but they did make living at the Belchertown State School more tolerable for some. Also, like stages everywhere in all times, they let a few lucky souls soar temporarily as if they were something they were not.

In his official role as school dentist, Westwell confronted a recurring assortment of dental issues among the residents—diseased gums and decaying teeth—that were exacerbated by the great difficulty of the feeble-minded to practice good dental hygiene. Add to this that teeth were often the weapon of choice among the most profoundly retarded (biting, literally, the hand that fed them or, in the case of the school dentist, the hand that treated them), and one begins to comprehend, if not sympathize with, Westwell's growing frustration. In 1933 he determined to solve what he called "the dental problem of the real low grade patient" by extracting all their teeth, diseased or not. The care with which he explains, and justifies, his solution may bespeak a certain hesitation:

> This type [the "real low grade patient"] presents many difficulties: he cannot cooperate, he is incapable of expelling food particles from between the teeth, and he responds to the attempted use of the tooth brush by biting it. Such natural means of cleansing as come to the normal individual by the action of the tongue on conversation and exploration, are denied him as he sits for hours with tongue and jaw motionless. Into such a fertile field for infection

is also introduced every foreign body upon which he can lay his hands. . . . He chews his food but little and because of this and the danger of his choking all his food is ground finely before it is served. Thus when we find in a mouth a tendency toward infection, and a set of teeth which serve only as a harbor for food particles, we feel justified in removing such teeth and leaving the smooth surfaces where food is not so apt to collect. Much of this work has been done during the past year, and the results certainly justify the procedure. The aesthetics have not been outraged in the process.[63]

By the following year, Westwell has gotten comfortable with his solution:

One of the greatest problems of the department continues to be the very low grade patient. Non-cooperative, he swallows cleaning materials, bites at instruments, and gains little or nothing from his trip to the clinic. Experience leads us to believe that, as a rule, such a patient is far better off with no teeth at all. Filling them is out of the question and with the specially prepared diet which is supplied such a patient as a matter of course, he gets along very well without teeth.[64]

The practice of extracting healthy teeth continued long after Westwell retired. Eventually, many of the victims were fitted with dentures; most had difficulty adjusting to false teeth and flushed them down the toilet. An operator at the school's sewage plant collected the discarded dentures and stored them in a bucket, in case there were second thoughts. Apparently, there weren't any.[65]

Apart from dental problems, the institution's biggest health concern was contagious disease. Chicken pox, mumps, measles, whooping cough, and tuberculosis were widespread, necessitating frequent quarantines. The trustees' annual report for 1933 is typical—and revealing—in this regard. It reported, "In January there was an epidemic of grippe affecting half of the medical staff, 35 employees and 416 pupils [a third of the resident population]. During the course of the epidemic, there were five deaths among our low-grade pupils. The Nursery was quarantined early in the year on account of a mild epidemic of chicken-pox."[66] Less discussed in the annual reports, but surely a frequent occurrence during the life of the institution, were injuries suffered by the residents—whether accidental, self-inflicted, or the result of aggression by other residents.

Not surprisingly for an institution whose raison d'être was to ensure that the feeble-minded "do not propagate and make the problem worse," sexual activity, even among adults, was rigorously suppressed. "The boys and girls are at all times kept entirely separate," McPherson assured a reporter in 1935. "When they meet they are heavily chaperoned and are not allowed to talk together."[67] Male and female residents were seated in different sections of the auditorium at school entertainments. The only sanctioned socializing was at church services and school dances. At dances, boys and girls could only touch fingertips.[68] The consequence was a highly evolved network of clandestine communication between the sexes. Affection was expressed mostly in writing, via notes or cards to a special friend. Those who couldn't write or read prevailed on those who could to pen messages or read them. "Lovers Only" was the endearing phrase most often used in this furtive correspondence.[69] The notes might be exchanged in the service tunnels that connected the various buildings or delivered by resident helpers whose jobs (shoveling snow, for example) took them regularly from building to building.[70]

Notwithstanding the vigilant segregation of the sexes, there were unwanted pregnancies. We do not know if abortions were performed at the school.[71] We do know from the annual report for 1930 that the trustees were becoming "favorabl[y disposed] toward the enactment of conservative, humane laws for sterilization in selected cases, in order that young women, particularly of child-bearing age, may not carry the responsibility of parenthood for which they are obviously unfit."[72]

There is no mention of homosexual behavior at the school in any of the sources relating to the McPherson era, but one may infer that it existed. A resident of the school in the 1950s, as well as an administrator in the 1970s, told an interviewer that homosexual behavior did occur at the school during their time there, although it was sometimes severely punished when discovered. Both viewed such behavior as inevitable—often a substitute for heterosexual relationships in an environment where heterosexual relationships were rigorously suppressed and the sexes strictly segregated. We have seen that such suppression of heterosexual relationships and segregation of the sexes was no less strict during the McPherson era, and there is no reason to think that the sexual needs of these earlier residents were any less.[73]

One of the difficulties of assessing what life was really like for the school's residents, especially in the formative years when McPherson was superintendent, is that there is little direct testimony available from the residents themselves. Most of the testimony is hearsay, comprised of accounts by employees and visitors. The party line, set by McPherson early on and echoed by reporters who visited the institution, was that the "children" were "happier" at the state school "than at any time in their lives." "Here," according to McPherson, "they are among their own people. A pupil with a low mental intelligence can play 'London Bridge Is Falling Down' and no one will laugh at him though his physical age may be more than 20 years." In 1929 he told a reporter that "60 per cent of our children were never so clean, well fed, clothed and cared for as at the present time."[74]

The occasional reporter who visited the school for some length of time would invariably reassure his readers that the residents were "happy." In 1927 a reporter for one of the Springfield papers wrote: "One must not suppose that the life of a Belchertown state school pupil is one of monotonous routine. The children have their moving pictures, their dances, and dramatics and picnics, as well as school, church and work. . . . As one passes for the first time through one building and then another, from one classroom to the next, and from the boys' industrial department to the girls, one cannot help but notice the dominant feeling of happiness. For these children are truly happy. They are well fed, well clothed and well housed."[75]

The frequent escapes, overcrowding, and discarded dentures may tell a different story. Eileen Staples, who began working at the school in 1947, told an interviewer many years later that the place was "pretty regimented," adding, "It was not a very happy life for most of them, I think."[76] Still, we should not be too quick to assume the worst. Albert Warner, a resident at the school in the 1920s and 1930s and one of the few from that era who has testified from personal knowledge about life at the school, told another interviewer, "We had some good times up there. Everything wasn't bad." For example, he loved baseball and recalled playing it often with the other boys and staff. He spoke fondly of McPherson and Westwell and called many of the school's other employees "caring people" who "kept us from falling apart." After attending classes to the sixth grade, Warner worked for a number of years on a construction crew that maintained the school grounds, and then became a mail carrier (a job he enjoyed because, he said, it got him around the school). He was released on parole in 1937, got work as a house painter, and eventually married another former resident.[77] While Warner's story should not make us complacent about the grim life of many at the school, it does offer reassurance that not all lives there were lost ones.

During the first three years of its operation, Belchertown State School "graduated" thirty-five men and women. These graduates, comprising less than 5 percent of the school's resident population at that time, left the institution, obtained jobs outside, and earned their own living. The women graduates were mostly employed as housekeepers, the men as helpers in the trades or as farm hands. One male graduate, employed as a mechanic's helper, reportedly earned $24 per week—a very decent wage for the 1920s.[78] According to McPherson, the goal was to graduate 20 percent of the school's residents and secure employment for them in the outside world. In reality, most residents, once admitted, never left.

The reasons for this are not entirely clear. Evidently, it wasn't for lack of family or friends wanting custody. In 1934 the school's trustees reported that they were confronted "continually [with] requests on the part of family and friends for discharging of pupils," but "in spite of the continued pressure and with the desirability of providing for a long waiting list, discharges have been relatively few and on the most conservative basis." Fear of sexual promiscuity and of the feeble-minded giving birth to new generations of mentally defective offspring probably explains this "most conservative basis" for discharge. As early as 1927, a local reporter wrote that "many of the children here will never become dischargeable because of sex delinquencies or other anti-social tendencies."[79] More ominously, as we've seen, the trustees stated in 1930 that they were beginning to favor establishing "conservative, humane laws for sterilization" in certain cases.[80]

Whatever the reasons, the rate of discharge between 1926 and 1940 averaged less than 5 percent and new admissions exceeded discharges by almost two to one. But a small number of those enrolled, probably less than 5 percent, were eventually "paroled," meaning that they stayed on the books as part of the school's official enrollment but were allowed to live and work in the local community. Typically, paroled girls did housework and paroled boys did farm work.[81]

Another group of enrollees was transferred to the community under the so-called family care program, instituted in 1937 to relieve the pressure of the school's growing wait list and make more room for younger, "trainable" students. Under this program some older residents, not otherwise eligible for parole, were boarded out to families in the town.[82] According to Gladys Meyer, a psychiatric social worker employed at the time by the school's outpatient clinic, the catalyst for the program was a widow, dying of cancer, who had devotedly cared for her Down syndrome daughter, Emma, for thirty-two years. Now facing imminent illness and death, and with no one to care for Emma, she sought to have her daughter admitted to the state school but was turned down for lack of space. Meyer knew there were likeable older residents at the school, in good health, who were able to take care of themselves if regularly supervised. She also knew of a family care program for such persons that existed in New York State under the supervision of the Newark State School, and she proposed to McPherson that a similar program be established at Belchertown. McPherson was supportive. He obtained permission from the Department of Mental Health and the program was launched in November 1937, despite the concern of some skeptics that participants would become more anxious if removed from their familiar institutional environment.[83]

The school identified forty men and women between the ages of forty and fifty who were deemed suitable for the program. Initially, six of them—all men—were boarded with farm families that had previously employed farm hands from the school under the parole program. According to Meyer, "These men adjusted extremely well and were absorbed into the family unit."[84] The homes were still in use twelve years later.

The boarding out of women proved more problematic, for reasons never fully articulated. Certainly there were sufficient families in town looking for boarders—even feeble-minded boarders, as 1937 was the depth of the Great Depression and many were eager for extra cash. In the end, the school selected the homes of two former female employees, both of whom had left the state school for personal reasons and both of whom, initially, were reluctant to participate. Curiously, neither had homes large enough to accommodate ten boarders (the number thought to be appropriate because it was large enough to provide the requisite financial incentive but small enough to allow proper supervision) and both therefore ended up buying new, larger homes for the purpose with financing from the Federal Housing Administration. The acquisition of sizeable debt in the middle of a depression, to take on feeble-minded boarders, must have been daunting for the two former employees. They did it, however, and it seems to have worked out for them; twelve years later they were still boarding women from the state school in their homes.

During the first twelve years of the family care program, the number of men and women from the school who were boarded out averaged forty-seven and varied from forty-two to sixty, depending on the year. Although a few participants were unable to adjust to their new environments, most did, and there is no reason to doubt Gladys Meyer's measured judgment, looking back on the program she initiated, that the men and women who participated in it were "physically and emotionally healthier" than their counterparts at the school and "comparatively happy." No one, in any event, was reported ever to have tried to escape from a boarding home.[85]

For the vast majority of those enrolled in Belchertown State School, however, the only alternatives to permanent residency were escape or death. Between 1926 and 1940, the school reported 111 escapes and 165 deaths. Little is known about either. Escapees, if caught, were punished—sometimes severely. All were "marked"—typically, by having their heads shaved in a distinctive pattern.[86] Some displayed a sense of humor about their experience. One man, who had gotten as far as New Haven before he was captured and returned, took a peanut butter sandwich with him but forgot water. Afterward he cautioned never to run away without water, "especially if you're going to eat peanut butter."[87]

Pneumonia and tuberculosis were the most frequently stated causes of death. Other reported causes included diphtheria, bronchitis, gastric ulcer, inflammation of the kidneys, and stroke. One resident starved to death due to regurgitation of food. There were also, from time to time, fatal accidents such as falling out a window. Beginning in 1926, the dead were buried in a small pine grove at the southeast corner of the school property, not far from McPherson's house. The farm boys dug the graves.

In 1942, shortly before the Fourth of July, George McPherson fell ill, missing for the first time the school's annual Independence Day celebration. He was not able to resume his duties full time, and he retired in June 1943. Two years later he was dead.[88] Arthur Westwell stayed on a few more years—shepherding, among other things, the school's acquisition of a Stein & Goldstein carousel in 1948. In 1949 he left Belchertown to become superintendent of the Montana State Training School, near Helena, and the outpouring of regret for his departure and good wishes for his future was heartfelt. He remained at the Montana school until his retirement in 1962.[89]

The McPherson era was over. The state school, now a permanent fixture of the local landscape, had become Belchertown's largest employer—and principal financial crutch during the Great Depression. School and town coexisted comfortably. Early crises (foremost among them the town's sale of its poor farm to the school) had long since been resolved. Routines of admission and daily life were well established. Minstrel shows, Fourth of July parades, and annual industrial exhibits reassured those on the outside who cared that life at the institution was good, that its residents were contented, well clothed, and well fed. Any hints of crises to come lay buried in unread reports and charts.

The *Sentinel*, commemorating the state school's quarter-century mark, was pleased with the seeming success of the enterprise:

> Friendly cooperation between the school and the town has marked the first twenty-five years of its history. . . . This cooperation was most apparent at the time of the [1938] hurricane. When public utility electric service here failed, the town could easily have been up against it as to water, were it not for the emergency electric line from the state school pump house to the water district pump house, enabling electricity generated at the school to be used in running the district pumps. . . .
>
> Be it also said that the town could never have weathered the financial depression as well as it has, were it not for the State school payroll.
>
> There have been human factors involved, too, for the school is not just so many buildings. The annual exhibits at the school . . . have been presentations of which to be proud, the entertainments open to the public bring back pleasant memories, while the Fourth of July parades have been quite marvelous. On the afternoon of the Washington Bi-centennial celebration, some of the best floats that day were permitted to come up the street to enhance the beauty of the town parade. And of course the participation of the school personnel in the life of the community has been most pleasing.
>
> "Belchertown may have turned down Amherst College," the *Sentinel* concluded, "but it wasn't quite feebleminded enough to let the State School slip through its fingers."[90]

CHAPTER 4

Working at the State School

For seventy years, Belchertown State School was the largest employer in town. As we've seen, one of the Board of Trade's principal objectives in 1916 in lobbying for the new state school was to create jobs, and within months of its opening in November 1922, the school employed 125 people—30 percent of them residents of Belchertown itself.[1] (Most of the rest came from nearby towns and villages.) This number grew steadily over the years, to approximately two hundred in 1930 and three hundred in 1940. In 1989, when Mary McCarthy, the commissioner of the state's Department of Mental Retardation, announced that the school would soon close, the number of employees was 1,400, including 440 Belchertown residents.[2]

To put these numbers into perspective, the official population of Belchertown in 1920 was only 2,062. This number grew to 3,139 in 1930 and 3,503 in 1940 (due, principally, to the growing resident population of the state school); in 1990 the number was 10,579. Not only was the state school the largest employer in town by a sizeable margin, but its employees represented a significant percentage of the total working population. Indeed, Henry Tadgell, the superintendent from 1943 to 1960, once remarked that it seemed to him (on looking through employees' files) that "most of the people in Belchertown have worked at the institution at some time or other."[3]

There were, broadly, two classes of employees: a small group of administrators, and a much larger group of what today might be called support and direct care staff (such as cooks, seamstresses, farmers, and attendants) who interacted with the school's residents on a daily basis.[4] Many of the direct care staff (particularly in the early decades) lived at the school in one of the employee cottages; most were blue-collar workers with, at most, a high-school education. Hollis Wheeler, a college volunteer who also worked briefly as an attendant and wrote a master's thesis on Belchertown's attendants in 1977, maintained that they came "not just from the working class but from among that group of working class people to whom few if any other jobs are available."[5] This may have been true, especially at the time Wheeler was writing, but it does not mean that the lower-paying positions were wanting for applicants or that those employed in such positions always disliked their jobs. Certainly in the earlier decades, especially for those who received room and board as well as salary, employment at the state school could be sufficiently remunerative as well as challenging. Mickey LaBroad, who went to work at the school in 1932 shortly after graduating from high school, was paid $10.35 per week plus room and board—not a bad compensation package for the time.[6] One former employee, who left his family farm to make more money and worked on the school farm in 1939–40, was paid $12.50 per week plus room and board—good money for the depression years.[7]

Moreover, accommodations at the school were decent by the standards of the day. Rooms in the employee cottages on the main campus (there were singles and doubles) were small but neat and immaculately maintained. A typical double contained a small table, two chairs, two dressers, and two narrow beds; each cottage resident also had a personal closet with a lock.[8] At the farm, employee accommodations were similar. A former farm employee remembered having a private room with steam heat; his room was furnished by the school and cleaned daily by a school resident. There was also a card room downstairs where the farm employees played lots of poker.[9] Meals were served on campus, and at the farm, in dining halls reserved for employees. The food was routinely described by the employees as "abundant," "hearty," "good"—at least by institutional standards.[10] All in all, the former farm employee recalled, it was not a bad life.[11]

Room and board—that is, living on the grounds—meant being on call twenty-four hours a day, seven days a week. When the need arose (fire, snowstorm, missing resident), the employees housed on the grounds were the first to be asked for help. Joe McCrea, the school's head farmer during the 1960s and '70s, lived at the school. His recollection of a Christmas-morning sewer blockage at the infirmary is both representative and a well-told story:

> By noon, there was a full crew of Maintenance men at the building, trying to unplug the sewage system. Shortly after Christmas

dinner . . . my phone rang. The crew had failed to clear the lines and the next step would be to dig up the sewer system outside the building. For this to happen, they needed me to plow the snow off the outside line. . . .

When I got to the site, I went to the second floor to talk to the man in charge [the chief engineer]. He told me to delay the snow plowing because they were in the process of one last attempt before digging. They had their ace man, Jim, a Mechanical Handyman, on the job. Jim had been through this type of trouble before and could work wonders. He seemed to "see" inside of pipes and into every elbow in the building.

When Jim had a free minute, I asked him what was the matter and why the blockage. Then he told me the story of a 12 year old patient who, in the bat of an eye, could flush his blanket down the toilet and cause the whole building to flood. Jim also told me that he tried on numerous occasions to do the same, that is, to flush a blanket down the toilet and could not get half of it into the drainage no matter how hard he tried. Plus, to get half the blanket down, took considerable time. This was a big factor because it was known who the patient was that flushed his blanket and he was under surveillance on all shifts. . . .

"Who is he, Jim?"

"Right over there, Mandrake, the Magician."

I saw a normal size boy standing in the corridor, leaning up against the wall, watching [the] proceedings. He was quite handsome with a sharp eye. He lost some of his normal looks when he would flash his eyes from side to side, drop his head and began shaking his hands and arms rapidly. But, oh how he had foxed the staff and created a show, here on Christmas afternoon. . . .

Within an hour, Jim, a Mandrake in his own right, freed the blanket and all sinks and toilets were back in working order. Now, the clean up would come after six hours of no flushing, water on the floor, foul air and 120 patients anxious to use the facilities. As for the blanket in the pipeline, that would be caught in the first settling bed at the Sewer Plant.[12]

That employment at the school could provide an acceptable career even among the lower-paying jobs is further evidenced by the relatively large number of long-serving employees—many of them married to fellow employees. As of 1944, almost half of the school's staff had been in state service (usually, though not always, only at Belchertown) for five years or more; one in four had been in state service for more than ten years.[13] Laura McLean was typical (though her tenure was longer than most). She worked in the school's clothing department (called the marking room) from 1935 until her retirement in 1967, except for a seven-year break to care for a young daughter. Her husband, Jim, also worked at the school, in the engineering department, for thirty years. When she retired, Laura was charge attendant with jurisdiction over all clothing for the school's 1,500 residents. Her responsibilities included acquisition (clothing was purchased either by the school from state funds, by parents and guardians, or by residents from personal funds), inventory management (all clothing had to be described, recorded, and labeled or marked—hence the name "marking room"), and sewing repairs. Christmas was an especially busy time for her, as the school received up to 1,200 gift packages of clothing that had to be opened, tried on, and inventoried. Laura supervised a staff of five outside employees and twelve residents. She was said to have few interests other than home, family, and work. (At home, she also helped care for a bedridden father.) She was apparently generous with her time— for example, taking older residents on weekly trips to Holyoke for shopping, lunch, and sightseeing. In 1967 she was awarded a plaque (one of five awarded in the state that year) for outstanding public service from the Massachusetts Citizens for the Advancement of Public Service.[14]

Even in the mid-1970s, when staff turnover (particularly in lower-paying positions such as attendant) was especially high, there was a core group of attendants with tenures ranging from ten to forty years (their mean age was fifty-five), as well as a sizeable intermediate group, perhaps a third of the total, with tenures of three to nine years (in this group the mean age was forty). Half of the direct care staff was said to have had a friend or relative working at the school when they took their jobs—not a bad rate of recruitment by word-of-mouth, and further evidence that there were good things to be said about working at Belchertown even in its darkest times.[15] Sometimes employees who left to work in the private sector would later return to work at the school a second time. One such former employee, after a stint in the private sector, went back to work at the school as a driver; he stayed for fourteen years, from 1967 to 1981, living off-campus in a nearby house and commuting by bicycle.[16]

What the direct care staff and support staff did in the course of a typical working day depended, of course, on the job. Most did what those having

comparable jobs outside the state school did. For example, an orchard-
ist might prune and spray fruit trees and pick fruit. A handyman might
plow snow and do other odd jobs around campus. A driver might chauf-
feur the superintendent, drive important visitors to and from the airport,
or transport residents to local medical offices and hospitals for scheduled
appointments and emergency visits.[17]

One "perk" that may have made employment at the state school more
attractive for some than comparable jobs outside the institution was the
availability of competent, unpaid (until the reforms of the 1970s) assistance from residents. "Walter" was typical of that group of residents who
served, unpaid, as "helpers" to the school's regular staff. How he came
to be institutionalized is lost history, but it was said by those who worked
with him that his IQ was "quite high." He worked in the greenhouse and
vegetable storage building. Joe McCrea recalled:

> [Walter] was a valuable asset to our work force. [He] loved to talk
> and it was known that if you worked with Walter, you didn't need
> a radio. He was also meticulous in his daily assignments. One of
> these was to inspect the many shelves of vegetables we had in stor-
> age. He'd go over bins of beets, cabbage, carrots, onions, squash,
> looking for anything that was spotty or needed throwing out.
> While performing this task [on] butternut squash, he had a melon
> scooper that would quickly get out any blemish before it got any
> worse, like a small soft spot or a bruise.
>
> After delivering a load of butternut squash to the Main Kitchen,
> our Vegetable Grower got a call to come to the Kitchen because the
> last load of squash had many areas that they said were "bitten by
> rats!" He quickly convinced them that it wasn't the work of rats,
> but the meticulous work of Walter.[18]

Many helpers became quite good at what they did. One former farm
employee remembers learning how to use a milking machine not from
another staff member but from one of the farm boys.[19]

The job that had no exact counterpart outside of similar institutions was
that of direct care attendant. The formal tasks to be performed by an attendant in a typical day were unremarkable: awaken the residents, supervise
or assist them in getting dressed, send them to the bathroom, dispense
medications, shave the men, mop the dormitory floor, make the beds, collect dirty laundry, serve meals to the residents, supervise or assist them at

meals, rinse dishes, mop the dayroom floor, supervise or assist the residents in showering and brushing their teeth, mop the bathroom floor, supervise or assist the residents in getting undressed, send them to bed, and update ward records and log books.[20] The difficulty—and (sometimes) danger—of this work becomes apparent when one considers the nature of the physical and mental disabilities of the residents being cared for (particularly the most profoundly disabled) and the small number of attendants employed to do such work, relative to the size of the resident population, during most of the school's history.

First, disabilities. Not every one, or even most, of the state school's residents were like the "farm boys" who worked on the school farm: sometimes slower to learn than those on the outside, but eminently teachable, physically healthy, reasonably self-sufficient, and hard working. Robert Francis, after his brief stint as an attendant in M Building in 1931, wrote about the first time he saw the residents of his building:

> They sat crowded on the bench that ran round the walls [of the building's lower day hall], and it needed but a glance to see that they were of all grades and varieties. . . . There were several Mongolian idiots, one little negro cripple who had had rickets, boys who could not speak, one boy who whimpered incessantly with a sound and an expression that was two thirds weeping and one third laughing, another boy who liked to totter up to me in order to caress the lapels of my coat and lay his head on my breast, dwarfs, clowns out of Shakespeare, and one pathetic figure with a long, narrow face who had been a chimney sweep in Dickens' day. It was this boy who had charge of a hapless tot whose nose was painted with mercurochrome. The only other very little boy sat grinning and seemingly trying to look at one eye with the other, while the boy beside him held his hands and kept them dangling.[21]

An area college student I'll call RB, who volunteered at the school in the early 1960s, later described some of the physical disabilities of the children with whom he worked: "There was a building [the infirmary] devoted to kids with major physical disabilities—hydrocephalic kids, severely Mongoloid, and an amazing number of kids whose disabilities were so unique and intense that I can't even think of words for them. Small birdlike infants; kids with stick-thin arms and legs and large heads who could not even sit up—disabilities so various and extreme that one would never have expected their existence."[22]

Ruth Sienkiewicz-Mercer, who was not mentally retarded but was severely crippled by cerebral palsy and unable to feed herself or talk, was a resident of Ward 4 of the infirmary in the early 1960s. She lived there with thirty other women, most of them suffering from a combination of physical handicap and mental retardation. Writing about her experience many years later, she called Ward 4, with its "staggering array of crippled bodies and damaged minds," a "human wasteland":

> There were many people on Ward 4 I will never forget because their behavior nearly drove me crazy. One of these was a girl I'll call Valerie, one of the ambulatory people on the ward. She was about a year older than me, and was very small. Valerie's bed was near mine and always smelled awful because of a particularly repulsive habit of hers: she liked to stick her hands into her diapers, extract her own excrement, and smear it all over herself, her bed, and whatever else she could reach. She also liked to eat soap.[23]

Hollis Wheeler, recalling her experiences as a volunteer and attendant, describes the behavioral problems of another group of mentally disabled adolescents she encountered (and the comments of an attendant who worked with them): "Two 'hyperactive' boys; a 'projectile vomiter' who can vomit at will; two 'grabbers' ('He may look small, but he's so strong if he grabs your hair, forget it, you'll [never] get his hand out, ya' just have to cut your hair'); an extremely self-abusive girl who tears open her own flesh; a self-abusive boy who has banged his head on walls several hundreds of times in a day (according to actual count)."[24]

William Fraenkel, the state's assistant commissioner of mental retardation (he later became the school's interim superintendent), spent twenty-four hours observing in Belchertown's back wards (where the most profoundly retarded persons lived) in 1969. He described a resident he met there who often ate floor tiles—as well as plaster, paint, toilet paper, and glass. He would crumble Christmas ornaments in his hand and chew them up. Another "urinate[d] throughout the day room over any one who [came] his way."[25]

In addition to such "sorry sights" and foul smells, there was noise. Ruth Sienkiewicz-Mercer writes:

> [Daisy] was a short, fat woman with heavy hips and large breasts. She liked to moo at regular intervals throughout the day. Every half hour she let go a moo-ooo-oo that would have fooled a farmer.

Daisy's mooing was so regular that the staff used to call her the alarm cow.

One ambulatory woman [was] called "the Siren." [She] was the most accomplished of the ward's sizeable contingent of screamers. Without any particular pattern or frequency, she would suddenly rip off high-pitched, ear-piercing screams.

About half the people on [the ward] talked to themselves, mumbling semi-intelligent comments to nobody in particular. "I am called Dad, I am called Dad" was what one woman said to herself all day long, day in and day out. Since some of the other residents were prone to echolalia—repeating what they had just heard someone else say—an "I am called Dad" chorus sometimes would bounce around the ward like some crazy version of "Row, Row, Row Your Boat." On other days I heard "Hello, goodbye, hello, goodbye" being repeated for hours on end.[26]

In short (to repeat RB's haunting phrase), disabilities so various and extreme that one would never have expected their existence.

Second, numbers. In 1970, after staffing levels had improved for several years, the staff-to-resident ratio was 1 to 2. This might sound like a very ample number, but it is not the ratio of attendant staff to resident population; it is total staff to resident population. Thus it includes managers and many support personnel (such as kitchen and maintenance staff) with little or no direct care responsibility. Round-the-clock direct care had to be provided seven days a week, on three shifts (day, evening, and night), and an employee working a forty-hour week could cover only five shifts. So although the overall staff-to-resident ratio at this time was 1 to 2, in the back wards the actual ratio of attendants to residents time was 1 to 40 during the day and 1 to 60 at night.[27] Now let's go back a bit. Until the late 1960s, the overall ratio of staff to residents was only around 1 to 5—in effect, for every hundred residents there were thirty fewer employees than in 1970. Even in the school's early years, when some employees worked sixty-hour weeks and didn't get vacations for three or four years at a stretch, the direct-care ratio must have been even worse than it was in 1970.[28]

And what was it like for a staff member providing direct care to residents at a time when the overall ratio was 1 to 2? Imagine a primary school teacher responsible for a class of forty. Now imagine that all forty have learning disabilities, some are hyperactive, many are actually physically mature men and women. Now add a projectile vomiter, a couple of grabbers, a self-abusive girl who tears her own flesh, a boy who bangs his head on the wall hundreds of times a day, perhaps a serial urinator. Now further imagine that you, alone, are responsible for awakening, bathing, shaving, brushing the teeth of, taking to the toilet, dressing, feeding, medicating, and putting to bed each of these forty individuals, as well as rinsing their dirty dishes, sorting their laundry, and mopping the day room and bathroom floors. Alone. (Well, not quite alone. There are two other attendants in the room with you, and the actual number of persons that the three of you care for is 120; 40 is just the average number per attendant.)

In these circumstances, it should not surprise us that education was a secondary concern of the attendants, that control—and personal safety—were paramount.

Control of residents was maintained in three distinct ways: by structuring their physical environment to restrict freedom of movement and individuality, by establishing routines and schedules that dealt with residents in groups rather than individually, and by punishing disobedient residents (and rewarding obedient ones).[29] In addition, mention should be made of tranquilizing drugs, the use of which became widespread by the 1970s and continued for many years; and the rhetoric of childhood, whereby grown men and women were routinely addressed and treated as children.

Everything about the physical environment of Belchertown State School emphasized control, beginning with the school's isolation on an eight-hundred-acre plot of land on the outskirts of a small town in a remote part of Massachusetts. Buildings were set far apart from one another; one needed a vehicle to move efficiently about campus. Many buildings were locked; unless one had a key, one had to ring a bell to gain entrance. Even within buildings, the doors to individual wards (as well as to closets, toilets, and other rooms) were closed and locked all day. Windows were covered with bars. Stairways were encased in heavy wire mesh. Rooms where residents lived were large and barren—dozens sleeping together in open wards on metal-frame beds set end to end with little space between them. "On occasion a resident with a bed in the far end of the room must crawl over the tops of other beds to reach it," Hollis Wheeler noted.[30] William Fraenkel reported that he once asked an attendant whether a room could be partitioned, to provide some privacy. The answer was no, because the staff would lose the ability "to control them. . . . If you do that, we'll need more manpower because you'll make them into smaller groups."[31] There were few wall decorations and no carpets. In the day rooms, televisions were secured inside wire cabinets; light switches were located high off the ground and often required keys to turn lights on and off. Even toilets needed keys to flush them. Outside, some playgrounds were locked as well as fenced in.

It has been said that the most efficient, though not humane, way to get done the many tasks that need to be performed in a given day in a residential institution for mentally retarded persons is to "establish structured routines and schedules whereby residents are treated en masse."[32] Certainly, for most of its history, Belchertown State School conformed to this pattern. Residents were wakened, bathed, dressed, fed, toileted, instructed, exercised, entertained, undressed, and put back to bed at the same times every day, together, in large groups. One observer recorded a description of lunch in the mid-1970s; the structured routine is emblematic, even though the numbers are unrepresentative (the number of residents at the meal is smaller than was typical for most of the school's history):

> At approximately 10:30 a.m., two staff members began to prepare for the meal, which is served on the ward. They line up three tables and 14 chairs by a far wall in the room. The tables are covered with bath towels. One attendant goes to the kitchen, a small room located off to the side of the dayroom and returns with bowls, spoons, and two large pitchers of milk. The other begins to call the 14 residents to the tables. This attendant proceeds to tie towels around the residents' necks as they sit down. He then goes to the kitchen, returning with two loaves of bread. The two attendants spread the bowls out on one of the tables. Each takes a loaf of bread and begins to break the bread into small pieces which they put into the bowls. After all of the bread has been distributed, they pour the milk into the bowls. Then they serve a bowl to each resident. Most of the residents eat quickly. One attendant prods slow eaters. He points to the one resident's bowl, and says firmly, "Eat! Eat!" He grabs the resident's spoon and forces one spoonful after another into the resident's mouth. He does the same with another resident. The attendants gather the bowls after the residents have finished their milk and bread, take them to the kitchen to be rinsed, and return with the bowls.

This routine is twice repeated, first with cake and water, then with stew and squash.

> When one resident refuses to eat [the mix of stew and squash]
> after being instructed to do so, the attendant feeds him, again
> rapidly, allowing only three seconds between the large spoonfuls
> of food. As this attendant feeds the resident, he remarks to the
> observer: "Are you gonna tell them what to do or are you gonna let
> them tell you; you gotta show them who's boss. . . ."
>
> After the residents have finished, the attendants send them
> from the tables, collect the bowls . . . and spoons and take them
> to the kitchen to be washed, throw the towels into a large laundry
> bag, clean the tables, and sweep the floor. It is now 11:15.[33]

The utilization of structured routines and schedules was not confined to meals; it pervaded every aspect of life at Belchertown. Fraenkel used language befitting a car wash to describe the bathing routine he witnessed in 1969: "See fifty nude men huddled together in the shower. Two showerheads go full blast. The cleaners wash the men. Soap and brush do their job. Two other men sit on the floor, waiting to be cleaned up."[34] Entire wards of residents would be "tripped" to the bathroom at scheduled times during the day.[35] Instruction, therapy, exercise, recreation, and entertainment were done mostly as group activities. According to Ruth Sienkiewicz-Mercer, even walks outdoors only occurred en masse, at least in the early 1960s: "Nobody left the building, even to go out for some fresh air, unless the whole ward went out, and that happened only two or three times all summer."[36]

A third mechanism for maintaining control was to punish disobedient residents and reward obedient ones. Forms of punishment included physical force (slapping, hitting), physical restraint (straitjackets, tying to chairs), seclusion rooms, confinement to back wards, forced maintenance of uncomfortable positions for long periods of time, and withholding of privileges. Robert Francis described one common form of punishment he witnessed that was routinely administered to boys in his building who made too much noise:

> "Shut up!" cried Miss L again. "Shut up and fold your arms!"
>
> In a twinkling she had grabbed a boy and pulled him to his
> knees on the floor.
>
> "Hold up your hands and keep them there until I tell you to take
> them down!" she snapped in a breath.
>
> The supervisor had told me that the boys could be effectively
> punished by depriving them of desserts and other privileges. Miss
> B had told me not to punish boys myself but to report them to

her or to whoever was in charge. But the other attendants seemed
uninterested either in reporting boys or in depriving them of privileges. It was quicker to fling a boy to the floor and threaten him to
hold his hands up. Striking a boy was against the law, but pulling
him to the floor was not interpreted as "striking." It was a frequent
sight to see one or more boys on their knees in the middle of the
room, pilloried against the air.[37]

Residents who wandered off the grounds or tried to escape were always
treated as "escapees" and punished if they were caught. Typically, until the
1970s, punishment included solitary confinement in a "seclusion room"—
a bare, unpadded cell with no toilet, not even a bucket for human waste—
for at least three days. The escapee would also be "marked" in some fashion
and have "privileges," such as watching movies or getting passes to go outside, restricted. "Marking" meant having one's head shaved in a distinctive
pattern like a pie-shaped wedge, or, in later years, wearing striped overalls
for a month. The most notorious example of punishment for wandering off
involved a relatively intelligent male resident who was confined to the back
ward for profoundly retarded men for two years (see chapter 6).[38]

Even if punishment was not always egregious or excessive, it was common. The state commission that investigated the school in 1971 reported
that incidents of punishment and prolonged discipline were "frequent,
open and notorious."[39] Punishment was administered, or threatened,
even for the most trivial matters. For example, an attendant on one ward
was overheard threatening a resident who sat slumped in his chair as fol-
lows: "Do you wanna be tied in the chair? You'd better sit up or I'll tie
you in that chair!"[40] Being tied into chairs was, apparently, a particularly
common form of punishment (or preventive detention). Fraenkel reported
"six women tied by the waist to a bench."[41] Another observer described
how a woman who stole food from other residents was tied up: "One leg
was bound to the bench, the other leg was crossed over the first. A rope
was tied to her arm, then tied again to the bench. Her other arm was tied
behind her to the back of the bench."[42]

Even residents who weren't actually tied down might be forced to stay
in a specific place for long periods of time. On one ward, an observer in
1975 reported that all but three of the fifteen residents were required to
stay seated all day, except when they obtained permission to move, to prevent them from "caus[ing] trouble."[43] There is a remarkable continuity
here between 1931 and 1975.

The use of drugs to tranquilize—or control—residents of the school is not well documented. We know, however, that tranquilizing drugs were widely used at similar institutions elsewhere, and there is anecdotal evidence of their widespread use at Belchertown as well.[44] The state's investigative commission reported in 1971 that "until recently, Belchertown had the highest reported incidence of physical and chemical restraint of any State school."[45] A researcher in the mid-1970s reported that a "sizeable number" of residents—one-third at least on some wards—regularly received tranquilizing drugs to "calm them down." Additional sedatives were administered as needed to deal with "problematic" behavior.[46] Whether drugs were also prescribed merely to control residents—that is, to keep them docile and easier to handle for the convenience of the staff— is less clear but seems likely, as an exchange between one researcher and a member of the staff suggests:

> (Staff) They (physicians) tend to order medicine just from what we tell them without seeing the patient first. I'm pretty observant when it comes to knowing that something is wrong with the inmates, but I'm not the doctor.
>
> (Observer) Are medicines used to control the patients' behavior?
>
> (Staff) Yes, and sometimes that's not good. . . . These kids need something to control their behavior other than the constant use of drugs.[47]

That residents were in any event often overmedicated may be inferred from a passage in the school's annual report for 1974, stating that after review with physicians of all medications then being dispensed to residents, "a number of them have been reduced or eliminated."[48]

Indeed, dispensing tranquilizers and others medications may have been an even larger part of an attendant's daily routine than the foregoing discussion would suggest. William Fraenkel reported that giving out medications was the first order of business at 5 a.m., after the residents were wakened. A former employee, asked to describe daily responsibilities, mentioned medications almost at the top of the list, ahead of feeding.[49]

Employing the rhetoric of childhood—that is, talking to and treating adults as children—whether or not it was intended as such, was one more technique to control residents. Regardless of age, successive generations of residents were referred to and treated as children by employees. A twenty-year-old attendant would scold a resident "easily 25 years her senior": "You just sit right there and don't move, little girl."[50] Whether they were eight or eighty, residents were always "girls" and "boys."

(Staff to resident) Now, now. Give those shoes to me like a good boy and go downstairs now.

(Staff to observer) He's such a shy boy, but good.

(Staff to residents) Boys! Do you remember yesterday? Let's all remember yesterday and do our best to be good today. OK?

(Staff to resident) If you're gonna act like a baby, I'm gonna treat you like a baby.

(Staff to resident who puts clothes in a laundry bag) Good boy! Good boy! (Pats resident's head).

(Staff to observer) They're all good kids here.[51]

Adult wards, when decorated at all, were decorated with paintings of cartoon characters. Adult residents were given toy cars, trucks, dolls, and soldiers to play with; for some, these were their only personal possessions. Often, adults were allowed outdoors only in large groups—there to engage in "kid" activities: to ride the swings or carousel or use the playground slide. Clothing, too, was often, as one observer noted, "age-inappropriate." Adults who were not able to use the toilet on their own weren't allowed to wear underwear. Elderly men and women were dressed in tennis shoes, bobby socks, "loud" slacks, and t-shirts with slogans. Clothing, even when it was age-appropriate, was often baggy and ill-fitting.[52] Women were all given Buster Brown haircuts because it was "easier" to do than anything else.[53]

Maintaining control, of course, had legitimate purposes beyond staff convenience or getting one's job done more efficiently. Belchertown State School could be a dangerous place to live and work. Violent residents might harm themselves, other residents, or staff. Personal safety—of residents as well as employees—was, therefore, a proper concern.

Certain residents were prone to dangerous self-abuse. Head banging seems to have been a not infrequent problem. Ruth Sienkiewicz-Mercer tells of two nine-year-old girls, Carla and Patty, who lived on her ward during the first summer she was at the school. Like Valerie, the female resident Sienkiewicz-Mercer described in a passage quoted earlier in this chapter, these girls would reach into their diapers to extract excrement that they would then smear over themselves and their surroundings, and they also repeatedly banged their heads against the wall. The staff, needing to prevent the girls from seriously hurting themselves and unable to curb their behavior in any psychological way, improvised a solution: "They placed boxing gloves on their hands to keep them from going into their diapers, and they strapped hockey helmets on their heads to prevent them from cracking their skulls open." According to Sienkiewicz-Mercer, it took three years of wearing the gloves and helmets, but the targeted behavior did eventually stop.[54]

Residents could also be violent to one another. William Fraenkel reported seeing residents repeatedly "shoving and hitting each other." In another instance, a resident ward worker could not get his shoe off to clean it; he put his shod foot in a toilet bowl to wash it, then removed the shoe and used it "to hit [other residents] to get them to sit together to get ready for breakfast."[55] Those prone to violence against other residents (as well as those who were not necessarily violent but whose behavior could be intimidating to others) were sometimes kept in straitjackets for long periods of time. Though such restraint seems cruel, the potential victims were often grateful. Again, Ruth Sienkiewicz-Mercer provides useful perspective. Valerie, Carla, and Patty, the three women on Ruth's ward, all ambulatory, who regularly smeared excrement about the ward, fouling the air, were more generally intimidating to the nonambulatory residents merely by their presence. Patty was also a serial vomiter.

> These three very sick girls were placed in straitjackets in the fall of 1962, about four months after I came to Ward 4. They were still wearing them when I left the ward in June 1963. I can't say I was happy to see them restrained, but I was relieved by it. Although none of them ever harmed me or anyone else on the ward that I know of, I would have been an easy target if they ever got the urge to come visit. Lying on my back in bed, I was defenseless. The straitjackets offered at least a measure of safety for these girls, as well as for potential victims like me. The mere fact that they were no longer doing such terrible things eliminated one nightmare from the ward.[56]

Finally, residents could be violent toward the attendants who cared for them. Hollis Wheeler, the student researcher who worked for a time on the wards, was at first suspicious of what she thought was a "disproportionate" amount of time spent by the attendants discussing violent residents and how to manage them. But once she had worked for two weeks as an attendant, she changed her mind. "I learned that all attendants have personal experience with actual violence however 'mild,' as I came to have. More consequential . . . , violence is potentially *always* present and, like fear of 'catching something,' becomes part of the attendants' orientation to the residents and the job, and a perpetual problem to be coped with."[57]

The violence could be extreme; for example, a resident suddenly throwing a bureau drawer at an attendant.[58] But even lower levels of violence, or mere threatening behavior, could be intimidating. Wheeler relates three such incidents:

> We were all crowded around in the office including a couple of attendants from second shift, and Fannie (resident) got mad at Karina (attendant), so she gave *me* a sharp rap on the shoulder blade. Also, this morning Danny made me a little nervous, first pulling my hair softly, then harder and harder till it hurt, then grabbing my "granny bun" and ripping it apart.
>
> This morning Ricardo (resident), a huge hulking guy, was crying hard on his bed before breakfast. I said, "What's the matter, Ricardo, what is it?" and lightly touched his shoulder, but kept my arm extended. He jumped out of the bed screaming at the top of his lungs, ran halfway across the room and hurled himself onto the floor, sliding a couple of feet. I tried to stay cool, but he was between me and the two doors and he weighs about 250 pounds. . . . [After Ricardo ran off down the stairs] I went to the clothing room and told Gloria, with my heart pounding.[59]

Were the attendants cruel? Some certainly were, although indifference rather than cruelty was the more prevalent abuse. A former employee who worked at the school from 1942 to 1976 told an interviewer in 1992, "They had rules down there, and regulations, and [none of the employees] went against those. The abuse of a patient came up from time to time, but that was dealt with."[60] The description quoted earlier of how certain residents were fed is one small example of indifference and cruelty commingling.

There were also acts of kindness. Ruth Sienkiewicz-Mercer remembers a tiny sixteen-year-old resident on her ward named Debbie who awoke one night screaming, for no apparent reason. She continued screaming for hours, keeping everyone awake, until sheer exhaustion wore her down to a whimper. Then an attendant took Debbie tenderly in her arms and rocked her "like a baby for over an hour until she quieted down completely."[61] Similarly, the "light touch" of the attendant on sobbing Ricardo's shoulder was surely a gesture of sympathy and concern. Albert Warner, whom we met in the previous chapter, suffered his share of abuse when he was a resident during the 1920s and '30s, but nevertheless years later remembered many of the school's employees as "caring people" who "kept us from falling apart."[62]

A story recounted by Joe McCrea, the school's head farmer, shows how "caring people" who took the time could keep one from "falling apart." The resident called here T had no known family and only one person outside the institution who ever contacted him (T called her his "aunt"); once a year, at Christmas, this woman would mail him a card. The card, McCrea reported, would transform him; he'd carry it in his back left pocket everywhere he went, until "by the Fourth of July, the card (and envelope) would show the ravages of time." T worked on the school farm.

> I drove into the Farm yard after lunch one day and heard a lot of shouting. Four patients were trying to talk at once. There was a problem. [T] refused to go to work with [BR, another resident] and the team of horses to pick up brush. All of the crew were getting their two cents into the shouting. The main concern: if [T] didn't go to work, he'd soon be doing anything he wanted and would end up a lazy nothing and a million more inequities. No one could figure out what had caused [his] problem and with [his] quietness, no one was ever going to find out. Something triggered his deep, dark mood.
>
> I got out of my pickup truck and entered into the fray.
>
> "You've got to do something with him," came the general consensus. . . . "Take him up the Hill to the Doctor. He'll fix him!"
>
> [T] remained still and only added a few of his "B'gawd's." He started most of his sentences with "B'gawd—" . . .

McCrea ordered a startled T to "get in the truck." But instead of taking him "up the Hill," McCrea took T for a long drive around town and around the town lake, bought him a large ice cream cone, and gradually calmed him down.

> We came back into the Institution the back way and I told him it was time to get back and help [BR]. B'gawd, he fully agreed and was anxious to get back. There was a lot to do. We drove down to our dump, where [BR] and the crew were piling brush high in the center where it would wait for a rainy day and a fire permit to burn.

> Out jumped [T] and he went right over to the wagon and began
> throwing brush up onto the pile. I turned and left.[63]

As in many workplaces, coffee breaks were a welcome respite from the
pressures of working at the state school. In addition to providing a little down time in which to unwind, they were the chief means by which
information and gossip about the school was communicated among the
employees. They also fostered camaraderie, particularly among the old-
timers. The day staff got two breaks, one in the morning and one in the
afternoon. Popular venues for these breaks included the basement of the
infirmary, the storehouse, the main kitchen (especially on doughnut-mak-
ing days) and the blacksmith shop located at the bottom of the maintenance building. "Dan, our Blacksmith, was quite eloquent and had a 'million' stories about the Town, old friends, drinking buddies, events, fairs,
harness horse racing and on and on," McCrea recalled. "His shop made
an ideal place to swing by for a coffee break or just to get the news, fresh
and correct. On a hot summer day, Dan would have his big fan on and in
winter, he'd fire up his forge with coke and have the Shop toasty warm."[64]

Dan made coffee the "cowboy" way: in an Army canteen cup with
brazed-on handle, water heated by an acetylene torch "brought to a rolling
boil and ready to serve." You brought your own cup; Dan provided milk
and sugar, free of charge. (Some brought their own coffee, too; apparently, the "cowboy" brew wasn't everyone's favorite.)

Another anecdote related by McCrea, a frequent visitor to the forge,
nicely illustrates the camaraderie that could flow from daily coffee breaks
like those in Dan's blacksmith shop:

> One Monday in November, Dan brought in a big wooden crate.
> . . . His blond Labrador Retriever would need shelter for the winter
> and Dan began by tar-papering the top to keep out the rain and
> snow. A Carpenter, there on break, said, "That's a flat roof and
> it won't shed water. You wait. I'll fix that." So, during his noon
> hour, he sawed out 2" by 2" sticks to make the roof rafters for the
> dog house. The next day, up went the rafters at a 45 degree angle
> and the roof was finished with ½" marine plywood, complete with
> good overhang on all sides. When the Roofer saw this, he said,
> "I've got a square of blue shingles home and I'll put them on. It
> will look better in your back yard." Before shingling, he did all
> of the roof's edging with aluminum sheeting, used caulking and

tar when needed and proceeded to do a first class job of roofing, complete with drip edge and a solid cap.[65]

Someone then insulated the crate with material from an old freezer unit. Another contributed an old rug with thick pile for the floor so that the retriever could have a warm, soft bed. The school's electrician wired the house, installing a 40-watt light bulb for heat "if needed" and a small attic fan "for warm summer days." "The men thought the original box didn't have a good enough finish for the outside, so material was cut for the sides and ends and fully edged to form a fine seal against any wind. A Plexiglas door was made to allow light, and it was hinged at the top so that the dog was free to come and go from his new home."

The construction crew was still not finished. They placed the structure on a base of two 4x4 fence posts, to which they screwed four brass handles so that the whole thing could be easily lifted or moved. Finally, they painted it a "pleasing gray," to complement the blue roof, added white trim, and painted the door frame beige.

> Winter came, as always. Dan told us how happy he and the dog were to have such a Taj Mahal. The coffee breaks were back to routine, too much so.
>
> Someone spread the false story that Dan had poisoned the dog and sold the dog house for a huge sum. This tale would not go to rest until Dan, using vacation time one day, brought his dog in for evidence and a picture of the dwelling, set really in his backyard.

If the rhetoric of childhood infantilized the school's residents, creating a parent-child model of authority between them and their caregivers regardless of physical age, it also implied other, more tender attributes of a parent-child relationship, including nurture, caring, love, teaching, expectations of growth, and a measure of protectiveness.[66] It was common, for example, for attendants to have favorites or "pets." Some would even take favorite residents home with them for a day, to give them a break from the school, or otherwise pay them special attention and do special favors for them.[67] Ruth Sienkiewicz-Mercer remembers as "one of the best days" of her life a Christmas shopping trip that an attendant took her on to a Springfield mall (see chapter 7). As much as getting out, the event was probably memorable for being a rare moment of sustained, one-on-one attention.

A difficult time for sensitive members of the staff was when expectations of further "growth" for a particular resident were dashed. It was hard in such circumstances for attendants to sustain enthusiasm; when they didn't see continuing development, they sometimes lost interest in the individual. One young attendant told Hollis Wheeler that her attitude had changed from "initially being idealistic and spending virtually all her time trying to interact, work with, and teach residents, to eventually getting frustrated with the infinitesimally small return on her huge input of physical and emotional energy."[68]

Employees were prohibited from giving residents gifts. For a number of years, in lieu of gifts, they would pool their funds and sponsor an annual Christmas entertainment. One year there was a magician and banjo player, another an acrobatic troupe from Holyoke that also sang, danced, whistled, and played bagpipes.[69] In 1928 the *Sentinel* reporter who covered these events was particularly smitten with a violin and harmonica performance by a certain Andrew Minnie. "No matter in what position he placed himself, the violin still kept going and no matter how hard he danced, the harmonica kept playing." Apparently, though, the residents preferred an (unnamed) comedian who performed with Minnie, wearing a size 25 shirt, size 15 pants, crumpled hat, and long hook nose. Two shows were given so that all could attend.[70]

Sometimes the employees entertained the residents themselves. For example, in the spring of 1932 they staged their own minstrel show, distinct from the annual minstrels featuring resident performers. Dr. Westwell, "in costume," directed.[71] They also had their own orchestra or band, which provided music for theatrical productions staged by the residents and played at school dances.[72] Finally, the employees would, on occasion, take up collections for particular causes, such as the $90 they raised in 1946 to promote scouting at the school.[73]

Employee morale varied widely, depending on the period; it was relatively high in the early years, relatively low in the 1970s. But even in the darkest times, there seems to have existed a genuine camaraderie, especially among the longer-serving staff. An early illustration is a scavenger hunt in the mid-1930s: a group of thirty employees in two teams participated in the hunt (conducted in the town itself), followed by a trip to nearby Ludlow for a steak dinner at a restaurant called The Homestead (where their booty was displayed and explained) and a game of Consequences after dinner.[74] A later example would be the building of the doghouse for

Dan the blacksmith's Labrador retriever. And, throughout the years, the employees would hold farewell parties for departing or retiring colleagues.

Morale was probably at its lowest in the 1970s, as an excerpt from a later blog by one of the school's former direct care workers attests. The blogger is Charles Caron, a college graduate with a bachelor's degree in psychology who went to work at Belchertown as a direct care attendant in 1976. He calls his years at the state school some of the most difficult of his career—not because of the work itself, but because of the constant battle he says he was engaged in to protect the residents from "the system" that was supposed to be protecting them:

> We had corrupt management. We had a corrupt union. We had corrupt law enforcement. We had supervisors beat[en] down by the failure of higher powers to hold management accountable. If you did as I did and brought attention to problems, you were harassed and threatened. The residents had no voice, the staff was silenced, and authority was corrupt. It was institutionalized corruption.
>
> The real tragedy was [that] without the institution, the residents had nothing. They were at the mercy of numerous little "institutions" with little oversight. Many were "communitized" and fell through the cracks. There was no central place of refuge. Quality of life was seriously in decline. There was an alternative.
>
> The facility should have been turned into a real school. A place where real skills and abilities could be acquired. For some it would be a place to learn employability/life skills and others a place to learn how to take off their socks. It would be a refuge from the outside world, a place where they could be with others accepting of their conditions. It could have been a place of inspiration and rehabilitation.[75]

This may be an extreme example of low morale, but it is not unrepresentative of the 1970s—which, as we will see, was a period of intense public scrutiny and criticism following sensational revelations of inferior care at the school.

Building K, shown here under construction in 1922, was the first men's dormitory built at the Belchertown State School. Originally designed for 145 beds, it eventually became the notorious men's "back ward" and was demolished in 1977.

Early school administrators insisted that much of the labor performed by residents was done in the spirit of play rather than work. "Kill the Kaiser" was a game invented by Arthur Westwell, the school's dentist, for clearing a field of stones. Boys would pick up stones in a given area and throw them at an effigy of Kaiser Wilhelm until all of the stones were collected near the effigy, and then "bury" the Kaiser by piling the stones into a makeshift marker.

—COURTESY CLAPP MEMORIAL LIBRARY, BELCHERTOWN.

The entrance to Belchertown State School's first administration building, completed in 1928. One of the women's dormitories, Building D, can be seen in the distance.

—COURTESY CLAPP MEMORIAL LIBRARY, BELCHERTOWN.

Dinner in one of the women's buildings in the late 1920s or early 1930s. Food was prepared for residents at a central kitchen and delivered to the various dormitories. Note the Buster Brown haircuts on most of the women—the preferred style because it was said to be easier for the staff to do than anything else.

—COURTESY CLAPP MEMORIAL LIBRARY, BELCHERTOWN.

Fourth of July float, 1928. For a quarter century, beginning in 1924, the school staged a yearly Fourth of July parade. Floats, drawn by horses or cattle and manned by school residents, were a regular feature. The parade was watched by school residents and employees and their friends and families, as well as by town dignitaries.

—COURTESY CLAPP MEMORIAL LIBRARY, BELCHERTOWN.

"Priscilla and John Alden" float, around 1928. The "parading" of residents before the town may have disturbing undertones for modern-day observers, but no such discomfort was expressed at the time. Also unremarked was the irony of residents who were strictly segregated by sex in their daily lives posing as the lovers immortalized in Longfellow's famous poem.

—COURTESY CLAPP MEMORIAL LIBRARY, BELCHERTOWN.

Prizes were awarded each year for the best floats. The second-place winners in this photo, taken around 1928, seem to have been part of an Indian-themed float.

—COURTESY CLAPP MEMORIAL LIBRARY, BELCHERTOWN.

For many years the school regularly staged musical productions using resident performers, the most extravagant of which was an annual minstrel show. Anywhere from 36 to 140 residents participated, and the public attended in large numbers. Shown here is a production from the early 1930s, probably the minstrel show; starting in 1928, performances were also staged outside the school for patients at state and veterans' hospitals in the area.

—COURTESY CLAPP MEMORIAL LIBRARY, BELCHERTOWN.

A curtain call at a 1930s musical—possibly the minstrel show. Productions were originally staged in a makeshift assembly hall that was part of the school's laundry building. In 1932 the school built a new schoolhouse with a permanent assembly hall seating twelve hundred. It included a large stage, dressing rooms, storage rooms, and up-to-date stage equipment.

—COURTESY CLAPP MEMORIAL LIBRARY, BELCHERTOWN.

Opening day of the school's carousel, October 17, 1948. The Belchertown State School acquired a Stein & Goldstein carousel for the residents in 1948. It was originally set up in a pine grove beyond the employees' parking lot but was later relocated to a prefabricated metal pavilion to protect it from inclement weather. After the school closed in 1992, the carousel's horses were auctioned off and the proceeds deposited in a trust fund to support former residents.

—COURTESY MASSACHUSETTS DEPARTMENT OF DEVELOPMENTAL SERVICES.

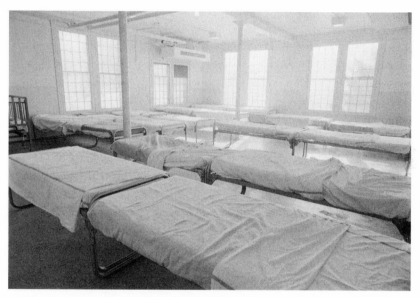

James Shanks reported in his 1970 exposé of conditions at Belchertown State School that men slept in large barracks, beds touching head to foot, with only a narrow twelve-inch aisle separating rows. Sometimes residents had to climb over one another to get to and from their beds.

The state school was closed in 1992. Most of the buildings on the main campus are now boarded or bricked up, abandoned, and overgrown with weeds. Efforts to reuse or redevelop the facility have so far failed.   —PHOTO BY WILL HORNICK.

Albert Warner and his wife, Agnes, former state school residents, successfully lobbied to restore the school cemetery, where over two hundred residents, many of them friends and acquaintances, were buried.

A monument naming those buried in the Warner Pine Grove Cemetery was erected in 1987 at the behest of Albert Warner. Still not satisfied, Warner continued to lobby on behalf of his interred friends until, in 1994, the state of Massachusetts agreed to place a granite marker on each gravesite with the deceased's name and dates. —PHOTO BY AUTHOR.

CHAPTER 5

Family and Friends

Benjamin Ricci and his wife, Virginia, were expecting their first child. It was May 1947 and Ben, who had finished high school in 1941 and served his country honorably in World War II, was now a freshman at Springfield College in western Massachusetts. Like most expectant parents, he and Ginnie were full of hope and expectations for their future life and the life of their soon-to-be-born child. Robert Simpson Ricci was born May 12. "We soon settled into our small, Springfield College trailer home with our new baby," Ricci later wrote. "In a scene strikingly similar to those on thousands of American college and university campuses during those immediate post-war years, the campus trailer parks and Veterans' Villages were abundantly populated with babies and small children. In just such settings, comparisons with the kids next door were inevitable. . . . [Our] pediatrician confirmed our suspicion that Bobby was 'not progressing normally.' "[1]

Among other physical and neuromuscular disabilities, Bobby could not suck through the nipple on his formula bottle. In order to feed him, his parents would have to press thumb and index finger on the sides of his cheeks, causing him to purse his lips over the nipple and, if the maneuver worked, ingest the contents of his bottle. The process was "laborious and slow." It often failed. The parents grew frustrated. Two pediatricians whom they consulted offered sharply contrary assessments. Don't worry, one said; Bobby will "become a basketball star." He isn't normal, the other said; when he's older he should be tested at Children's Hospital in Boston.

Meanwhile, stress levels in the Ricci trailer home were high. Bobby required constant attention—so much so that Ginnie almost missed Ben's

[69]

Springfield College graduation ceremony in 1949 because sitters were
reluctant to stay with the boy even for a few hours. The subsequent birth of
two other sons in October 1949 and May 1952—both "robust, alert, quick-
to-learn, abundantly cheerful" boys—further heightened family tensions.
Bobby's hyperactivity increased. A family physician recommended glu-
tamic acid, available at the hefty price of $28 per gallon. They had to force
feed it to Bobby, who gagged with every sip. The exercise was physically
and emotionally draining on both sides; Bobby showed no improvement
and the "treatment" was abandoned.

In 1952, when Bobby was five years old, the Riccis took him to Boston
for evaluation at Children's Hospital. Three staff physicians performed a
detailed medical examination of the boy and administered numerous psychological tests over a two-day period. When they were finished, the doctors asked Ben and Ginnie to join them in a nearby examining room:

> The spokesman for the group started off with a statement that
> caused my hopes to rise. "It is our considered judgment," said the
> senior physician, "that you have a choice. . . " I took advantage of
> the slight pause in his delivery to ponder that statement. A choice.
> Not bad, I thought. At least we have a choice. What a precious
> opportunity. Then came the measured words, delivered without
> emotion by the doctor who had obviously delivered bad tidings
> before. "You have a choice which involves your family." The choice
> was between us—the family unit—or Bobby's continued presence
> with us. "The stress upon a growing family that the presence of a
> hyperactive, retarded child exerts is often intolerable and in most
> cases causes undesirable psychological and emotional harm. Your
> choice is between a somewhat normal family life and a hectic
> future with likely detrimental effects upon all family members."
> The doctors were of one opinion: they strongly recommended that
> Bobby be "institutionalized."[2]

What is most striking about the doctors' recommendation is its focus
on what was best for Ben, Ginnie, and their other children rather than on
what was best for Bobby. Of course, it may be that the doctors also believed
their patient's well-being was better served by committal to an institution.
But if so it was an unspoken belief. More likely, they simply assumed that
the life of a mentally retarded person was less worthy than the life of his
or her parents and normal siblings, therefore justifying the sacrifice. If
that was their assumption, the doctors were perfectly consistent with the

prevailing opinion of their day. Starting in the early 1940s, the threat of the
feeble-minded came increasingly to be seen as more psychological than
sexual in nature. Marriages would be sundered, careers would be compromised, the lives of otherwise normal children would be wrecked and
broken, unless the parents "chose" wisely and removed the threat.[3]

The pressure of choosing whether to institutionalize a disabled child must
have been excruciating for the thousands of families to whom it was offered,
time and time again, in doctors' offices and hospitals all over Massachusetts
and the rest of the United States. The Riccis, who were by then settled in
Amherst, where Ben was teaching at the University of Massachusetts, saw
no viable alternative. Their home had already become, in Ben's words, a
"facility," with gates installed across all doorways and barrier bolts on all
doors, and the household was "constantly in turmoil."[4] Moreover, Bobby
would soon be of public school age, and the superintendent of schools had
told them there was no place for him in the Amherst public school system.

The only "school" to consider, conveniently located a few miles from
Amherst, was the Belchertown State School. At first the Riccis requested
a day program there; they were prepared to drive Bobby to Belchertown
every morning and return for him in the afternoon, so that he could live at
home. But this was not allowed. Belchertown was a residential institution
only. Moreover, they were told that their son would have to be committed
involuntarily, not simply enrolled, in the school. For the first thirty days,
they would not even be allowed to visit him.

The Riccis reluctantly accepted these terms and Bobby was formally
committed to the state school in September 1953.

> The day we accompanied Bobby [there] was traumatic; it has seared
> an indelible memory into my brain. We were heavy-hearted. As we
> reached the foot of the granite steps leading into the administra-
> tion building, my wife and I placed Bobby between us, each taking
> hold of one of his small hands.
>
> Waiting on the landing to receive Bobby was a burly woman
> dressed in a white uniform. Ten granite steps separated us. . . . We
> climbed slowly. At the landing, the woman in white took Bobby's
> hand and turned toward the door. Simultaneously, we turned
> away, not daring to look back at Bobby as he disappeared into the
> institution. . . .
>
> We traveled the most circuitous route home to Amherst, sob-
> bing all the way. . . .

> The month following Bobby's commitment was indescribably hard to bear. Practically every joint in my body ached. My head ached constantly. My appetite left me. . . . It was without question the most difficult, soul-searching decision I have made in my life. . . . Bob was now institutionalized at the Belchertown State School. Those words from the mouth of the senior physician at the Children's Hospital in Boston were heard once again, "It's either your family or your mentally retarded son."[5]

Similar scenes, similar agonies must have played out time and again on the front steps of the Belchertown State School, in the buses and automobiles transporting bereft parents home, and in the reflective quiet of their bedrooms and kitchens.

The admissions routine was, indeed, that there could be no parental contact for thirty days. It was thought that the child would acclimate to the new environment more easily, get to like it, and not want to go home. Once the thirty days passed, visits were allowed, the visitation rules varying somewhat over time. For example, the Riccis were initially permitted to take Bobby home between 9:30 a.m. and 4:40 p.m. any day except holidays. Later, such visits were also allowed on Easter, Thanksgiving, and Christmas. The procedure for "checking out" a son or daughter to go on visit was somewhat cumbersome, at least during the Riccis' time. There was no parking near the dorms, only in the visitors' parking lot adjacent to the administration building. So regardless of weather, the visitor would likely have a substantial walk to and from the dormitory. Once in the dormitory, he or she would be escorted to a small, narrow, rather sordid waiting room whose principal decoration was a sign forbidding visitors to enter the sleeping area.[6] There one sat until someone on staff brought the son or daughter out for the visit.

How did parents regard their children, once institutionalized, other than as afflicted sons and daughters? Were they "students" at a boarding school? "Patients" at a hospital? "Inmates" in a detention facility? What did parents know about living conditions there, schooling, vocational training, work? How often did they visit their loved ones? Did they ever try to enter the sleeping areas or other off-limits locations? Did they ever talk about the development of their sons and daughters with the officers or staff—as one might with teachers or counselors in the public school system? Did they ever complain or try to change things?

There is too little evidence, direct or indirect, to suggest answers to these questions for the first thirty years at the Belchertown State School. We know that some parents and family members visited the school during this period and took their sons and daughters home with them on visits, because Superintendent McPherson noted in his annual reports the number of residents absent from the school "on visit" at the end of each year. This number is material but not large (for example, 9 of 768 enrolled in 1925; 38 of 1,487 in 1941). We know that between 1937 and 1940, several dozen residents were "discharged" from the school while out on visits, implying that some visits were for periods substantially more than a day. Perhaps parents learned or inferred things about the school during these visits—favorable or otherwise. We also know, because the trustees frequently enough remarked on it in their annual reports, that some parents sought, but were usually refused, discharge of an enrolled son or daughter into their custody and care. Perhaps this indicates disenchantment with conditions at the school. Alternatively, maybe these parents simply missed their children and wanted them back.[7]

There was newspaper coverage of the school during this period, particularly in the local *Sentinel*, but it seems unlikely that parents, most of them from other towns, would have read the *Sentinel*. Even if they did, the stories were largely flattering and congratulatory—nothing to give parents reason for discomfort.[8] The occasional longer stories in the Springfield papers were similarly reassuring about daily life at the school.

There were, of course, also the public events to which parents, family, and friends would be invited: the minstrel shows, the Fourth of July parades, the industrial works exhibits, Christmas. These were reported on regularly and glowingly in the press. It seems unlikely that parents who attended such events would have seen them any differently. Certainly, as loving parents, they would have wanted to believe that their sons and daughters were well cared for and that what was happening to them at the school was in their best interests. These public displays of normalcy were calculated to reassure, and probably did so.

Finally, there were the trustees' annual reports. Perhaps a committed, diligent reader of these reports—one used to reading small print and between the lines—would have had questions. In 1923, for example, the trustees remarked on the "salutary effect" that removing a "delinquent group of boys" between the ages of seventeen and twenty-five had had on the rest of the population. They then "heartily endorsed" removing similarly delinquent boys under seventeen years of age, as well as "defective delinquent girls" in both age groups. Were the delinquent groups that had not been removed terrorizing other residents? Did they absorb dispropor- tionate amounts of staff attention, thereby depriving other residents of needed supervision and care? In 1925, writing about the school's needs for the coming year, the trustees said: "These [needs] continue to be the same as for 1924 and 1925. We are hampered by lack of bed space. Our children, particularly the boys, cannot be properly classified on account of lack of room. We need an Administration and a School Building in particular."[9] Just how serious was this problem of overcrowding, only three years after the school opened? What sort of schooling was going on in a school with- out a school building?

This thirty-year period of apparent passivity on the part of parents ended in 1954 with the formation of the Belchertown State School Friends Association, whose stated purpose was to "establish a closer relationship between the institution, parents, relatives and friends of the children at the B.S.S. and to carry out programs or projects, which will be of mutual ben- efit to all concerned."[10] It is unclear whether the organization was formed in response to a particular provocation. The decade following World War II was, generally, a time of increased parent activism in the United States, and similar groups were forming around the country, so it is not surpris- ing to find a parents' organization starting up at Belchertown as well. A friends group already existed at the state school in Waltham.[11]

Benjamin Ricci writes that Dr. Henry Tadgell, the school's superin- tendent at the time, was unhappy with the group's formation and viewed it as a threat to his authority.[12] If so, there is no indication in the public record. Tadgell himself was named honorary president. Other school offi- cers were invited to, and regularly attended, meetings of the association— often as guest speakers. In the June 1957 issue of The Bell (the association's internal newsletter), in which the editors summarized the group's accom- plishments to that time, they noted, "We have also been gratified to find our association and our objectives accepted wholeheartedly by the entire school staff."[13]

Certainly the group's initial agenda was not in any way threatening. At their first meeting, the members listed various projects that they might undertake. Their top priority was assisting at school parties. This was fol- lowed by replacement of radios (the school needed some twelve replace- ments each year) and TV maintenance. Other projects mentioned included sporting equipment, outings, equipment for the treatment of polio, transportation of parents, and toys for infirmary children.[14] The top priority—assisting at parties—is perhaps revealing. It suggests a desire on the part of some parents to be more engaged in the lives of their children. Indeed, at the close of the group's first meeting, many parents reportedly came forward to talk privately with the head of the elementary school, who was the evening's guest speaker, about the progress of their children. Equipment for treating polio aside, most of this seems no different than what one would have encountered at a typical PTA meeting at any public school in America.

Membership in the Friends Association grew rapidly—from 41 at the start to 215 in 1955, 334 in 1957, and 425 as of June 1958.[15] The number of participating members was always substantially less, however, and meetings were often poorly attended. In September 1955, at the group's first meeting of their second year, attendance was so poor that the president announced they would not be able to carry on. Someone suggested that attendance might improve if meetings were scheduled not on Monday evenings but rather on Sunday afternoons at the school, when parents would be either visiting their sons and daughters or returning with them from weekend visits home.[16] This was done, attendance improved, and the group survived.

Collecting dues was also a perennial problem. For example, as of September 1957, at the start of the group's fourth year, only 47 of 334 members had paid their dues for the prior year.[17] In addition to dues, money for the group's activities came from special fund-raising campaigns, such as bazaars, Christmas corsage sales, and card parties.[18]

Early in its history, the Friends Association adopted several small but telling amendments to the purposes clause of its bylaws. Whereas the original bylaws spoke of establishing a closer relationship among the school and parents, relatives, and friends of the "children" at Belchertown, the revised bylaws referred to "patients" instead of children. In part, this may reflect the reality that substantial numbers of the school's residents were physically adults, not children, although of course it was still called a "school" and many of the Friends were parents, not merely relatives or friends. But also, and more tellingly, it no doubt reflects the way these sons and daughters were in fact seen by their parents. These were, after all, mothers and fathers who had been dealing mostly with medical establishments in relation to their afflicted children since birth: pediatricians, consulting physicians in children's hospitals, state school superintendents and staff who were also physicians, psychologists, and nurses. Is it any wonder that they saw their offspring as patients in need of medical care?

The other amendment of interest addressed who should benefit from the Friends' efforts. Originally, the bylaws spoke of carrying out projects of "mutual benefit to all concerned"—meaning, presumably, the institution, staff, parents, relatives, and friends of residents as well as the residents themselves. But in the revised bylaws the notion of mutual benefit was dropped. Instead, the purpose of the group's programs and projects would be, simply, to "benefit . . . the patients." This single-minded focus on the "patients" made clear what might have been blurred before: that the Friends Association was not a social club. It was a benevolent association whose sole function was to improve the lives of those persons required by nature or circumstance to board at Belchertown State School. It is one of the few times in the school's history that the needs of its residents were so straightforwardly made a priority.[19]

Throughout the 1950s and 1960s, the Friends Association diligently pursued its primary agenda of dormitory parties, radio replacement, TV maintenance, and the like. The expenditures for fiscal year 1956–57 were typical. Of $4,152 spent, two-thirds was for dormitory parties ($619) and TV purchases and repairs ($2,131). Other expenses included $348 for steam irons, ironing boards, and covers, $200 for athletic equipment, $195 for sewing machines, and $32 for sleds.[20]

Dormitory parties were sponsored monthly ten of twelve months per year—one party for each residential building each year. Typically, the school provided refreshments while the Friends provided "frills" such as birthday cakes, balloons, prizes, and candy. Sometimes there would also be a small band or other special entertainment. Of course, it was the presence of the residents' relatives and friends at these parties that made them special. A paragraph in the March 1969 issue of The Bell is particularly poignant for what it suggests about family-deprived residents: "At the last building party in F Building, the children had a wonderful time due largely to the fact that so many parents and friends came. Very often we find that in spite of our efforts to give them a good time some of the children remain sad and unhappy because neither their parents or relatives are present. Won't you try to attend at least the party in the building where your relative is a resident?"[21]

While dormitory parties and TV purchase and maintenance were always a large part of the association's annual budgets, there was an ever-changing list of other expenditures that shows the group's practical orientation. This eclectic list included things such as electric floor polishers, electric razors, an audiometer, a portable bed lift, washing machines, stoves, Plexiglas protection for TV screens, sanitary napkins, draperies, farm horses, fences, and paint.

The decision to buy fences illustrates an important internal debate the group had early on about whether they should wait for the state to provide needed physical facilities for the school that were, technically speaking, the state's responsibility, or instead do it themselves by association projects "for the children's sake."[22] The school had repeatedly asked the state for fences at the nursery grounds and infirmary, to make it easier—and safer—for the residents of those buildings to spend time out of doors. These requests were ignored. The association decided it would raise the money for nursery fences itself (some $2,000)—and did so. In the end, though, it did not have to make the expenditure because the state took over the project and put up fences at both nurseries at its own expense. According to Superintendent Tadgell, "the authorities' decision to take over was due to the push given by the Association."[23]

The issue of whether and to what extent the Friends should fund projects that should have been the state's responsibility was never fully resolved, and the debate about fences was repeated from time to time in other contexts. For example, at a meeting in 1957 there was a discussion about installing ventilating fans in two of the buildings. Apparently, false ceilings (to make room for the ducts and fans) had been included in the school's budget for several years, but nothing had happened. "In the meantime," someone said, "the kids suffer."[24] This issue was discussed again at a meeting the following year, together with concerns about the need to replace many of the school's mattresses. According to the *Sentinel*, "In some of these matters it was felt that the state should bear the expense, and it was thought desirable to contact the powers that be in Boston to make them more conscious of the situation."[25]

If parties and procurement was the chief mission of the Friends Association, they were not its only—or even its principal—accomplishment. During the 1950s and 1960s, there was a sharp increase generally in transparency and volunteerism that seems directly attributable, at least in part, to the Friends. There was also a secondary political agenda that grew in importance as the years passed.

First, transparency. As we've seen, from the beginning there were reports about the state school in the *Sentinel* and, occasionally, in the Springfield papers or one of the other area journals. For the most part, however, these were "story" pieces about annual events such as minstrel shows, industrial exhibits, Fourth of July parades, Christmas festivities, retirement parties, construction projects, storm damage. There were also annual surveys published each January, highlighting events of the past year, and, once in a while, more substantial pieces in which a reporter would visit the school farm or some other department for a day and write about it (always laudatory) in more depth. In 1948, following publication of an article in the *Woman's Home Companion* titled "Take Them Off the Human Scrap Heap," which told of dreadful conditions in many of the nation's state institutions and called for more intelligent care and financing for the mentally deficient, the *Sentinel*'s "Steeple" columnist reassured his readers that there was "No 'Scrap Heap' Here" and wrote that "this would be a good time for Massachusetts papers or magazines to tell readers how progressive the Bay State is in its care of the feeble-minded."[26]

Perhaps it was, but newspaper coverage of the state school—particularly by the *Sentinel*—did not increase substantially until 1954, when the Friends Association was formed. The *Sentinel* began reporting in some detail each and every association meeting—this in response to direct efforts by the association to obtain coverage, for example by providing the paper with regular information about its meetings and copies of its newsletter. Now, for the first time in the school's history, the general public was made aware of deficiencies in the care of the residents at Belchertown: missing fences, broken radios and televisions, inadequate ventilation, ruined mattresses. But the increased coverage did not stop there. Starting in 1958, the *Sentinel* also began publishing a weekly column titled "State School News." The inaugural column noted, "Since its establishment, the life of the State School has touched the life of Belchertown at many points. However, it remains essentially a self-contained unit, a town within a town. To many of the newer citizens it may be chiefly a landmark, vaguely perceived as a custodial institution. These items, which we hope to be the first of a series, are submitted to present the State School as a means of education and rehabilitation, as well as physical care."[27]

This increased transparency did not provide sudden insight or revelation. But it did add rich new detail to the unfolding story of the school. Perhaps most important, it "moved" the state school from a (somewhat unsavory) place on the edge of town where a number of locals worked to a central feature of the Belchertown community—something worthy of regular attention and discourse. Henceforth, what happened at the state school would matter every week—whether it was Miss Madeline Fitzgerald, a 1958 graduate of American International College, giving piano lessons to boys and girls, or a cookout for one hundred "men" of Building L on the lawn facing the school building, at which volunteers (Mr. and Mrs. Louis Shumway, Mr. and Mrs. James Mulane, Mr. and Mrs. Frank Grover, and Mr. Rod Valliere) and assisting staff grilled and served hamburgers and hot dogs along with hard-boiled eggs and potato, macaroni, and tuna salads provided by the service building staff, or the darker disclosures of later years.[28]

There also developed a small degree of frankness between parents and staff. A few employees began talking with relatives about the institution's shortcomings and needs. Some staff members even began to suggest ideas for particular projects. For example, in 1969 one of the new projects that the Friends Association considered was installation of continuous music for the infirmary. The request came from an attendant in the infirmary who thought the music would be soothing to the patients "and bring much happiness."[29]

Although volunteerism increased dramatically after the Friends Association was formed, it was not a new phenomenon. Even in the early days, volunteers occasionally contributed time and materials to the school. In 1927, for example, the men's club of the First Congregational Church of West Springfield put on an entertainment for the "children." It was reported that "thunderous applause . . . brought the soloists back again and again to repeat their numbers."[30] In 1929, the Amherst Theatre hosted 250 of the school's residents for a complimentary showing of Harold Lloyd's first talking picture, *Welcome Danger.* The Amherst Rotary Club transported a hundred residents to the theater; D. D. Hazen himself transported twenty-five.[31] As I mentioned earlier, the school's employees were prohibited from making Christmas gifts to individual residents, but they annually pooled personal funds to hire professional talent to put on a special show for residents.[32] There were also occasional gifts in kind, such as the piano that an anonymous donor presented to one of the nurseries.[33] Such individual contributions could be substantial. In 1945, Richard J. Coleman of Middletown, Connecticut, who had operated concessions at the annual Belchertown Fair since the 1920s, began providing free amusement rides to state school residents the afternoon before the fair officially opened. In 1947, nine hundred pupils were accommodated—3,600 rides in all. This program was hugely popular and continued into the 1960s.[34]

Most of these early volunteer contributions had two things in common.

They were random, unsolicited events, and they did not require the contributor to spend much, if any, personal time at the school. By contrast, the Friends Association was an organized, sustained volunteer effort. Also, besides making regular contributions of goods paid for from annual dues and periodic volunteer fund-raisers, members of the group spent personal time at the school with the residents.

The very existence of the Friends Association seems to have spurred other volunteer efforts, including (to name only a few) those of the Birthday Box, the Westover Officers' Wives Club, the Women's Guild, area college students, the Hampshire County 40/8 Club (a veterans' group), and various church groups. In 1957, the school established a formal volunteer program, headed by Barbara Valliere, to coordinate these activities. By 1965, more than eight hundred people were actively engaged in doing volunteer work at the school—a number of them performing a hundred or more hours of service per year.[35] The volunteer services performed by these individuals and organizations were rich in variety and detail:

> The Birthday Box, organized in 1957, provided individually chosen birthday gifts for each resident regardless of age. The group was also responsible for Project Birthday Bus—possibly the most audacious volunteer program undertaken at the school—which involved the collection of 3,840,000 trading stamps to exchange for a new, sixty-passenger school bus.[36]
>
> The Officers' Wives Club of Westover Air Force Base in nearby Chicopee sponsored a variety of projects. For example, they painted a drab classroom in Nursery 2 bright colors and decorated the walls with characters and scenes from various cartoons and children's stories, such as Bugs Bunny, Donald Duck, Smokey the Bear, and Bambi. From time to time the Wives Club also took small groups of girls out for shopping tours and luncheon that included visits to a grocery store, department store, and five and dime.[37]
>
> The Women's Guild of the Congregational Church in Belchertown sponsored a "substitute parent program" in which volunteers would "adopt" individual residents, visit them, write letters to them, and take them home for a visit.[38]
>
> The Holyoke Musicians' Union regularly donated their time to play at school dances.[39]

Students from Mount Holyoke College set up a canteen on Friday nights for Building C girls and Building L boys. Residents were permitted, but not required, to attend—thus introducing an element of choice into the otherwise strictly regimented life of the school's residents. The canteen included records for dancing and singing, a bowling game, cards, Chinese checkers, and refreshments of soda and cookies.[40]

University of Massachusetts undergraduates held "sock-hops" on Saturday afternoons in the school gym, complete with all the top tunes on tape.[41]

Graduate students from the university joined the school's "I on I ratio" program, which involved taking disabled residents from the infirmary out of doors twice a week for a ride in a wheelchair or to roll around on a blanket—or just to spend time outside.[42]

Tom Yawkey, owner of the Boston Red Sox, periodically treated residents to a day at Fenway Park for a Red Sox game.[43]

This burst of ancillary volunteerism was facilitated in no small part by the special talents of Barbara Valliere, who headed the school's volunteer program for a number of years. She also authored the *Sentinel*'s weekly "State School News" column for a time. The column provided her with a unique platform from which to promote the numerous volunteer efforts. Her perky writing style ("Snow, snow, beautiful snow . . . to be perfectly candid it's nearly all I can remember about February '61") seems also to have attracted readers, thereby ensuring her the widest possible audience for a town paper.[44] But if Valliere was the master chemist, the Friends Association was surely the catalyst. It was the Friends' very existence—and persistence—that inspired others in the community to want to help and that impelled the state school to establish an office of volunteer services in the first place.[45]

Finally, the early Friends era saw a growing consciousness of the value of political action in bringing about reform. The Friends Association was established as a benevolent association, not a political movement. The intent of the parents, other relatives, and friends who founded it was to obtain information about, identify needs of, and provide goods and services for their loved ones at the state school. Some of them also simply wanted to spend more time with their institutionalized children, siblings, or acquaintances. Nevertheless, given the circumstances (not least the drive and motivation required to sustain such an effort), it was probably inevitable that the group would develop a political agenda as well. As Al Dumas, the association's president, gently put it in a "message" to the membership that he sent out at the start of the 1957 fiscal year,

> As I personally see it, we have two duties to the school residents, both of equal importance. On the one hand, we want to take care of immediate local necessities, such as living conditions at the school, and entertainment for pleasure and relaxation. On the other hand, we must actively participate in a long-range program designed to secure the gains we have made in the last few years. We must also continue to educate and inform the public and government alike regarding the necessity of increased activity in the program. The role of the [Friends Association] in this cooperative State-wide and Nation-wide movement must be determined by the membership at some future time.[46]

The political agenda manifested itself in several ways. Early on, the Friends associated themselves with MARC (the Massachusetts Association for Retarded Children, now known as the Arc of Massachusetts), a state-wide organization founded in 1954 to promote the interests of the retarded. Friends' representatives regularly attended MARC conventions and reported back to the membership on the proceedings.[47] At the second annual convention held in Springfield in May 1957, the Friends served as one of two hosts.[48] The executive director of MARC was a guest speaker at one of the Friends' meetings.[49]

The Friends also monitored executive and legislative branch developments affecting the retarded. In the January 1956 issue of The Bell, the membership was exhorted to appear at upcoming hearings scheduled to determine whether a special commission to study problems of "retarded children" should be extended. Only three members attended. A frustrated editor, after reporting the poor attendance, exclaimed, "How can we interest others if we are not interested ourselves?"[50] Evidently, politics did not come easily to most of the Friends.

The exhortations continued. A year later, when the final report of the Governor's Commission for Retarded Children was to be read in front of the Committee on Public Welfare, The Bell urged members to contact their legislators, appear before the committee to record their support for the commission's recommendations, organize car pools, bring friends.[51]

Apparently they did. A few months later, summarizing these first tentative political efforts, the president wrote with seeming satisfaction, "We can ... take pride in the fact that we have recognized the necessity of providing long range improvements at the school by affiliating ourselves with MARC and by personally appearing before legislative committees and going on record as an Association by endorsing various items of legislation."[52]

One of the recommendations of particular interest to the parents of residents at Belchertown, which aroused a number of otherwise politically complacent association members to action (that is, contacting their state legislators), was that parents should be freed from any financial obligation to the state school. Under the system then prevailing in Massachusetts, parents were required to pay some or all of the cost of maintaining their children at the institution. In 1957, the total cost was about $20 per week; the amount of the required contribution varied, depending on the family's financial situation. Approximately 7 percent of parents statewide were required to pay the full amount. This recommendation was the subject of animated discussion at one of the association's meetings. Why, it was asked, should state school parents (whose offspring had committed no misdemeanor) have to pay, when parents of children incarcerated in state penal institutions did not?[53]

In June 1969, Benjamin Ricci was elected president of the Belchertown State School Friends Association. Cumulatively, parental advocacy, the surge in volunteers and volunteer projects, the increased transparency, and the parents' growing political savvy heralded a new awareness of and sensitivity to the plight of the mentally retarded at the state school. The Friends Association had, it seemed, brought about meaningful reform— directly through its own actions and indirectly through the ancillary programs and efforts that it inspired. Concerned parents, relatives, and friends were at last making a difference in the individual lives of the institution's residents.

CHAPTER 6

The Tragedy of Belchertown

The front page of the *Springfield Union* on March 15, 1970, was packed with grim news. One article reported the misfiring of rockets by a U.S. helicopter into American troops north of Saigon, killing three and wounding nineteen. But it was another front-page story, published above the masthead with the banner headline "The Tragedy of Belchertown," that would rock residents of Belchertown to their core, changing life there—and at the state school—forever. The first of a six-part series by a staff writer, James Shanks, "The Tragedy of Belchertown" sensationally exposed what were said to be "conditions so bad some legislators touring the institution become physically ill and cannot continue or refuse to enter buildings."

According to Shanks, after penetrating the double-locked doors of Building K—the men's "back ward"—one entered a "stench created by 48 years of neglect, urine and human wastes." "Smell and sight are overpowered by the stink. But if that's bad the sight of men—other human beings, but retarded—standing around naked or holding their pants up because the laundry ruined the fastener, is worse. Physically grown men roll on a cold tile floor, sit in grotesque positions motionless, or rock rhythmically back and forth. Others are bent in strange poses on stark prison-made benches."[1]

About 120 men lived in Building K. The youngest was fifteen, the oldest over eighty—mentally, all two-year-olds in the physical bodies of grownups. There was no privacy. They slept in large barracks, beds touching head to foot, a narrow twelve-inch aisle separating rows. Clothing and other personal effects were kept on small, open shelves in another room. There were two bathrooms, each with six toilets—no toilet seats and no partitions. A single open shower stood at one end of each lavatory. Only three attendants cared for the men during the day and only two at night. Each day attendant, responsible for forty men, was required to dispose of night soiling, bathe and feed the men, send out laundry and linen, sort and bag the laundry when returned. The residents, many of them nude, sat all day on benches, or on the floor "in strange and grotesque positions, sometimes in pools of their own waste." Their only outside stimulation was a TV set boxed into the wall; the men stared at it for hours whether it displayed a picture or rolling blur.[2]

Conditions in the women's back ward, Building A, were, if anything, worse. Whereas the men of Building K had recently begun eating their food with utensils from a plate (thanks to a year-long effort by the chief attendant to teach the men how to feed themselves), each woman still ate like an animal from a deep aluminum bowl in which soup, meat, vegetables, and dessert were all indiscriminately mixed in a single porridge. Two of the women, who were said to be taking food from the others, were "restrained": "One woman was tied in a grotesque and uncomfortable position. One leg was bound to the bench, the other leg was crossed over the first. A rope was tied to her arm, then tied again to the bench. Her other arm was tied behind her to the back of the bench. The other woman was in a homemade straightjacket, one leg also bound to the bench."[3]

Besides being "warehouses" for the profoundly retarded, Buildings A and K were, according to Shanks, sometimes also used as places of punishment for minor misdemeanors of the brighter residents living elsewhere at the school:

> A Springfield man considered intelligent and able to repair radios and televisions, walked away from the grounds several times. He wasn't attempting to escape, just scavenging the town dump for electronics parts. He was ordered sent to Building K where the "two year old men" live for an "indeterminate sentence" as punishment. He was sent into the filth, squalor and monotony of sub-human conditions for exhibiting his intelligence. This "prisoner" remained in Building K for two years, his plight coming to light only after his family called [the regional administrator for retardation] to ask why he wasn't allowed home for the Christmas holidays.[4]

Shanks summed up life in the back wards by quoting M. Phillip Wakstein, a regional administrator for the state's Department of Mental

Health, who reportedly said, "The only difference between Belchertown and Auschwitz is the lack of gas chambers."[5]

Shanks's indictment of the back wards should not have caught the school's administration unawares. In 1964 a special commission established by the state legislature to investigate training facilities in Massachusetts for the mentally retarded reported that the Belchertown school was overcrowded by 20 percent (applying standards of the American Association of Mental Deficiency) and that it was "conspicuous[ly] neglect[ful]" in the provision of attendants and therapists. There was also a "flagrant lack of social service workers, psychologists and psychiatric personnel," a "desperate need for doctors [and] nurses," a "manifest shortage of teaching personnel and rehabilitation specialists," and a "lack of music, speech and art therapists and physical education."[6] In 1968 the American Association of Mental Deficiency (AAMD), in a report especially prepared for the Belchertown State School, concluded that the school was still "seriously" overcrowded despite recent transfers to other institutions and the completion of a new dormitory. This overcrowding, it said, when combined with a shortage of resident care and nursing personnel, "seriously limit[ed] the personal care of the individual residents, particularly the severely and profoundly retarded."[7]

More recently still, in January 1969, after William Fraenkel, the state's assistant commissioner for mental retardation, visited the back wards for twenty-four hours, his account included a compelling description of what he had observed. Of Building A he wrote:

> I saw several nude women eating food from a metal bowl using a spoon. Others were on the floor. Some parts of the walls and floors bore evidence of feces. The smell of urine was strong.
>
> Look at the Buster Brown haircuts! Two women beauticians come in once every six weeks to cut hair. [An attendant says], "It is easier to give Buster Brown than anything else—they're quicker too."
>
> Look at the benches in the day room, so aligned that they form a barricade separating women from women. One crawls over the head of the other to get to the other side. Many women are in a back room. Look at the six women tied by the waist to a bench. See the towel-restrained jacketed girl walking in the day room.
>
> See the residents shoving and hitting each other. Most everyone

is in some type of motion. The women scream. One woman lifts her garment, exposes herself and then rips it off. The attendant rushes over, puts it back on, and off it comes again. See the nude woman sitting on the floor, hunched over near the door, touching herself.

In K building:

An attendant says: "We have ninety better grade moderate and forty severe-profound in this building." All forty men in the second group are without clothes twenty-four hours a day [because, according to the attendant, they won't keep their clothes on, and] "it is easier to keep them clean that way. . . . All we do is scrub them down after meal time in the shower room. What a mess it would be if they had their clothes on and a lot more work for us."

[Middle of the night.] What is that noise? A man sits up in bed, tearing his sheet, strip by strip. Another is banging his head, another cries out, another begins to eat his blanket. By 5:00 A.M. it is half eaten.

[Early morning.] One nude man urinates throughout the day room over anyone who comes his way. Another urinates, then defecates and then crouches over near the floor, statue-like. Another nude man crouches next to him. They don't talk. All the urine and feces is cleaned up by another resident who grumbles as he mops up the floor with a bucket and rag. The bucket is emptied and then used by someone else to clean off a table. . . .

[An attendant says,] "Volunteers? They never see what you have seen. We don't show them this part of the building."[8]

In his "Tragedy of Belchertown" series, Shanks wrote about conditions elsewhere at the school as well, particularly in the two nurseries where young children were housed and in the infirmary where persons with multiple disabilities lived. A careful reading of the series shows that he distinguished between conditions elsewhere and in the back wards. Regarding the other buildings and programs, his indictment was more of the regimentation and emptiness than of the degradation or filth. He also had good things to say about the overworked and underpaid staff, laying blame on state officials who failed to fund the school adequately, rather than on the employees. "The staff itself can't be blamed for the conditions at the institution," he wrote. "Most are dedicated to children. Some have performed near miracles with the young." Rather, Belchertown provided "such a harsh negative environment" for its residents "largely because the staff budget and needed construction" were "so long . . . ignored by the legislators."[9]

For example, in Nursery 2 there were only three daytime employees to care for thirty-four children of ages six to twelve. This small staff spent two hours per day playing with the children and trying to develop their minds, but it was not enough time; necessary housekeeping and other daily chores like taking the children to the bathroom consumed most of the day. The children themselves spent most of their time unsupervised in a large day room with a cold stone floor, no rug, and no chairs—just hard wooden benches ringing the walls—where they watched television and played with plastic bottles. There was also a basement classroom with bright murals on the walls. A single dedicated teacher taught classes there but complained she was ineffective because there were too many children for one teacher to provide the individual attention necessary to teach the mentally retarded.

The situation was better in the Tadgell Nursery, where infants and the youngest children resided. Although the physical conditions were similar to those in Nursery 2, there was more staff—seven adults for forty-eight children. Most of the children had learned to feed themselves, and some were even learning numbers and the alphabet. There was also a jungle gym and more toys—although most of the children, like those in Nursery 2, simply sat around on the floor not really using the jungle gym and toys because, according to Shanks, no one had taught them how to do so. Intensive, long-term play therapy was not available.

Regarding the infirmary (itself a back ward of sorts for the severely, physically disabled), Shanks reported "startling strides forward" despite the grim conditions. "In one section, children who used to be completely bedridden now walk, crawl or sit in wheelchairs. The nursing staff has taught many to feed themselves. Others in the infirmary are making progress never before believed possible at Belchertown."[10]

These hopeful stories of nursery children learning to feed themselves and formerly bedridden residents of the infirmary now walking, crawling, or sitting in wheelchairs for the first time, while no doubt reflective of reforms undertaken at the school in the late 1960s, were overwhelmed by the horror stories of the back wards. In most quarters, the impact of the horror stories was immediate and profound.

Curiously, the *Belchertown Sentinel* was not one of those quarters. One might have expected that a scandal like "The Tragedy of Belchertown" series, which implicated the town's largest employer and publicly disgraced the town's good name, would merit coverage—indeed, considerable coverage—in the local paper. (The importance of the story to the town's future well-being was obvious; the *Sentinel* was also uniquely positioned to interview town officials as well as school administrators, employees, parents and friends.) Not so. This venerable publication, which had regularly reported on events at the state school for fifty years, fell silent. There was no news coverage whatsoever of the exposé or its aftermath and no editorial comment for more than a year.[11] The only reference to the scandal was by a *Sentinel* columnist—the author of "From the Middle Chair"—in the April 17, 1970, issue, four weeks after the Shanks series was published. Complaining that the town had lately been targeted by "several 'kickers,' 'squawkers,' and 'belly-achers'" in "a bunch of politically motivated articles" published by the *Springfield Union*, the columnist reassured readers that the town had "nothing to do with" the alleged "atrocities" at the state school. The series was "full of half truths" that were "worse than useless to base an opinion upon"; a "large percentage" of the school's employees "render care that is better than the average home care." In short, "the Springfield papers [can] be used to wrap garbage in, but otherwise [should] not . . . be taken seriously."[12]

The school itself could hardly stay silent—or limit its response to a dismissive injunction about what to wrap garbage in. On April 23, 1970, the administration issued a report titled "An Objective Review of Belchertown State School." Defensive in tone, it comprised several quotations from "The Tragedy of Belchertown," each followed by a comment. For example, in response to Shanks's allegation that the women in Building A ate from pots like animals, the report stated, "The majority of residents in A and K Buildings are served family style in dining rooms. Some profoundly retarded residents are served pureed food in bowls. At the time of the newspaper articles eight residents in A Building were eating pureed food in bowls while in K Building all residents were eating out of sectional food trays or dishes." Some of the comments read more like admissions than rebuttals. In response to Shanks's claim that large numbers of residents were being supervised by a small number of attendants, the report said, "Belchertown has [been] and in all probability will continue to be confronted with the problem of not having sufficient personnel to meet the needs of all residents. Shortage of personnel at all levels is a problem of a most serious nature."[13]

The school also promised a series of further reforms, prodded by William Fraenkel, the assistant mental retardation commissioner. Fraenkel had written to the school's superintendent, Lawrence Bowser, shortly after the exposé was published, lamenting the "half-truths, mistakes and innuendo in the articles," but also making suggestions for "immediate change" and urging Bowser to give such changes his "highest priority and backing." These suggested changes included: visits to every building at least once a week; scheduled priority for building clean-ups; reevaluations and appropriate programming to be written for each resident; the elimination of all seclusion rooms and reduced use of restraints; a crash program to expedite building repairs; a publicly declared intention to eliminate all back wards; building matrons to begin keeping daily written reports indicating that each resident was supplied with necessary toilet articles, clothes, and bedding; establishment of more sanitary food handling procedures; sex education; and creating opportunities for residents to walk, jog, and exercise. More generally, Fraenkel also recommended that promising programs be extended to other parts of the institution, that efforts be stepped up to discharge working residents or release them into community employment, and that volunteer programs be expanded. Finally, he noted that Belchertown was lagging behind all other state schools with regard to "unitization" (the state's then preferred method for organizing residents of state mental institutions into units based on behavioral level and chronological age) and urged Bowser to speed up the unitization process.[14]

The school's trustees also had their say. In their annual report for the 1969/70 fiscal year, they recorded their "profound disapproval of the irresponsible series of articles published by the *Springfield Union*." They too lamented "the wide dissemination of the many false statements and half-truths contained in these articles" and referred their readers to the school administration's recently issued "Objective Review" for validation. The trustees took special umbrage at Shanks's charge that commitment to Belchertown was the etiological factor in the development of severe depression and insanity among the residents. "There have been no severe depressions reported," the trustees wrote, "and relatively few residents have been diagnosed as psychotic. We do not believe the reporter or his consultants, whoever they may be, are competent to express such theoretical insinuations." Lastly, the trustees said they were "greatly distressed by the damage to the morale of our capable, conscientious and devoted employees and the fears, doubts and grief suffered by concerned parents and relatives with the publication of 'Belchertown, the place without affection, the place which turns people into vegetables or caged animals,' and the odious statement attributed by the reporter to Dr. Wakstein that 'the only difference between Belchertown and Auschwitz is the lack of gas chambers.' Such sensationalism seems entirely unwarranted whatever the motives of these articles may have been."[15]

The state legislature, in no mood to give Department of Mental Health bureaucrats, school administrators, or school trustees any benefit of the doubt, moved quickly to do what legislatures do in such situations: investigate. On April 16, 1970, it set up a joint commission to study operations and conditions at the Belchertown State School and Monson State Hospital. The commission, chaired by Senator Philip Quinn of Spencer, was comprised of four senators, seven members of the House of Representatives, and two citizens appointed by the governor. Benjamin Ricci, the recently elected president of the Belchertown State School Friends Association whose son Robert had been a resident at the Belchertown school since 1953, was one of the citizen appointees.[16] Over the next twelve months the commissioners visited the institution, gathered reports and memos, and held hearings. It issued its first report on March 24, 1971.

The report was an indictment of conditions and operations every bit as damning as "The Tragedy of Belchertown" series had been. The school, it said, was a "product of monumental administrative neglect, inertia and malpractice," a "near total failure" that needed "immediate and direct attention." Citing (and appending), in addition to public testimony, the earlier report by the AAMD as well as Fraenkel's account of his twenty-four-hour visit, the commission condemned every aspect of life at the school. It highlighted gruesome detail after gruesome detail. It ignored or buried in appendixes any ameliorating action, such as the recent improvements at the nursery and infirmary that Shanks reported, or the community placement and volunteer programs that AAMD (and Shanks) complimented. It excoriated the school's administration for the "Objective Review" it issued in response to Shanks's series—noting, correctly, that "surprisingly few of the charges made by the newspaper and selected by the institution for comment were denied." Instead, the administration treated problems "such as deaths, inability for the residents to be habilitated, and psychotic symptoms among the residents . . . as natural to large residential institutions for the mentally retarded for which little more could be done."[17]

Going further than Shanks, the commission also criticized the state's Department of Mental Health. The department, like the school, had responded to "The Tragedy of Belchertown" more in self-defense than self-criticism. There was, to begin with, the assistant commissioner's letter to Superintendent Bowser (mentioned earlier) lamenting the "half-truths, mistakes and innuendo in the articles"—thus seeming to align the department with the school's administration rather than its residents.[18] In January 1971, the department fired M. Phillip Wakstein, the regional administrator who had cooperated with Shanks's exposé and likened Belchertown to Auschwitz, on trumped-up charges—thus blaming the whistle-blower for the foul. The commission called the department's justification for the dismissal "of such a poor nature and scope that it could be applicable to most other Department officials responsible for conditions at Belchertown" and said it was "unnecessarily harsh" even when viewed in "the most favorable light." Regarding the twelve-member Committee on Belchertown that the department had established in December to "assist the Superintendent in improving the care and treatment of residents at Belchertown in every possible way," the commission noted dismissively that the committee was inadequately staffed and funded, and derided it as a mere "rubber stamp for existing administrative policies."[19]

In February, shortly before the commission's report was published, a group of seventy-one Belchertown State School employees petitioned the commission, seeking Bowser's dismissal. "The undersigned feel," the petitioners wrote, "that the Superintendent has shown a deplorable lack of concern for the well being of the Mentally Retarded and the physically handicapped for a number of years. We strongly urge that he resign or be replaced by a more capable and concerned administrator."[20]

This was a shocking, unprecedented act of insubordination by a normally docile group of state employees. It foreshadowed the end for Bowser. On March 31, 1971, one week after the report was published, Bowser resigned.[21] Most of the board of trustees followed suit.

Not everyone cheered Bowser's departure. Peter Dearness, the editor of the Sentinel, finally roused from a year of silence, wrote that the resignation of Bowser, together with the firing of Wakstein, "may turn out to be the real 'Tragedy of Belchertown'—for somewhere between their two goals lay the real answers." "The study commission would have found the truth without the continual repetition of half the story," he wrote. "Changes underway since my first contact with B.S.S. in 1956 as a student, and those underway when the 'series' began, along with those announced this past week, were not a result . . . of the Union crusade. The Commission report, while it may have been entirely correct, said little that school officials and employees did not know. We hope that they now provide the means to implement these proposals."[22]

Aside from the quotation marks around "series" (is their purpose to distance the editor from the series? to disparage it?), this passage is astonishing in several respects. First, despite complaining that only half the story was being told, Dearness concedes the truth of that half-story; there may have been more to say that wasn't said (more bedridden patients now walking, crawling, or sitting in wheelchairs than Shanks had reported? frustrated school administrators lobbying the legislature for more aid?), but existing conditions and operations were as appalling as charged. Second, school officials and employees knew that it was so. Third—and this is the part that most astonishes—reforms that were initiated in the aftermath of the "Tragedy of Belchertown" series would have happened anyway without it.

This last claim deserves a respectful hearing; it would be unfair in the extreme to condemn school administrators and trustees for perpetuating horrific conditions that they were in fact capable of and intent on ending swiftly, without public humiliation. But it is worth a skeptical frown at the outset. Of all the impressions and facts packed into the commission's report, three are especially damning in this regard. First, per capita expenditures at the Belchertown school ($3,100 in 1969) were almost 15 percent lower than at the Fernald School in Waltham ($3,600). Second, since 1960 the school had returned, unspent, *twice* the percentage of funds (in non-personnel accounts—for example, for educational programs and rehabilitative services) appropriated to it than other state schools. Third, in the fiscal year preceding the commission's report, the school received 100 percent of its requested appropriation from the legislature.[23] This does not, at first blush anyway, look like a school administration committed to substantial, sustainable reform.

Whether the Bowser administration should be blamed for creating the horrific conditions at the school that were exposed by the Shanks series or merely for perpetuating them, it must be conceded that Bowser effected some significant changes during his tenure, especially in the latter half of the 1960s. For example, he reduced the resident population by 20 percent, built the first new nonspecialized residential dormitory in more than thirty-five years, added staff, and expanded volunteer programs.[24] Further changes were undertaken in 1970 shortly after the "Tragedy of

Belchertown" series was published, most importantly additional volunteer programs and the opening of a halfway house in nearby Springfield to facilitate the transfer of eligible residents to community homes.[25] Bowser also struggled, under the prodding of William Fraenkel, to put together what would become, the following year, a more substantial set of changes that came to be known as the ten-point plan of reform.

These reforms (and others like them) notwithstanding, the special commission was surely correct in broad outline if not in every detail. The reforms undertaken in the late 1960s may have eased some of the overcrowding and ameliorated some of the egregious conditions at the school, but they did not effect any systemic change. Similarly, the additional reforms instituted in the twelve months following publication of "The Tragedy of Belchertown" series were neither sufficient nor sustainable. Moreover, there is little evidence that substantial reform would have happened without the *Springfield Union* exposé. One of the suggestions Fraenkel made in the letter he wrote to Bowser after his one-day visit to Buildings A and K in January 1969 was that that residents of the back wards be clothed and taught to feed themselves. Some progress was made on this front; when Fraenkel revisited the school a month later, he noted with satisfaction that men he had seen during his earlier visit "sitting denuded and eating out of metal pots with spoons [were] now seated at the same table, clothed, eating from trays."[26] But other suggestions of his were never heeded. M. Phillip Wakstein, whom Fraenkel had instructed to monitor further progress in this area, never reported any. The Joint Commission determined that, as of July 1970 (shortly after the exposé), only four of Fraenkel's fourteen suggestions had been acknowledged or implemented by Bowser.

One profound difference between the *Springfield Union* series and the joint commission's report was the degree of blame assigned to the state's Department of Mental Health for conditions at Belchertown. Shanks was highly critical of the state legislature for inadequate funding of the school, but he did not, in so many words at least, criticize Department of Mental Health officials for conditions there.[27] Indeed, as we have seen, both the assistant commissioner and the regional administrator for Belchertown seem to have facilitated the newspaper's investigation—in the case of the regional administrator, even accompanying Shanks on his initial visit to the school and providing him with one of his most memorable (and inflammatory) quotes—the comparison to Auschwitz. The impression from the *Springfield Union* series is that state administrators were complicit in the exposé—regarding it as a necessary instrument of reform following their own failed attempts to bring about change.

The joint commission, by contrast, was highly critical of department officials. Perhaps this was no more than a politically motivated effort to divert attention from Shanks's harsh words about the legislature's failure to provide adequate funding. Perhaps it was sincere—and legitimate—criticism. (Certainly the department was legally responsible for administering the state schools.) But for our purposes what is of interest is not the legitimacy of the criticism but the consequence it had on reform efforts. Instead of enlisting the Department of Mental Health as a natural ally of reform, the joint commission report treated the department as part of the problem, thereby putting it (together with school officials) on the defensive and leaving no obvious alternative that could be trusted to implement change. As we will see, this void would ultimately be filled by the federal courts.

The department's response to the commission's criticism was at first nuanced and multi-tiered. In mid-April 1971, shortly after the report was issued and Bowser resigned, the commissioner of mental health, Milton Greenblatt, issued a statement emphasizing the "sharp changes in concept and practice" that the department had undergone since its reorganization in 1966.[28] He sought to distinguish between two types of facilities—the large, older state hospitals and state schools that continued to exist, and the many newer, community-based programs that had been established for providing treatment and care to the mentally ill and mentally retarded since 1966—and he maintained that the newer programs represented the "proper direction for the future," which, when fully developed, would "obviate the need for the large, outmoded institutions" such as the Belchertown school.[29] Sidestepping the allocation of blame ("Only a serious historian would be able to unravel the complex factors that in their totality have given rise to the shameful conditions we all have tolerated"), Greenblatt emphasized that the department had recently adopted a "crash program" for change at Belchertown (what came to be called the ten-point plan of reform).[30] "It should be possible," he concluded hopefully, "to make Belchertown an institution of pride within a few years."

Several weeks later, in June 1971, Dr. Arnold Abrams, the Mental Health Administrator for Region III, issued a longer, more reflective statement in which he sought to educate the public on the history of state schools in Massachusetts (starting with the aspirations of Samuel Gridley Howe)

and the special burden of caring for "profoundly retarded" individuals who, although making up only 10 to 15 percent of the total number
of residents in the institutions, required an "inordinately larger propor-
tion of the institutional resources." Abrams wrote, "Seen in this light, the
Belchertown 'scandal' is no surprise to those of us who are familiar with
these institutions. Indeed, many of the things stated in the Report of the
Special Commission no doubt are, unfortunately, and—to our never-end-
ing dismay—true."[31]

But if "many" of the things stated in the commission's report were true,
it was also true, according to Abrams, that there were enough persons in the
department committed to and capable of effecting reform. Inflammatory
newspaper stories, however well intentioned, could not do the job. Rather,
"improvements are dependent upon a well-informed, concerned public
which gets behind those who are trying to solve these problems and which
provides, not only human interest and commitment, but, through the legislature, the monies necessary to build the proper kinds of staff for those very
profoundly retarded who will need a lifetime of residential care."[32]

Neither Greenblatt nor Abrams sounds overly defensive. Their statements are nuanced and thoughtful—more so, certainly, than those of the
school's administration and trustees or the *Sentinel*. Moreover, the department responded promptly to Bowser's resignation with what looked like
an inspired, interim appointment to replace him: William Fraenkel.[33]
Who better combined commitment with clout than the department's
second-ranking administrator, who had actually spent twenty-four hours
in Belchertown's back wards, reprimanded Bowser for conditions there,
recommended a program of reform, and established a timetable for
implementation?

In early July 1971, Fraenkel—only three months on the job as interim superintendent—held a general staff meeting at the school to give a "progress
report" on implementation of the ten-point plan of reform.[34] More than
a hundred supervisors and employees attended. Members of the press
were also present. A summary of the progress report will serve as a useful
benchmark against which to measure and evaluate what would follow:

- Back wards. Building A would be shut down by Labor
  Day and Building K by Christmas of that year.
- Unitization. The school was being reorganized into
  five units: children's, adolescent, adult, geriatric, and

medical-rehabilitation, consistent with the state's mandate for unitization.

- Individual assessments. The school was reassessing the condition and capabilities of each resident, with priority to residents of Buildings A and K.

- Transfers. An undisclosed number of residents were in the process of being transferred to one of fifteen other locations, ranging from halfway houses and group homes to nursing homes, state hospitals, and other state schools—thus further reducing the population of the school.

- Additional staff. Fifty new attendants were being hired to work with the most profoundly retarded residents of Buildings A and K.

- Student interns. Fifty interns from area colleges were being hired to work twenty hours per week in special programs such as speech and hearing, vocational rehabilitation, and recreation.

- Building repair. Special budgetary requests had been made to the state for building maintenance and repairs.

- Campus beautification and revitalization. Part of the special budgetary requests would be used to develop hiking trails, bike-riding paths, and other outdoor recreational facilities on the school's eight-hundred-acre campus for use by residents, families, staff, and the public at large.

- Community program services. Work had begun with local citizen groups to develop needed community services.[35]

Although Fraenkel acknowledged that serious problems still had to be addressed (such as severe overcrowding in Buildings L and G for men, insufficient staff to extend the benefits of new programs and services to more residents, buildings in need of extensive repair and renovation, lack of adequate privacy for residents (particularly in the toilets, showers, and living areas), and a need for additional administrative staff including a new superintendent and new department and unit heads), his report was upbeat and optimistic. A corner seemed to have been turned, a new direction set. At an employee recognition ceremony in September, further progress was reported.[36]

Neither Greenblatt nor Abrams had promised miracles overnight. Greenblatt's stated timetable for making Belchertown "an institution of pride" was "a few years"—not, to be sure, an aggressive schedule, but perhaps a realistic one in the circumstances. The expectation seems to have been that if an ambitious reform agenda could be established, if some progress could be periodically demonstrated, and if the most egregious outrages of the back wards could be eliminated promptly, then the public and the legislature would be patient.

It was not to be. Whether Greenblatt miscalculated or Fraenkel underperformed (as we will see, not everyone saw progress where Fraenkel did), the condemnation of the department's reform efforts was swift and substantial—further isolating the department as part of the problem instead of the solution. The special commission made a surprise inspection tour of the school in September and quickly issued a scathing "evaluation report" that blamed the department for continuing bad conditions at the school. "This commission is astounded that the full resources of the Mental Retardation Program of the Department of Mental Health, when focused on one institution, could accomplish so little," the report stated. "We are led to the inescapable conclusion that the answers to Belchertown's problems lie beyond the institution and are to be found within the personnel and structure of the central office of the DMH."[37]

The report charged that the department had responded to the appalling conditions at the school with "poorly planned, publicity-oriented programs which have had little impact on the permanent structure through which the institution provides services for the residents." According to the commission, the actions taken had actually *lowered* living conditions for 90 percent of the population—as well as the morale of most employees. (Apparently, the commission meant that by focusing its efforts on the back wards, the department was ignoring the remaining ones to the detriment of the great majority who lived there.) It complained that the fifty new attendant recruits were serving only twelve of the most severely retarded residents of the institution. It blamed Fraenkel by name for unsanitary and unhygienic conditions on the wards, alleging they were even worse than they had been before, and it otherwise dismissed the department's ten-point reform program as nothing more than the (insufficient) ten-point program recommended to Bowser a year earlier.

Fraenkel went ballistic. "I can't believe what I'm reading," he began an official statement responding to the evaluation. He insisted that "much progress" had been made toward improved care, humanization, and overall treatment of residents during his five-month tenure. He called the evaluation report "generalized and vague" and criticized the commission for ignoring the fact that five items of the ten-point program had been fully realized in those five months (including the closing of Building A, the individual assessment of all back ward residents, the hiring of the fifty new attendants and fifty student interns, and the expansion of the volunteer program). He noted that two of the five remaining items (building main-tenance and repair; campus beautification and revitalization) were await-ing legislative action, while others were in various stages of completion. He proudly touted the school's new transparency policies ("The School has been fully opened to the public, the press and to all family members of residents") and concluded by demanding that the commission provide documentation to back up its negative comments and meet with him so that he could "explain our achievements to date and . . . hear whatever programs they may recommend."[38]

What is going on here? Was Fraenkel a fool—or worse, a fraud? Were his ten-point program and progress reports merely a publicity scam? Certainly Benjamin Ricci thought so. In his book *Crimes against Humanity*, which recounts his efforts—and those of the Friends—to improve condi-tions at Belchertown, he derides Fraenkel as a flamboyant, bombastic, and ineffective "relief pitcher" for Commissioner Greenblatt, heaping upon him bucketfuls of ridicule and scorn.[39] He mocks what he calls Fraenkel's "first official act"—"the painting of dozens of fifty-gallon steel drums in psychedelic colors," which were then distributed about the campus. "By so doing," Ricci writes, Fraenkel "demonstrated he could also provide comic relief through the unveiling of Trash Container Art." More seriously, he criticizes Fraenkel for "discourag[ing] parents from becoming involved in the [school's] internal affairs," in particular from "monitoring the goings-on."[40] He dismisses the closing of Building A as a publicity stunt, saying the effect was merely to move its residents from one building to another, re-creating in the other (already occupied) building the same squalid and overcrowded conditions that had characterized Building A. "The inexpe-rienced and unquestioning news reporters" who played up the story were unaware that Fraenkel "conveniently and artfully omitted mentioning his creation of two additional back wards because of the necessary doubling-up of residents. With one bold administrative stroke, he severely *over-crowded* several residential buildings . . . further dehumaniz[ing] the resi-dents." Most damning of all, from Ricci's perspective, was that Fraenkel brought with him to the school a public relations professional whose "handsome" salary was allegedly paid from the same account meant for hiring badly needed attendants. "Contrived propaganda was deemed to be more important than direct care services."

Ricci concludes his hatchet job by describing a meeting that the Friends' board had with Fraenkel in the early fall of 1971, portraying Fraenkel at that meeting as a sniveling, unmanly sycophant:

> We had many important matters to question and to fully discuss. He . . . carried with him into our meeting room large-sized "chips" on both his shoulders. He had misjudged us; he was not in the least prepared for our serious questioning. His was a very bad start. It was apparent that he was playing in a different kind of ball game. This was hardball, not softball.
>
> Immediately following my introduction—even before I announced the agenda—after all, it *was* our meeting, and he had been invited as our guest, Dr. Fraenkel had the audacity to ask for a "vote of confidence." His was an emotional appeal; tears filled his eyes. Our board members remained calm and focused. We rejected unanimously his plea for a vote of confidence. The Belchertown Friends had had their fill of his buffoonery and enough of his fraud and incompetence.[41]

Ricci is a towering and complex figure in the later history of the Belchertown State School. Sincere, impatient, tenacious in the extreme, he was an intrepid advocate on behalf of the men and women, boys and girls, who lived at the institution. He was also, one suspects, riven by guilt at having committed his son Robert to the school in 1953. Perhaps this guilt accounts for his stark, black-and-white worldview. There are no shades of gray, just good folks and bad (mostly the latter). While his judgments cannot be lightly dismissed, they should sometimes be questioned. It is difficult to reconcile the Fraenkel of "A Twenty-Four-Hour Visit to a State School for the Mentally Retarded" with the buffoon of Ricci's narrative.

Ricci, still teaching at the University of Massachusetts in Amherst, had been on sabbatical in Norway during the turbulent first eight months of 1971 when the report of the special commission was published, Bowser resigned, and Fraenkel took over as interim superintendent.[42] Armed with a 35-mm Leicaflex SL camera and ten rolls of Kodak color film courtesy of the Friends board, Ricci toured a number of facilities for the mentally retarded in Norway, Sweden, and Denmark, saw firsthand the renowned care provided by the Scandinavians, and took hundreds of photographs of what he saw. Old buildings, otherwise identical to Belchertown's dormitories on the outside, were attractive, comfortable, and inviting on the inside. Sleeping quarters had no more than four beds to a room. The air smelled fresh. The sounds were soft and happy. Residents were gregarious and well mannered. Coffee, tea, and light snacks were readily available to the residents, as were a variety of fruit juices—all served on china or glassware. In one facility a resident invited Ricci to have coffee, pastries, and sandwiches—unthinkable at Belchertown.[43]

To see the kind of high-quality care his son Robert might have had for eighteen years, but did not, must have tormented and enraged Ricci. Is it any wonder that he returned from Norway itching for a fight? Within days, he persuaded his colleagues on the special commission to make the surprise inspection tour mentioned earlier and to produce the interim evaluation report. Whether or not a corner may have been turned at the school or new directions set while he was away was of no interest to him. Everything was contrast, and the contrast was unacceptable. This is not to say his assessment of Fraenkel was wrong. It is to say that Ricci's mood, when combined with his temperament, left no room for nuance. Nothing that could have been done in the five months Fraenkel had been acting superintendent would have assuaged him or begun to approach the quality of care he witnessed in Scandinavia.

Still, the question must be asked: was Fraenkel a fraud? Was his alleged progress merely a publicity scam? Probably not. The preponderance of evidence suggests that the ten-point program was a meaningful agenda for reform and that Fraenkel was indeed motivated to change things—that some things had begun to change for the better. One had to start somewhere; surely it was not wrong to prioritize the back wards and the profoundly retarded persons who resided there. The back wards were the focus of the *Springfield Union*'s exposé. The residents confined to them had long been the most egregious victims of inadequate care. It is curious that the special commission, in its interim evaluation report, would single out for special reprobation the assignment of fifty new attendants to these wards—on the ground that "only" a small number of individuals were being benefited while the majority was not. To some degree this would necessarily be the case no matter where the new attendants were assigned.

The criticism of the closing of Building A is also curious. If all that was done was to move its residents to another building that was already full (as Ricci asserts), then of course the criticism would be justified. But transfers out of the institution were also taking place, reducing the net number that had to be accommodated within. The evidence that Ricci cites of over-crowding elsewhere is actually a memo dated more than a year later from one of the unit directors to the chief engineer (by then, unitization had been mandated and implemented), long after Fraenkel had been run out; the unit director says G Building is in violation of state law because there are more than sixty-five residents living on the first floor of the building and that he himself is not responsible for this violation. He then asks what can be done to alleviate the situation.[44] It hardly seems fair to nail Fraenkel for a violation reported many months after his departure, which does not name him as the cause or otherwise link him in any way. Moreover, during the months that Ricci was in Norway and Fraenkel was starting his reforms, there was unprecedented transparency at the school. There were follow-up news reports, television and radio broadcasts—even talk-show discussions—about what was going on there. All reported some degree of progress. That Fraenkel was assisted by a public relations professional does not detract from the reliability of these third-party witnesses or prove a scam.

In the end, though, it didn't matter. No one—interim or otherwise—could withstand such withering criticism by a special commission of the state legislature. The special commission, with Ricci leading the charge, had determined that the state's mental health bureaucracy was the prob-lem, not the solution. Fraenkel was finished. He was replaced in October 1971 by Dr. Roland Nagle, at the time an administrator for the state's com-munity-based programs in western Massachusetts.

Ricci complains in his book that Commissioner Greenblatt never sought the prior input of himself or the Friends Association before appointing Nagle, and he has only slightly kinder words for Nagle than he did for Fraenkel. In fact, though, Greenblatt did ask the Friends for their views on the Nagle appointment—if not beforehand, then shortly afterward—and Ricci responded by letter on their behalf, saying that the association's view was "that we support his candidacy."[45]

Nagle, who lasted only eleven months, will be discussed in the next chap-ter. The appointments and resignations of state school superintendents would be greatly overshadowed by a singular event never before attempted in the history of Massachusetts: the filing of a class action lawsuit on behalf of residents of a state school against the mental health bureaucracy of the state, requesting that all residents of the state school be provided with adequate treatment and humane living conditions, and seeking to place the school under the supervision of a special magistrate until the requisite treatment and living conditions were provided. The lead plaintiff in the case was "Robert Simpson Ricci, by his father and next friend, Benjamin Ricci."[46] The lead defendant was Dr. Milton Greenblatt, Commissioner of the Department of Mental Health of the State of Massachusetts.

Endings

The idea of suing the state's mental health bureaucracy to obtain redress for the appalling conditions at Belchertown State School was Ben Ricci's. It isn't clear when the idea first took form in his mind—whether before or after his sabbatical to do research in Norway during the first half of 1971. Perhaps he had read about the lawsuit filed in October 1970 on behalf of residents of the Partlow State School and Hospital in Tuscaloosa and other state-run mental health facilities in Alabama.[1] He may well have thought about a lawsuit, and started to gather photographic and other evidence for it, before going to Norway, although his sabbatical there (during which he saw that first-rate care could be, and was being, provided to mentally retarded persons in Scandinavia) surely was the catalyst for doing so.

Ricci says in his book about the case, *Crimes against Humanity*, that he interviewed fifteen lawyers, all of whom turned him down, before attorney Beryl Cohen agreed in early October 1971 to take on the case. Cohen, a former Massachusetts state representative and state senator, was counsel to the special commission established by the legislature a year earlier to investigate conditions at Belchertown, which had issued a scathing report in March 1971. He therefore already knew a great deal about conditions at the school, knowledge that would soon be supplemented by Ricci's own independent fact gathering.

Cohen determined that the lawsuit should be a class action. He and Ricci met frequently over the next several months, drafting the complaint and debating what remedies to seek. Apparently Ricci had told no one except the lawyers he interviewed about his idea of a lawsuit—not the

Friends Association, not even his wife. He justified his secrecy by saying that his fellow parents on the Friends' board, though "dedicated and wonderful human beings, were fundamentally conservative in their thinking."[2] Now, however, it would be necessary to make full disclosure. A class action required a class of plaintiffs, not just an individual.

We have only Ricci's account of the fateful board meetings. They must have been spirited. All members were present at the first meeting. "I came right to the point," Ricci writes; "I wanted us to consider filing a lawsuit on behalf of our children." The board had many questions: "Where is the money coming from? Can the state sue us in return? Will our kids suffer from this? It was a lively evening, but clearly they seemed ready to proceed. . . . Only one board member disagreed with the lawsuit idea: he wished 'not to buy into it at this time.' "

Ricci had determined not to introduce Cohen to the group unless they agreed to proceed with the lawsuit, so a second meeting was now necessary to introduce the attorney. Both Ricci and Cohen wanted to maintain secrecy. They also wanted to expand the list of invitees to include other potential class members than the board. Therefore, instead of scheduling a larger meeting at the school that would surely call attention to itself, Ricci invited this larger group—some thirty-five in all—to his home in Amherst. Hot coffee, tea, homemade shortbread, and homegrown strawberries with freshly whipped cream were served to this standing-room-only crowd. When dessert was finished, he announced that the purpose of the gathering was to discuss bringing a lawsuit against the Department of Mental Health on behalf of the invitees' relatives and friends at Belchertown State School. He then introduced Cohen. "Beryl began by noting that a class action lawsuit had never before been filed on behalf of institutionalized, mentally retarded persons in Massachusetts history. This would be precedent-setting. It would also be surprising. It would be the Belchertown Friends' way of using the proper and legitimate forum to address its grievances against the State of Massachusetts" for the appalling conditions at the school and for "the state's crimes against humanity."

In response to questions, Cohen explained that the remedy being sought was not monetary damages but rather "the immediate amelioration of living conditions, the hiring of adequate staff persons, and basic improvements in the quality of medical and nursing care." He said he would not bill for his services. "Just send me what you are able to when you are able to." He sought to alleviate concerns, which were considerable, about possible retribution by state officials. At the end of the evening, most attendees had been won over; the board voted, with one abstention, to hire Cohen and proceed with the lawsuit.

As signatures were solicited over the next several weeks from potential plaintiffs' representatives, there was some resistance—particularly to the idea that the superintendent of the school, Roland Nagle, would be a named defendant. "How dare you even consider thinking of suing such a wonderful superintendent," one parent responded. Occasionally, the hostility was personal to Ricci: "You are a disgrace to the teaching profession," another wrote. In the end, though, most of those solicited eagerly agreed to be plaintiffs' representatives. Ricci got commitments from forty-eight people, of whom twenty-six were ultimately selected.

The class action was filed in federal court in Boston on February 7, 1972. The forty-two-page complaint began by quoting various findings of inadequate care at the school set forth in the American Association on Mental Deficiency's 1968 final report, William Fraenkel's 1969 twenty-four-hour-visit report, and the joint special commission's 1971 report. It then alleged numerous violations of the First, Fifth, Eighth and Fourteenth Amendments of the U.S. Constitution, including:

> overcrowding
> grossly inadequate furnishing of buildings
> unsanitary lavatories and inadequate bathing facilities that
>   lack privacy
> unclean and unsanitary buildings and facilities
> pest infestation
> delayed repairs
> inadequate clothing
> lack of medical and dental treatment
> lack of proper food and nutrition services
> insufficient preventive health services
> lack of physical therapy services
> poor psychological services
> insufficient speech pathology and audiology services
> regimented impersonal environment
> shortage of staff
> lack of personal hygiene
> brutality of the environment
> aberrant sexual climate

    denial of basic civil rights
    improper restraint and punishment
    knowing denial of treatment[3]

Although not intended at the time, the beginning of the end of the Belchertown State School was at hand.

Roland Nagle had replaced Fraenkel as superintendent in the fall preceding the lawsuit, after the joint commission's interim evaluation report, issued in September, excoriated Fraenkel for lack of progress in improving conditions at the school. We do not know what prompted Nagle, an obscure administrator of community-based mental retardation programs at the time, to seek the position of superintendent (if, indeed, he sought it), or to accept it at a moment when morale at the institution was low, public scrutiny was intense, and the big guns of the state legislature had the school in their sights. He survived for eleven months—from October 1971 to September 1972—although he submitted his resignation a few months earlier.

Nagle took office with the cautious support of Ricci and the Friends Association.[4] He began by hiring a wheelchair consultant to make a complete survey of the wheelchair situation at the school. As a consequence, the school ordered twenty-seven new chairs; an additional seven were purchased with private funds.[5] He reorganized the Education and Training Department, emphasizing training rather than production, and established the Occupational Therapy Department as a department separate from Education and Training, with emphasis on occupational therapy treatment techniques rather than education. The volunteer program also expanded on his watch: more than 1,100 volunteers contributed some 20,600 hours of service.[6] Overall, though, his regime was very much a continuation of Fraenkel's themes and ideas.

Probably Nagle's most important legacy was the completion of "unitization"—the reorganization of the school into seven residential units based on behavioral level and chronological age.[7] Unitization had been mandated by state regulation some years earlier but was not begun until Fraenkel took charge. Although it can be dismissed as little more than a shell game (the Adult Living and Learning Unit and the Adolescent Living and Learning Unit, for example, were merely new names for the back wards), there was logic to the new structure. Among other things, it established new lines of responsibility that made supervision and accountability easier to track—key elements of any sustainable reform program.

In June 1972, less than nine months into the job, Nagle tendered his resignation, to become effective September 2. Nothing became him so much as the style of his departure. Pressed to explain his resignation publicly, he wrote a reluctant, thoughtful, self-effacing letter to the editor of the *Sentinel* that was quite unlike anything any administrator of the Belchertown State School had written or said before. It is worth quoting in some detail:

> My original preference was to avoid any public statements, for I earnestly dread being drawn into open displays of reciprocal "blaming," which news media often are skilled in precipitating. Actually I have no person or group of people upon which I could place any specific blame, unless it be myself for my self-deception in the summer of 1971 that I could somehow perform satisfactorily under the myriad demands of this position.
>
> The field of mental retardation is in a state of great stress currently. Indeed, there exists a concern and demand for changed and/or increased services for needy people, i.e., inhabitants of prisons, persons addicted to drugs, persons suffering from mental illness (without retardation), as well as those afflicted by mental and physical handicaps, and those unfortunate enough to have been born into economically and socially deprived classes or races. It is awesome to think of their needs, and absolutely numbing to think of the public treasury which must be collected to meet them.
>
> And that's the rub. The existing treasury is not sufficient. . . . The money isn't there, and yet the demands multiply and grow louder constantly. . . . I don't have the stamina of the few exceptional people who can tack into the teeth of the gale. Positions such as I occupy require this level of courage and determination and I don't possess it. My resignation is unequivocal.

Nagle did not end his letter there. Indeed, he wasn't yet half finished. He went on to propose what he called a "radical departure from the system of delivery of services to handicapped people." His proposal was to replace the existing system of large, state-owned facilities with "small private, profit-making entrepreneurs [who] would be able to compete with one another to offer habilitative services." His idea was for the federal or state governments (or a combination of the two), or a large-scale health insurance plan, to provide funds to the handicapped, who, protected by parents or legal guardians, would purchase services from these private providers.

"In this way guardians of handicapped people could use monies granted directly to them to purchase the help required by their needy charges—the needs to be determined by qualified professional evaluators, whether medical, residential, vocational, social, psychological, or other."

Competition would ensure that the more effective, needs-fulfilling providers would survive while the less efficient would suffer economic extinction. Ombudsmen would be created "to assure redress for consumers and their advocates" and to help assure "an even speedier elimination of those who are less prepared than others to deliver services at effective levels." The cost of such a proposal would, Nagle admitted, be difficult to estimate in advance. He hoped, though (and here Nagle finally tips his hand as far as identifying who he thinks is at fault for the poor care of the mentally retarded—he engages in the blame game after all), that

> it would circumvent central bureaucracies whereby most operations are controlled by people who are often completely out of touch with evolving patterns of needs. Such controls often cause the efforts to provide services to the handicapped by present field managers to be relatively ineffectual. Every proposal such managers make is so circumscribed by centralized authority that it often is reduced to the status of a mere intellectual exercise. The job becomes one of trying to outwit the authorities in Boston and the possibility of success in such efforts are very limited.[8]

There are echoes here of Ricci and his colleagues, although Nagle may have meant to cast his net wider than they did: "Boston" sounds bigger than the state's mental health bureaucracy.[9] Probably Nagle had in mind his recent budget battle with the state authorities for the 1972/73 fiscal year. He had asked for a whopping $10,647,431—almost double the prior year's expenditure. His request included $389,000 for "consultant services." Most of those who staffed the school's new speech and hearing center, for example, were "consultants," not salaried employees. Also, a substantial part of this amount was meant to maintain the growing college-student work-study program at the school (for expenses such as payments to the consultants who supervised the program and to interns). According to a staff psychologist at the school, college students were now providing 1,200 hours of service there each week, including 500 hours by paid interns. Nagle, a tireless advocate for this program, declared in an interview with the *Sentinel* that the students demonstrated "exuberance, innovativeness, psychological inspiration for the residents, who theretofore had functioned in a depressed and withdrawn state." He pointed out that the interns "free up some of the full-time staff people for supervisory and other types of planning duties that would be difficult for them to carry out without the help of the interns," and added, "In many cases the paid interns develop levels of skill and competency almost equal to the paid staff members who have graduate training and experience."[10]

The state's governor, Francis Sargent, though, in his budget recommendations to the legislature in March, slashed the Belchertown State School request to $6,098,000—even less than the prior year's appropriation. Only $120,000 of this was earmarked for consultant services—not a third of what Nagle had sought. Ricci, of course, was outraged too, telling the *Sentinel*, "They're putting humans below highways. . . . It's not a sign of integrity and good will. It's a mean trick."[11]

Perhaps the third branch of government really was the only solution.

The class action got off to a fast start. Four days after the case was filed, Francis J. W. Ford, the ninety-two-year-old federal judge to whom it was originally assigned, issued a preliminary restraining order prohibiting further admissions until a plan for the orderly reduction of the resident population was presented, prohibiting transfers of residents to any state facility for the mentally ill, directing the Secretary for Human Services to make a complete evaluation of the medical needs of each resident within thirty days, and calling for the preparation of various plans to provide better care. Beginning in February, the same month the suit was filed, medical evaluations were conducted by a special team of physicians and ancillary personnel, in accordance with the court order. In June, the state presented a 140-page "Care and Treatment Plan for Belchertown," also mandated by the court order.

But there things stalled. First, Judge Ford retired; the case was reassigned to seventy-two-year-old Judge Anthony Julian, who soon retired as well; it was reassigned to Levin Campbell, a much younger U.S. district court judge in Boston, but Campbell was shortly thereafter promoted to the Court of Appeals. Once again it was reassigned, this time to Judge Manual Real of the U.S. district court in Los Angeles, whose out-of-state residence presented its own set of challenges. Finally, in April 1973, fourteen months after the complaint was filed and Judge Ford's temporary restraining order was issued, the case was permanently reassigned to Judge Joseph L. Tauro of the U.S. district court of Massachusetts.

During this fourteen-month interregnum, further tragedy was to befall the residents of Belchertown State School. On the afternoon of November 19, 1972, Linda Buchanan, a thirty-nine-year-old resident of Building F who had been committed when she was sixteen, wandered off and got lost on the grounds. She died of exposure early the next morning, and her body was not found until some hours later. On November 20, John Abbott, a spastic paraplegic living at the infirmary who was unable to speak and who had the mental age of nine months, died after swallowing an open safety pin that punctured his esophagus and carotid artery. On November 24, Christopher Adams, an eighteen-year-old resident of Building G who had lived at the school for ten years, died from asphyxia caused by food inhalation. On December 3, Rena Aubin, twenty-three years old and a resident of the school since she was twelve, died from a spontaneous rupture of her stomach as a result of overeating and bronchial aspiration of stomach contents.

These deaths, occurring so close together and at a time when the school was under intense public scrutiny, served to heighten the sense of a leaderless institution run amuck. The state secretaries of human services and public safety were asked by the governor the following January (1973) to investigate the deaths.[12] They determined, in the case of Linda Buchanan, that there had been culpable negligence. The search procedures in effect at the school were called "totally inadequate." (For example, a state policeman had called off the search on the evening of Buchanan's disappearance only three hours after it began.) Disciplinary action was recommended against several school employees. No blame was assigned for the other three deaths; however, the report is meticulous in recounting the details of those deaths, including relevant events preceding each and the actions taken by various staff personnel afterward.[13] It also included a number of sensible recommendations to minimize the likelihood of such deaths in the future. Even Ben Ricci, not given to saying nice things about public officials in the state of Massachusetts, described the secretaries' 104-page investigate report as a "thorough masterpiece."[14]

At the time of the four deaths the school's de facto superintendent was Dr. Aran Kasparyan, who was also the chief physician. Kasparyan was the third superintendent in less than twelve months, and he acceded to the position by default: he was next in the chain of command when Nagle's resignation became effective. Nagle had given enough notice of his resignation that, in ordinary circumstances, there would have been enough time to find a replacement other than Kasparyan. These were not ordinary circumstances. According to Ricci, Commissioner Greenblatt had in mind for the job the former superintendent of a facility for the mentally retarded in Miami. Ricci got wind of the name, uncovered scandalous details about the man's prior performance, and managed to thwart the appointment.[15] Then, in July 1972, Greenblatt established a superintendent search committee. He invited Ricci to join. Although Ricci was only one of half a dozen or more appointees on the committee (the others were Department of Mental Health loyalists, including one of the school's former superintendents, William Fraenkel, and two staff members), he took the job very personally.

To say that Ricci was a thorn in the search committee's side does not begin to describe the torment that he inflicted on them. He viewed the group as a rigged jury and acted accordingly. The initial chair was a Department of Mental Health, rather than Division of Mental Retardation, administrator. Ricci objected—and succeeded in having the man replaced. At the first committee meeting, he demanded that the superintendent vacancy be advertised in professional journals nationally *and internationally* as well as in major American newspapers. (Although the committee agreed to do so, this was never done.) He dismissed four of the six resumes presented at the first meeting (how, he wondered, had resumes been procured without advertising?), two on the grounds that they were musical-chair bureaucrats seeking lateral transfers and the other two as "barely worth a second glance." He refused to interview any of them. At a subsequent meeting he insisted that the vacancy be advertised at the International Congress on Mental Retardation in Montreal, to be held in late September. A perfunctory notice was posted at the congress. Not a single person expressed interest in the position. (Ricci himself attended the congress and gave a talk on the pending class action lawsuit. One cannot help but wonder at the inhibiting effect his no doubt enthusiastic description of the lawsuit must have had on prospective applicants; the successful applicant would find himself on day one a defendant in a most contentious lawsuit in which the zealous Ricci was lead plaintiff.)

With a reluctant interim superintendent, Kasparyan, now in place, and no serious candidate yet identified, Ricci decided that the problem lay in the nature of the search process itself. He complained to the governor. In November, after a private meeting among Ricci, two of Ricci's compatriots from local advocacy groups, and the governor's special assistant, the governor rebuked Greenblatt for a flawed search process and barred him from further participation in the search. (Ricci says a furious Greenblatt, who was also a trustee of the University of Massachusetts, where Ricci taught, threatened to have him fired from the faculty in retaliation.) A new hiring process was put in place; henceforth selection committees would include parents of retarded persons, vacancies would be advertised in appropriate professional journals and newspapers, and solicitations would be mailed to major colleges and university professional schools. Ricci was told that he, personally, would have the decisive say in filling the Belchertown vacancy.[16]

The candidate who received Ricci's blessing was William E. Jones, an assistant dean in charge of curriculum and research development in the School of Education at St. John's University in New York City. Jones was appointed Belchertown's superintendent in December 1972 and served until 1986.[17] He would eventually be credited with implementing the reforms sought by the Ricci lawsuit and establishing deinstitutionalization as the ultimate goal of the school.

The lawsuit filed on behalf of the school's residents in February 1972, which had languished for more than a year while it was being assigned and reassigned to a series of federal judges, finally landed on the desk of U.S. District Court Judge Joseph L. Tauro in April 1973, three months after Jones took office. Tauro, who had recently been appointed to the federal bench, wasted no time taking the case on. Having read the complaint, he wanted to see for himself what conditions at the school were like. He asked the plaintiffs' attorney, Beryl Cohen, along with Ricci in his capacity as plaintiffs' representative, and Terence Patrick O'Malley, the Massachusetts assistant attorney general who represented the defendants, to accompany him and his law clerk on a visit to the school.

Their unannounced visit took place on a sunny, warm, humid morning in early May. Many years later, Tauro would reminisce to reporters about his impressions of that day. "What a waste of time this is," he thought as he drove onto the grounds and viewed the rolling lawns. "It look[s] like a prep school. . . . This is beautiful." Inside, though, Tauro was quickly disabused of first impressions; what he saw next remained with him for life. "I saw a little girl drinking from a feces-filled commode; bare rooms with no partitions between beds. People were lying on the floor half naked in their own excrement and urine. They had no closets, no doors on toilets."[18] Altogether, Tauro spent nine hours at the school, touring the Tadgell Nursery, the infirmary, and Buildings G and K, among others. His law clerk took extensive notes. At the end of the day, he invited his fellow visitors to go with him across the street for sandwiches.

Accounts vary a bit as to what happened over sandwiches. Ricci recalls Tauro asking O'Malley how many times he had visited the school; when

O'Malley replied that this was his first visit, the judge, "visibly upset," directed him to inform Governor Sargent and the state's attorney general the next day that he had now done so, that conditions there existed as expressed in the complaint filed with the court, that he intended to waive trial, and that a consent agreement would be achieved.[19] Judge Tauro, when asked about the event some years later, had a less ad hominem, but equally pointed, recollection: "I told them that I didn't see how it would be possible at all for the commonwealth to come up with . . . any sort of expert opinion that would convince me that little girls are supposed to drink out of urinals, that there were supposed to be welts all over people's bodies, that there were supposed to be feces all over the floor, that people were supposed to be unclothed, writhing around in obvious pain."[20]

Shortly thereafter the state advised Judge Tauro of its desire to settle the case rather than try it. Negotiations ensued, and six months later, on November 12, 1973, the parties signed their historic consent decree. The signing ceremony took place in the Hearth Room of the Lord Jeffery Inn in Amherst. Benjamin Ricci, intrepid advocate and father of one of the school's long-term residents, signed on behalf of the plaintiffs.[21]

The consent decree ushered in a new era of reform at Belchertown State School, one in which the state was obligated by agreement and court order to implement substantial change. The decree addressed three broad areas of concern: the physical plant, staffing, and community-based alternatives to institutionalization.

Under the terms of the agreement, the Department of Mental Health was to seek an immediate appropriation from the legislature of $2.6 million, to be used for the renovation and improvement of the physical plant: the school's buildings, including furnishings and equipment. Detailed guidelines were provided as to how this money should be spent. For example, each resident was to be given a set of personal furniture, including a chest of drawers, a table or desk, and an individual clothes closet with accessible racks and shelves as well as a place to keep personal recreational and prosthetic equipment. Bathrooms were to be upgraded to ensure privacy, promote personal hygiene, and eliminate offensive odors. Each toilet and shower would be partitioned. All toilets would be equipped with toilet seats and toilet paper. The ratio of bath fixtures to residents was set at one toilet and one washbasin for every six residents and one shower fixture for every eight residents. More generally, sleeping, living, and dining areas were to be ventilated, redecorated, and made more homelike.

The defendants agreed to hire eighty new domestic workers within sixty days to work in the cleaning, food, laundry, and maintenance services and to add thirty-six professional specialists, in areas such as physical and speech therapy and vocational training, within ninety days. In the area of community alternatives to institutionalization, the defendants committed to support various community residence and day programs for at least seventy-five residents—this number to be increased to ninety-two the following year. Perhaps most important, the court retained oversight responsibility for implementation of the decree, and the parties were obliged to meet and report to the judge at regular intervals about any additional or desirable programs.

The consent decree would prove instrumental in improving the quality of care available to the residents of Belchertown State School during the final years of its existence. But before we examine these improvements more closely, two other events no less important to the outcome should be noted: the commencement of lawsuits similar to *Ricci v. Greenblatt* with respect to other state institutions in Massachusetts, which also gave rise to consent decrees, and the sudden availability of large sums of federal money for state mental retardation programs.

First, the other lawsuits. *Ricci v. Greenblatt* proved to be only the first of several lawsuits brought on behalf of residents against state institutions for the mentally retarded. During 1974 and 1975 (partly at the urging of Ben Ricci), similar class actions were filed against the authorities with respect to the Fernald State School in Waltham, the Wrentham State School, the Dever State School in Taunton, and the Monson State Hospital.[22] These cases were all assigned to Judge Tauro and consolidated with *Ricci v. Greenblatt* in a single action. Like *Ricci v. Greenblatt*, they were settled by consent decrees whose implementation was subject to the oversight of Judge Tauro. The decrees, which together covered all of the institutions in the state of Massachusetts caring for the mentally retarded, reinforced one another and gave the plaintiff class, collectively, substantial leverage vis-à-vis the state authorities that no individual class would have had standing alone. The dedication and political savvy of Judge Tauro further assured strict compliance. (Tauro revisited the institutions regularly, condemning shortfalls when he found them and praising compliance.) Moreover, although Tauro could not force the legislature to appropriate the funds required to implement the decrees, the legislature did, in the end, always do so.[23]

Second, federal money. In 1972, Congress amended Title XIX of the Social Security Act to allow states to obtain reimbursement from Medicaid for up to 50 percent of eligible costs relating to the care of mentally retarded persons. To be eligible, the states were required to comply with detailed federal standards regarding such things as physical design of facilities, staffing, and programs. After some initial hesitation, Massachusetts decided to participate. Uniform standards based on Title XIX were incorporated in the various consent decrees (including, retroactively, Belchertown's). Beginning in 1974 and accelerating subsequently, substantial funds were obtained under Title XIX—for example, over $118 million in fiscal year 1987. The impact of this federal money cannot be overstated.[24]

As we've seen, the superintendent of the Belchertown school at the time of Judge Tauro's visit was William E. Jones, who was personally approved by Ben Ricci to fill the job after Roland Nagle resigned. Interestingly, unlike Nagle or Nagle's predecessor, William E. Fraenkel, both of whom were criticized by Ricci for nonperformance after only a few months on the job (and, in the case of Fraenkel, excoriated by the joint commission of the Massachusetts legislature investigating conditions at the school), Jones, who had been on the job for only three and a half months when Tauro visited, seems to have escaped any personal blame for what Tauro saw. He was, in effect, given a honeymoon that the previous two were denied.

An early indication that things might be about to change for the better was the school's annual report for the 1972/73 fiscal year, issued six months after Jones became superintendent. For one thing, the report was much longer than before—a sign, perhaps, that there was more to talk about. Most astonishing was the unprecedented transparency and frankness. Each unit director, for example, was required to provide his or her own report. The report of the director for the new Adult Living and Learning Unit (which housed some of the former back ward residents) is illustrative of this new transparency and frankness:

> I have been concerned because we are the only unit without a psychologist and yet, behavior problems that were too difficult for other units were transferred to our unit.
>
> . . . It was disappointing to learn that the Basic Skills Program, directed by the Education Department, had been taken from this area and transferred to the vocational area. I wish that their program could be brought back to our unit. It appears that this staff could be utilized in this area so much more effectively than they are now.

> . . . It is difficult to cope with medical needs. . . . Much despair
> existed in the buildings for the staff and for me, as unit director,
> when we worked to respond to the urgent request with a prior-
> ity list of residents to be evaluated at once. [One of the medical
> doctors] left within about one week from my starting date and we
> continued for some time with physicians coming and going.[25]

This is not the language of someone fearful of reprisal. It is certainly
not the voice of cover-up. On the contrary, it is refreshingly straight talk
direct from a unit head to the superintendent and the school's board of
trustees.

The report for the following fiscal year, 1973/74, runs to 452 pages,
almost three hundred pages longer than the previous year's. It too is trans-
parent and frank, but there is also more in it that is positive. For example,
we learn that the trustees visited all the buildings at the school during the
course of the year and that they set up a new program: at each of their meetings, they interview a resident of the school and an employee. We learn
from the same unit head of the Adult Living and Learning Unit, whose
report the prior year was so despairing, that her unit now has 92 employees to serve 152 residents—a remarkable increase in the staff-to-resident
ratio of the back wards compared to a few years before. She is also, generally speaking, more optimistic than the year before. Precisely because she
didn't mince words earlier, we are that much more willing now to take her
word for it that things are better: "It is with greater satisfaction that I present this annual report; especially because I have just reviewed last year's
resume and feel that I am able to report some more positive feelings in this
narrative."[26]

She goes on to say that her unit now has a psychologist who has "worked
diligently to support the needs for the men and women of our unit, who
have lived here the longest, and suffered the most." Efforts are underway
to segregate the unit's residents into small groups, and employees are now
"responsible for providing more Love and Attention, and for stimulating
and teaching." Perhaps most impressive, she has begun a program for at
least five days a week that allows the residents of her unit—the most profoundly retarded at the school—to leave the dormitories "for a good por-
tion of the day, and have the opportunity to participate in a well-structured,
professionally-supervised program."[27]

Further anecdotal evidence to support this sense of improving conditions in the wake of the consent decree may be gleaned from the memoir

of Ruth Sienkiewicz-Mercer, the woman with cerebral palsy who had been confined in the school's infirmary since 1962. According to Sienkiewicz-Mercer, improvements in her own care, which had begun as far back as 1968, accelerated after 1973. For example, in 1970 a new employee started a speech, hearing, and learning center at the school. By the end of 1974 the center had a full-time staff of ten therapists and ten student interns, plus two supervisors and a director.[28]

Sienkiewicz-Mercer, who began therapy at the center in 1971, says it became the "highlight" of her existence at the school. "I wasn't treated like a State School resident at the clinic, nor was I considered a patient or even a client. Howard, Kathy [both student interns] and I were participants in an ongoing experiment. We were partners in discovering what worked and what didn't in developing the most usable and unlimited communication techniques for the verbally disabled." She acquired the ability to communicate with a word board, piecing together a message by using eye movements and facial expressions to direct a helper who held the board in front of her to particular words.[29]

Sienkiewicz-Mercer's memoir corroborates other changes for the better mandated by the consent decree and noted in various annual reports. In November 1974 she heard that some of the "easier" residents were being allowed to go on day trips with friends or staff. She asked a new attendant in the infirmary, eighteen-year-old Michelle Busquet, to take her and her sister, Shari, to a mall in Springfield to do Christmas shopping.

> Suddenly leaving the State School was easy. Michelle simply loaded me into the old car she was driving, threw my wheelchair into the trunk, and off we headed to my parents' house to pick up Shari. . . . [Eventually we] made it to the mall, where Michelle and Shari kept the jokes going full tilt.
>
> Our activity for the rest of the day was to laugh our way around the mall. In the process, we caught a lot of sidelong stares from other people. But I just laughed harder and harder as Michelle and Shari cracked jokes about everybody who gawked at us.
>
> Without a doubt, that was one of the best days of my life.[30]

The combination of unitization and renovation of the physical plant was also making life at the state school better for at least some of the residents. Sienkiewicz-Mercer recalls being moved out of the infirmary for good in 1975, first to "temporary" quarters (for one and a half years) in Tadgell (the former nursery), and then next door to Alpha House.

Although it was only a few hundred yards away [from the infir-
mary], Tadgell was drastically different. It was spacious, bright,
well lit, and recently renovated. It was a one-story building, with a
central kitchen, a TV area, and male and female sleeping quarters
divided by common bathroom facilities. . . .

Twenty people, ten men and ten women, moved to Tadgell from
the Infirmary. All of these individuals were physically handicapped
but either intellectually normal or at least high-functioning retarded. This setup gave me an opportunity to meet new people as well
as spend more time with friends I had made at the Infirmary. Also,
for the first time in my life at Belchertown, I was able to socialize
somewhat normally with male residents. The mingling of men and
women was a real improvement, part of a very new and different
concept: to allow at least some of the residents to live in a less institutional environment.

. . . I slept with four other women in an open area, with small
privacy screens around our beds. With a brighter group of people,
there were very few disruptions caused by roommates who were
unable to control their behavior, so I had more actual privacy than
at the Infirmary.

. . . Tadgell fell far short of community living, but it definitely
beat the Infirmary. At least I was halfway free. The attendants were
helpful and considerate, and several used my word boards regularly. All of them gave me the time and opportunity to communicate with them.[31]

It is difficult to verify meaningful reform, other than anecdotally. But
one statistic in particular—the staff-to-resident ratio—would seem to
corroborate the anecdotal evidence. Whereas in 1970 the school had one
employee for every two residents, by 1985 there were three and a half
employees for every resident.[32]

Even as the poor quality of care at the school was, finally, being redressed,
a new debate was starting about whether mentally retarded persons
should be cared for in large state-run institutions at all. This debate as
it related to the Belchertown school was foreshadowed in an acrimoni-
ous exchange between Ben Ricci and the Hampshire County branch of
the Massachusetts Association for Retarded Citizens (MARC) in March
1973. The exchange was published in the following month's issue of The

Bell, the monthly newsletter of the Belchertown State School Friends Association, of which Ricci was still president. In the February issue, Ricci had penned a long essay attacking the Department of Mental Health. Under the repeated refrain "How would you view the future if you knew that . . . ," he belittled the department for—among other things—what he called its "almost fanatical desire to reduce institutional populations without genuine concern" for the individuals involved. He said residents were "never" properly prepared for their transition into community life, that there was inadequate counseling, too little training, and too few homes where mentally retarded residents could be placed. He accused the department of maintaining halfway houses that did not meet minimum standards of public safety and of having recently released three alleged "trouble-makers" merely for the purpose of "disposing" of them; their relatives, he said, had neither been consulted nor informed of the transfers and were "shocked" when Ricci told them of the moves.

To be fair, Ricci was not attacking community placement per se but rather the method by which it was being pursued. Nevertheless, the response of the Hampshire County MARC—and others committed to "deinstitutionalization" (as it was called)—was sharp: "[We] take strong exception to your statements . . . regarding community residences and the attitudes of parents of institutionalized children concerning them," they wrote, adding "Without exception, parents of Belchertown children are convinced that the community home concept, providing services that are available within the community and providing a normal environment for their children, is far superior to any that can be offered in the isolated, poorly staffed, run-down, dehumanizing conglomeration called Belchertown." Citing, among others, the writings of the psychologist and researcher Wolf Wolfensberger ("Have you read the recent literature on institutionalization?"), the Hampshire County MARC went on to say: "These studies plus others done over and over regarding the effects of deprivation on children in institutions, should convince you that your emphasis on maintaining this large, unwieldy complex is poorly placed. . . . We feel that you have seriously misled parents of institutionalized children and that if you continue to champion the isolation of retarded citizens from the mainstream of life you will do them and their parents a great disservice."[33]

Ricci responded in the same issue of *The Bell*. He was skeptical that the state of Massachusetts would be any more likely to provide requisite funding and services for community homes than they had done for the state schools. He insisted that in fact the "overwhelming majority" of parents of state school residents were opposed to the community residence concept "as it is presently constituted" and that MARC did not represent the views and concerns of these parents. Acknowledging that the letter-writers had chosen to put their own children in a community home, he stressed that they themselves—not the state or a state school—had made the decision to do so, and that this was consistent with his underlying theme that parents should play a major role in decisions about their children. "In like manner, please permit other parents to solve problems in their own manner." The choice, he said, should not be between state schools as they were presently constituted and community placement, but rather between the community and "vastly improved institutions." Thus the battle lines were drawn.

Ricci's skeptical attitude toward deinstitutionalization was shaped by two events: his visits during his sabbatical to residential centers for retarded persons in Scandinavia, which represented for him an ideal of care that the community houses touted by the MARC letter-writers no more resembled than did the Belchertown State School; and the recent murder trial of Russell Daniels, a young black man who had lived most of his life at the Belchertown school and was convicted in 1972 of murdering an eighty-three-year-old woman in Springfield by sticking a butcher knife in her throat. At the time of the murder, he lived alone in a nearby apartment and worked part-time as a janitor in the victim's building. In 1970, as part of the state school's community placement program, he had been released to a halfway house in Springfield, where he lived for five months before moving into his own apartment and obtaining his part-time janitorial job.

Daniels's conviction was based solely on a confession obtained from him during police interrogation. Ricci and others maintained that Daniels, who read only at a second-grade level and whose IQ was 53, lacked the mental capacity to make a voluntary and intelligent confession to a crime. They also saw Daniels as the victim of an ill-conceived community placement program whose goal was merely to reduce the population of the state school by transferring residents to community homes without adequate preparation or follow-up.

> Where were the DMH legal experts . . . when Russell Daniels was arrested for murder? . . . His signature affixed to a confession statement *he could neither read nor comprehend* was used by the Commonwealth as primary evidence for his conviction. . . . Massachusetts distinguished itself by sending to the infamous

Walpole State Prison a 10 year old boy in a 28 year old body who happens to suffer the dual discrimination of being mentally retarded *and* black. Would you say programs and services were available for Russell Daniel? *They were not.* He was discharged following a five month stay in . . . a [halfway] house which failed to meet even minimum safety standards. Where were the "professional protectors" of the retarded? Where were Secretary Goldmark, Commissioner Greenblatt . . . ? Are they protectors?[34]

This debate or quarrel between the advocates of institutional reform and the advocates of deinstitutionalization would persist for another twenty years, framing the broader discussion of what should happen to the Belchertown State School.[35] Gradually, momentum would build in favor of deinstitutionalization and community living. New admissions to the school would be frozen; transfers to community homes would accelerate.[36] Even Benjamin Ricci would decide to remove his son from the school and place him in community living. The turning point, if there was one, probably came on a blustery Sunday in November 1983, when hundreds of demonstrators, including residents of the state school, gathered on the town common in Belchertown to show their support for deinstitutionalization. The Committee in Support of Community Living provided signs ("Label Jars, Not People," "A Building Is Not a Home," "End the Battle Between School and Group Homes," "Free the Belchertown 423") and speakers. Gunnar Dybwad, a professor at Brandeis University and a leader in the disability-rights movement, sought to change once and for all the premise of the debate. "I have a strong objection," he told the crowd, "to community living as an alternative to institutions. The opposite is the case, institutions are an alternative to community living."[37] The rally emphasized the humanitarian issue: community living was better for the mentally retarded. But the economics, too, had evolved in favor of deinstitutionalization: whereas the cost of maintaining a person at the state school for one year was $70,000, that same person in a community home cost the taxpayers only $35,000 per year.[38]

The ideological underpinning for deinstitutionalization and the community living movement was "normalization," a social principle developed by Bengt Nirje, director of the Swedish Association for Retarded Children, in the 1960s and popularized in the United States by Wolf Wolfensberger in the early 1970s. Normalization holds that there should be made available to all mentally retarded people "patterns of life and conditions of

everyday living which are as close as possible to the regular circumstances
and ways of life or society":

> Normalization means sharing a normal rhythm of the day, with
> privacy, activities and mutual responsibilities; a normal rhythm of
> the week, with a home to live in, a school or work to go to, and lei-
> sure time with a modicum of social interaction; a normal rhythm
> of the year, with the changing modes and ways of life and family
> and community customs as experienced in the different seasons
> of the year.
>
> Normalization also means opportunity to undergo the nor-
> mal developmental experiences of the life cycle: infanthood, with
> security and the respective steps of early childhood development;
> school age, with exploration and the increase of skills and expe-
> riences; adolescence, with development towards adult life and
> options. . . .
>
> The principle applies to all retarded people, whatever their
> degree of handicap and wherever they live.[39]

The premise was that if general living conditions were "normalized," then
retarded people would act and be more "normal."[40]

At the time the "Tragedy of Belchertown" exposé was published in 1971,
some professionals in the field had already become disillusioned with
large, state-run custodial institutions for retarded persons. They despaired
of reforming them and were looking for alternatives. "Normalization"
suggested an alternative. Several of these professionals already worked in
regional offices of the Massachusetts Department of Mental Health, which
had been set up following enactment of the state's Comprehensive Mental
Health and Retardation Services Act of 1966 with a view to creating local
community service systems. Initially these regional offices had very limited resources and only tiny program budgets. They provided almost no
services of their own, instead channeling their funds into private community service providers like the MARC. "Nevertheless," as a historian of the
community living movement writes, "they were the infant version of what
would become over the next several decades the rival system to the institutions and eventually emerge as the new dominant system."[41]

The focus of this small group of Massachusetts professionals—developing community-based alternatives to long-term institutionalization of
the disabled—was representative of a broader national trend. Beginning
in 1967, the number of residents in the nation's 190 public facilities for

mentally disabled persons had, for the first time, begun steadily to decline across a broad range of states—from 193,000 residents in 1967 to 181,000 residents in 1971. Analysis indicates that this "historic reversal" was due to "one factor only": more adult residents were being released to live in other settings.[42] Whether these releases nationally were motivated by new ideas like Nirje's normalization principle, by a growing recognition of the horrific living conditions at these institutions, or other factors, is less clear. But the trend was unmistakable and, as it turned out, irreversible.

Community living was a radical departure from the fortresses of custodial quarantine that the schools envisioned by Samuel Gridley Howe in the mid-nineteenth century had become under the tutelage of Walter E. Fernald and others—but not so great a departure from Howe's vision itself. One can easily imagine Howe, whose pedagogical goal was the reintegration of feeble-minded persons into the community as productive participants rather than charges, pleased by the new direction.

The movement to take mentally retarded persons out of large, isolated, rural institutions and care for them instead in apartments and small houses located in urban and suburban neighborhoods throughout the state could not have succeeded unless those communities acquiesced in their presence. This shift in the willingness of the public to accept, or at least tolerate, mentally retarded persons as neighbors is in itself noteworthy. It has been suggested that other changes occurring in society at the time may have facilitated this shift, including public acceptance of expanded government support for human services, widely publicized governmental programs to aid the disadvantaged (such as the war on poverty), the civil rights movement with its focus on equality, integration, and opportunity for African Americans, the rise of investigative and advocacy journalism and, more generally, the "protest culture" and "counterculture" of the late 1960s, both of which put premiums on experimentation, permissiveness, and challenges to orthodoxy.[43] Perhaps a more affluent world could now better afford more individualized care. Perhaps, too, the science that had for so long justified quarantine (for example, the purported inheritability of most mental retardation) was finally and irrevocably exposed as bogus.

Whatever the truth of these broader speculations, it is a fact that the community living movement proceeded at different paces in different places, and that Belchertown was the first of the state institutions for mentally retarded persons in Massachusetts to yield completely to the movement. This is curious—especially given the fact that Belchertown was the first state school subject to a consent decree and therefore the furthest down the road of genuine institutional reform at the time it was closed. Perhaps there really was some special tie between Belchertown and its state school—a tie beyond being the largest employer in town—that made it easier, finally, for its residents and those of nearby towns to receive the school's residents into their communities. Maybe the many decades of school produce and crafts exhibitions, minstrel shows, Fourth of July floats and parades, community parole, family care, *Sentinel* columns, and free rides at the annual town fair helped to humanize the men and women, girls and boys, confined at the state school. Perhaps the many student interns and volunteers from universities and colleges in the area who worked part-time at the school in its later decades helped to break down its walls more quickly than at other facilities where the volunteer commitment was less.[44]

The decision to close Belchertown State School had been anticipated as far back as 1979, when the town's board of selectmen appointed a study group to consider the impact on the town of losing 1,400 jobs (440 of them held by Belchertown residents) at the school if it closed and to devise a plan of action to counter the anticipated negative effects, both economic and social.[45] The formal announcement came ten years later, on March 8, 1989. Speaking at a group home in nearby Amherst where several former residents of the school now lived, Mary McCarthy, head of the Department of Mental Retardation, told the more than one hundred state officials, workers, advocates for the mentally retarded, and state school parents gathered for the occasion that the Belchertown State School would close by 1992. In the interim, the remaining 266 residents would be moved to community homes, and the existing staff of more than 1,500 state workers would be transferred to community programs throughout western Massachusetts or to other state institutions. "This is a historic occasion," said Ben Ricci, "a day we have looked forward to for many, many years."[46] There were a few dissenters—Barbara Konopka (also a state school parent), for one, who insisted that those needing "round-the-clock supervision and specialized medical care" were best served in institutions, not community-based programs. "The state's just trying to get out of the business of taking care of the mentally retarded," she said, just trying to cut costs at the expense of the disabled.[47] But hers had become, in the twenty years since the "Tragedy of Belchertown" exposé and the Ricci class action, a distinctly minority position.

The end came on a rainy day in late December 1992, when the last three residents of the state school—Mary Marshall, Theresa Dansereau (both in their sixties), and Andrew DeLiso (thirty)—boarded a van that would take them to their new home in Agawam, a small city about thirty miles away. Besides private bedrooms for each, their new home had living, dining, and kitchen areas; it was wheelchair accessible and equipped with a whirlpool bath for physical therapy. It would be staffed by nine direct-care workers (all former Belchertown employees), at least two of whom (including one nurse) would always be on duty, twenty-four hours a day. Lisa Almeidi and Ann Foth (a licensed practical nurse), two of the staff members who were transferring to the group home in Agawam and who had been working with Marshall, Dansereau, and DeLiso since the spring, boarded the van with them. Ben Ricci, standing nearby, wept.[48]

There was one final detail: the keys. At a ceremony on the last day of the year attended by some two hundred interested people, including former residents, the front door of the school's main administration building was locked for the last time and the keys transferred from the Department of Mental Retardation to the Division of Capital Planning and Operations.[49] Several dignitaries, including the commissioner and the secretary of health and human services, gave short speeches. The commissioner chose a historical theme: "Over the past 20 years, the state, families, and the court have worked together to radically change conditions such that they have really turned 180 degrees. The horrible conditions of the past can be contrasted with today's environments of small family-like settings where people have opportunities to make choices, form relationships with various kinds of people, receive training, participate in meaningful work opportunities, and be contributing members of their communities."[50]

The last to speak was Ruth Sienkiewicz-Mercer. She finally left the state school in 1978 and had recently published a memoir of her years there, *I Raise My Eyes to Say Yes*. Still confined to a wheelchair because of cerebral palsy, she spoke with the aid of a computer.

> This is one of the happiest days of my life.
>
> Perhaps the happiest day of my life was the day I moved out of Belchertown State School and into my own apartment in Springfield.
>
> When I think back to the years I spent here I am both angry and sad. I am sad about the many years of living which were wasted lying around in the infirmary. All of that time could have been spent learning the things we all must learn from household tasks

and daily living skills, to the ins and outs of human nature. I am angry that society in those days felt that the only way to deal with people with disabilities was to put them in an institution.

"I am so very happy and grateful that I was able to leave the Belchertown State School and to begin to enjoy my life," she concluded. "Now everyone who was living here will get the same opportunity to have a good life. We should celebrate this opportunity."[51]

CHAPTER 8

Ghosts and Graveyards

An eerie quiet settled over the former Belchertown State School. Boarded-up buildings stood abandoned. Thick weeds, brush, and small trees sprouted in the fertile soil, overgrowing pathways and lawns. Disrepair and decay spread. The occasional trespasser reported odd things happening: sharp fluctuations of temperature, an intense odor of flowers where none grew, lights flickering in the tunnels though the power was off, mirrors vibrating, running footsteps, random cries and moans. Some called it a haunted place.[1]

What could—or should—be done with the former state school? As we saw in chapter 7, as far back as 1979 the town, anticipating the eventual contraction or shutdown of the school, had established a reuse committee to study alternatives.[2] At a public meeting in 1991, seventy possibilities were put on the table.[3] Now the time was at hand. The Commonwealth of Massachusetts proposed converting the main campus to a 1,150-inmate medium-security prison. Some 350–575 new jobs would be created and local residents would be given preference in hiring. The state would also give the town four parcels of land, two buildings, and $10 million for capital projects as compensation.

The town was tempted. The selectmen visited nearby prisons in Gardner and Shirley to assess the impact and found that "they did not have a negative impact on the community as a whole." Still, there were reservations: the new prison would be relatively close to the center of town; the sixteen-foot-high fences with razor-wire coil seemed "intimidating"; prison lights would light up the night sky forever. Unsaid but no doubt deeply felt, the town had also, in a sense, been in the business of incarceration since 1922;

there was a certain fatigue. On June 22, 1992, in the largest turnout anyone could remember (71 percent), the town's voters emphatically rejected the proposed prison, by a vote of 2,675 to 1,067.[4] Whatever happened to the former state school, it would not again be a place of confinement.

Weapons of modern development theory were deployed in an effort to convert the abandoned facility into a productive town asset. Two entities, the Belchertown Economic Development and Industrial Corporation (BEDIC) and the Industrial Development Finance Authority, were established to develop, implement, and finance an economic development plan.[5] The town itself was designated an Economic Target Area under the state's Economic Development Incentive Program, and the school property was designated an Economic Opportunity Area for twenty years, making tax incentives available to prospective businesses. As with the Board of Trade a century before, the goal was to increase town revenue and create new jobs.

The New England Small Farm Institute (NESFI), a nonprofit organization whose mission is to promote small farm development, leased 416 acres of what had been the school farm. It renamed the leasehold Lampson Brook Agricultural Reserve (later called Lampson Brook Farmstead) and sublet smaller parcels to a number of independent small farm businesses. These enterprises have produced and sold a variety of farm products over the years, including berries, organic vegetables, herbs, annual and perennial plants, fresh and dried flowers, grains and hay, eggs, honey, cordwood, beef feeder calves, and breeding pigs. NESFI also subleases land to the Belchertown Community Garden, which provides small plots for gardening to families in the Belchertown area.[6]

The more vexing challenge was what to do with the former school's nonfarm acreage, including the main campus land and buildings. Five of the buildings (E and F, Tadgell Nursery, and Nurseries 1 and 2) were located on a twenty-acre parcel at the edge of the campus known as Parcel A. In the early 1990s, before the state school closed, the town leased Buildings E and F for use as elementary school classrooms. It leased Tadgell for the same purpose after the school closed. Then, in the mid '90s, it bought the parcel outright.[7] There the town developed, in addition to the elementary school, a new middle school, teen center, senior center, police station, public-access cable TV center, American Legion facility, indoor pool, and playing fields. But the bulk of the nonfarm acreage (approximately 263 acres, known as Parcels B, D, and E) was still owned by the state and remained undeveloped. The largest parcel, B, included thirty structures—the core of the former campus.

In 2002, BEDIC purchased the three parcels for $10.[8] It resold Parcel E, containing 43.7 acres, to a developer for an office park.[9] It leased Parcel D, containing 52.7 acres (including 20 acres of wetland), to the Pioneer Valley Transit Authority for development of a regional intermodal transportation center, but this did not work out, and as of 2011 Parcel D remains mostly undeveloped.[10] It resold ten acres of Parcel B to local businesses, including 3.3 acres to a van operator for storing and maintaining its fleet of passenger and wheelchair-accessible vans.[11]

BEDIC's biggest challenge was what to do with the remaining 156 acres of Parcel B—the core of the former campus. BEDIC was supposed to increase revenue and create new jobs for the town. How best could this be done? Various redevelopment proposals were considered, including a geriatric center for treatment and research of aging, a national center for retired musicians, age-restricted townhouse condominiums and assisted living facility, a self-contained community similar to the Disney-developed community of Celebration in Osceola County, Florida, an office complex, indoor soccer fields, and a garden center.[12]

The most ambitious proposal was for a resort and spa, recalling Belchertown's brief history as a tourist center in the nineteenth century. Elizabeth Taras, a Belchertown resident, proposed the resort idea at a 2000 town meeting, and she was appointed as BEDIC's point person for the project. Hunter Interests, Inc., a Maryland-based real estate company, was retained to study the project's feasibility and to recruit investors and developers. (The study was funded by a $185,000 grant from the state.) Hunter reportedly had worked on dozens of development projects and reuse initiatives around the world, including the former Pineland Center in New Gloucester, Maine, a state facility similar to Belchertown, now a successful mix of office, agriculture, education, and fitness facilities. "To some extent, this is right up our alley," said Ernest Bleinberger, Hunter's senior vice president and chief operating officer.[13]

Hunter proposed an $85 million redevelopment plan, to be called the Cold Spring Resort Hotel and Spa (after the town's original name, which commemorated a spring located nearby where weary colonial travelers were said to have refreshed themselves).[14] The resort plan was unveiled on August 4, 2005, at an event on the Belchertown campus. A tent, set up for the purpose amid the school's boarded-up buildings, provided cover for the assembled crowd. The centerpiece of the plan was the hotel itself, to be, according to Bleinberger, "architecturally reminiscent of the grand old hotels of New England."[15] Bleinberger flourished a picture from the 1880s of Belchertown's celebrated Highland Hotel. In addition, there would be a wellness center, recreational areas, retail and other small businesses, a cultural and performing arts center, a waterfall, and an equestrian center. The resort spa was expected to provide 130–175 full-time-equivalent jobs, 50–100 small businesses, and $1 million in new tax revenue, plus additional visitor spending.

Hunter prepared a short narrative, to convey a sense of their vision:

> The first time visitor turns right into the stately drive, passing through stone columns that support ornate, wrought iron gates that stand open in welcome. To the left, an historic viaduct, now an observation platform, rains a small waterfall down into a beautiful pond that is ringed with natural wetland vegetation. To the right, the vista is of the New England Small Farm Institute, which stretches out in emerald green splendor. Thick woods are beyond, and in the distance the Holyoke Range completes the frame. Continuing up the curving drive, white board fencing acts as a welcoming guide, and showcases horses grazing in the fields beyond. Directly ahead is the object of the journey, an elegant hotel, reminiscent of grand hotels of the past. A large veranda is visible facing the farmland to the west. A vision of the golden sunset to come enters the consciousnesses of the visitors as they pull into a wide port cochere that is flanked by mature flowering shrubs—now at the height of bloom. The ambience is calming and soothing, while at the same time exciting. The week ahead promises an invigorating spa experience, excellent food and drink featuring local products, and the chance to ride, hike, swim, play sports, or just read a book. A few day trips to attractions in the area are planned as well, but for now the well appointed lobby and Great Hall of the Cold Spring Resort Hotel and Spa beckon.[16]

The town officers were ecstatic, the rank and file excited but skeptical. Tom Fuller, a longtime resident, worried about the increased demand for police, fire, water, and sewer services as well as the additional traffic. "That's asking a lot from the infrastructure, the town," he noted. Irving Rosazzi, a seventy-nine-year-old resident, thought it was "a great idea" but had "doubts about it ever happening." "Why," he asked, "would anyone want to come to Belchertown when they could go to a hotel anywhere?" Another resident, Christine Jacobsen, summed it up this way: "It's just kind of hard to picture." Bleinberger was reassuring. "What does Lenox [the location of New England's premier Canyon Ranch spa] have that Belchertown doesn't?" he asked rhetorically, as if the answer "nothing" was self-evident.[17] Don Hunter, the president of Hunter Interests, dismissed the doubters. "Spa development is hot," he said. "There's an increasing awareness of the value of fitness. Baby boomers are approaching retirement age. The market is expanding."[18]

The town issued a request for proposals, to which twenty-three "interested parties" responded.[19] Bridgeland Development LLC of Chicago was chosen to be master developer. Its portfolio of projects around the country, according to a BEDIC press release, included the $150 million Orlando Performing Arts & Education Center and a $1 billion redevelopment in Glenview, Illinois.[20] "We've had a significant amount of interest in the Cold Spring project and we are delighted to have a qualified and experienced partner with which to move forward," said William A. Terry, chairman of BEDIC.[21] Paul McDermott, the president of Bridgeland, was "very excited." "The site is spectacular," he enthused. "When we drive it, we think of Colorado. People are going to want to come to Belchertown."[22]

Bridgeland submitted a revised and expanded concept plan, renaming it Quabbin Resort Development.[23] As many as feasible of the existing state school buildings would be preserved and remediated, including the former theater/school building, the kitchen/cannery, and the administration building. The anticipated 162-acre facility would cost between $144 million and $172 million to develop (up from Hunter's initial estimate of $85 million). The resort would include:

> a 200–300 room hotel and spa offering "5-star living"
> a conference center
> a hospital-affiliated health and wellness center
> a sports performance center
> a two-hundred-stall equestrian center
> a multi-use medical/office building
> restaurants
> boutique retail facilities
> a museum
> recreational activities, including miles of walking, bicycling, horseback riding, and cross-country ski trails, as well as canoeing, fishing, swimming, and tennis[24]

The seven voting directors of BEDIC unanimously approved the revised plan. On May 24, 2006, a festive signing ceremony took place on the

Belchertown common. BEDIC and Bridgeland signed a memorandum of agreement launching the project and a purchase and sale contract for the land and buildings. (The purchase price, not disclosed at the time, was $500,000.) Closing on the property was set for the following September. Construction would begin in the fall of 2007, and a grand opening was anticipated for spring 2009. The *Sentinel* declared the resort spa "a reality."[25] Town officials estimated that an additional $1.4 million in local tax revenue would be realized annually. BEDIC chairman William Terry proclaimed: "We've been working towards and highly anticipating this day for a long time and we really feel this is the highest and best use of this historic and beautiful land. The team that Bridgeland is selecting for this exciting enterprise will provide the best cross section of expertise available today and we can't wait to roll up our sleeves, get down to the final business over the next several months and see the ultimate product—Belchertown and the region deserves it!"[26]

Alas, the hopes of Belchertown would once again be dashed. Hints of trouble surfaced early. The scheduled September closing date passed without closure. A weekly *Sentinel* column ("Quabbin Corner") by Bridgeland's Paul McDermott, begun in August 2006, suddenly stopped in February 2007. That June, rumors circulated that people working on the project were not being paid; selectmen complained publicly that they were being "kept in the dark" about many of the recent details surrounding the project.[27]

It ended, finally, with a bounced check. The sale to Bridgeland of the school's land and buildings, originally scheduled to close in September 2006, had been postponed eight times. Now it was October 2007. The requisite financing was not yet in hand. An Illinois financial broker hired by Bridgeland produced a signed commitment letter from a Florida company called Indie Capital, said to be willing to lend Bridgeland $50 million (at a hefty interest rate of 22 percent); the loan, however, would not close before the end of November, and Indie had not yet signed off on the proposed security package. McDermott ("People are going to want to come to Belchertown") sought a ninth extension. BEDIC—frustrated, and worried about Bridgeland's bona fides—demanded a second, nonrefundable deposit of $100,000 as additional earnest money. Bridgeland sent a check. The check, deposited Monday, October 22, was returned for insufficient funds.[28]

The full BEDIC board met on Thursday night, October 25, to consider its options. Richard Kump, a BEDIC director, got a phone call from a

Bridgeland representative, requesting instructions for wiring the money. But it was too late. As Richard Barry, another BEDIC director, put it, you couldn't trust a man who was willing to write a bad check. The Bridgeland contract was terminated. Quabbin Resort Development was dead.[29]

The project's promoters had a hard time letting go. Elizabeth Taras, the town resident credited with conceptualizing the resort, said it was "not the project" that didn't work, "it was the developer. The plan is sound—two feasibility studies have shown that—and it remains the best option for the site. We just have to find the right developer." Kump concurred. He saw the Bridgeland debacle as merely a setback in the town's fifteen-year quest to redeploy, productively, the former state school's land and buildings. "We're well beyond stage one," he said. "A lot of equity has been established in this concept; we're so much better off than we were two years ago."[30]

For many months thereafter, the BEDIC website included a link called "Quabbin Resort Development," complete with site plan, master plan, map, photos, and news. But there was no further news to report. Eventually, the website was shut down.[31]

In addition to the boarded-up buildings, overgrown lawns, and deteriorating infrastructure, there could be found abandoned around the site numerous items of personal property—utensils, furniture, vehicles—all in various stages of disrepair. There was even a once-beautiful old carousel. It had been purchased for the school from a nearby amusement park in 1947 and refurbished over the next year with contributions from organizations and individuals throughout the state, including the American Legion, Veterans of Foreign Wars, Rotary Club, and Lions Club.[32] Its forty-two horses were hand-carved in 1922 in Brooklyn, New York, by master carvers Solomon Stein and Harry Goldstein—long celebrated by merry-go-round enthusiasts for their flamboyant style.[33] (Stein & Goldstein horses are said to be distinguished by their "big teeth and bulging eyes," the "huge and colorful cabbage roses which festoon their bodies," and their "real horse hair tails.")[34]

Set up in a pine grove beyond the employees' parking lot, the carousel was formally dedicated on a bright Sunday afternoon in October 1948 "to the boys and girls of Belchertown State School." Coffee and cold drinks were served to guests at a nearby refreshment stand. Edward Stowe of Middlebury, Vermont, a former employee who had supervised the setting out of the trees in the pine grove twenty years before, was present.

Superintendent Tadgell delivered the dedicatory speech. After the ceremony, the guests took rides on the new carousel. Then, according to the *Sentinel*, "the state school youngsters were given their turn at it, and did they make a dash for it. It reminded one of the phrase, 'food shot from guns.'"[35]

Unfortunately, New England weather took its toll on the uncovered merry-go-round. A pavilion that was supposed to house the apparatus never got built.[36] Although horses and benches were removed each winter and stored, the wooden turntable and machinery were left outdoors, unprotected. They fell into disrepair. The horses, too (kept in damp, unheated basements), deteriorated. After a few years, the device became inoperable.[37]

In the early 1960s the Friends raised more than $20,000 to restore the carousel. Great care was taken to replicate the smallest details: antique glass eyes for the heads, natural horsehair for the tails, paint colors perfectly matched to the original shades.[38] The carousel, though, was still out of doors and fell victim to the same New England weather that had ruined it before. A second restoration was done. This time, the carousel was relocated closer to the residential buildings and was housed in a prefabricated metal building that the Friends purchased. When someone complained that it was "rather gloomy" there on cloudy days, volunteers installed additional lighting "to make it more cheery."[39]

For several years, the restored carousel got a "good work-out"—9,800 riders, for example, in the summer of 1963.[40] But wear, tear, and untrained operators took their toll. The carousel suffered mechanical damage and, once again, fell into disuse. This time there was no enthusiasm to restore it; some even questioned whether merry-go-rounds belonged at state schools, arguing that they were "not age-appropriate for mentally retarded persons."[41] In 1978 the carousel was permanently removed from service. The site acquired an air of decadence—broken windows giving entry to starlings and pigeons, bird droppings covering the once gleaming horses.[42] Thieves tried to steal two of the horses, further damaging the apparatus.[43] When the school closed in 1992, ownership of the forty-two Stein & Goldstein stallions reverted, along with the school's land, buildings, and other assets, to the State Asset Office. The appraised value was $206,000.[44]

Ever practical, Ben Ricci's advocacy group pressed to auction the abandoned carousel and use the proceeds to support former residents in their new habitats. The state eventually agreed.[45] An auction date was set: April

24, 1993, a Saturday. David Norton, a specialist in historic carousels, was appointed auctioneer. An opposition group formed—Friends of the Belchertown Carousel. They feared the eventual buyer would dismantle the carousel and sell the horses individually, destroying its integrity. Their goal was to keep the carousel intact, in Belchertown.[46] "What better way to memorialize the residents of the former Belchertown State School and the heroic efforts of the Advocacy Network . . . than to have the carousel restored and retained on the former BSS site?" asked Doris Stockton, chair of the town's Carousel Task Force. They petitioned the state to delay the sale—or give them six months to try to match the highest bid.[47] The two groups exchanged charges and angry words. The day before the auction, a fire marshal suddenly closed the carousel building where the auction was to be held, alleging that it contained combustible materials and was a fire hazard. (The "combustible materials" were variously described as cans of oil-based paint and a small box of brochures.) The governor's legal counsel intervened, and the building was reopened in time for the auction.[48]

The winning bidder, wearing sunglasses and unidentified at the time, agreed to pay $440,000—a record price. Immediately following the purchase, he was whisked away from the site in an unmarked vehicle, guarded by state troopers. David Norton, the auctioneer, told the press it was his impression that the buyer did not plan to break up the carousel and sell the horses individually to collectors. By nightfall, though, the most valuable horses had been removed from the carousel platform and shipped away.[49]

The winning bidder was soon identified as Michael Moodenbaugh, thirty years old and part owner of a Michigan-based amusement park company. Moodenbaugh, who lived in Seattle, confirmed what the opponents of the carousel sale had feared: it was his intention to sell off the carousel piece by piece.[50] A second auction was held in San Francisco on October 17. Once again, David Norton was in charge. More than 150 dealers and collectors from as far away as Alaska, Pennsylvania, and New Mexico attended, and more than a hundred pieces of carousel art were on the block, including Belchertown's former horses.[51]

Moodenbaugh hoped to realize $750,000 to $800,000 on the sale. He got only $451,000. Taking his costs into account, he actually lost money.[52] (Moodenbaugh himself did not attend the auction. At the time he lay in critical condition in an Ohio hospital, after suffering severe injuries in a one-car crash the previous month.)[53] As for the residents of the former Belchertown State School, a check dated February 24, 1993, in the amount of $380,000 (the net proceeds to the state of the first Belchertown auction, after costs) was deposited into the Carousel Trust Fund—maintained for the benefit of retarded persons living in the four western Massachusetts counties.[54]

Nostalgia for the lost carousal persisted well after its sale. "How many times have you taken a ride on a Carousel?" asked Judy Walker, a nurse in the school's infirmary wards. "Wasn't it the most exhilarating feeling? The wind blowing in your face while you [were] riding the beautiful painted steed—hearing the hurdy-gurdy music, the waltzes, polkas and dreamy music for a few minutes. . . .You could be anyone you wanted to be."[55] At the first sale, Dana Anderson, a Santa Barbara contractor, browsing the many pieces of carousel art, seemed to speak for everyone when he said, "It's a reminder of childhood, when days were happy."[56] But for those with sons and daughters at Belchertown, the carousel was less a reminder than a prayer—for happiness, reunion, Sundays in the park—largely unanswered.

We can hope that the carousel gave happiness to those who rode it. Certainly the *Sentinel* reporter who wrote of the first "dash for it" by the boys and girls of Belchertown thought so. One wonders, though: was theirs a dash of the delighted or the doomed? The memories of Ruth Sienkiewicz-Mercer, the physically but not mentally disabled former resident who lived at the state school from 1962 to 1978, are not fond ones:

> The few times I was taken outside during my early years at the Infirmary, it was usually to the carousel, which blared out the same old stale music of the fifties all the time—the attendants loved Elvis, and the carousel played nothing else. Usually I would be parked nearby [in a wheelchair], where I could enjoy the outdoors and watch the merry-go-round or the trees or the sky. Then an attendant who didn't know me very well would run up and say, "C'mon, Ruthie, let's take a ride on the merry-go-round, you'll love it."
>
> I always responded with my sourest grimace and most negative sounds, my version of "No, anything but that." Without fail, the attendant would ignore my clearly stated wishes, lift me out of my wheelchair, plunk me down on a hard wooden bench on the carousel, scrunch me up in a terribly uncomfortable, sometimes painful position, and take me for a ride. Then he or she would tell me how much fun we were having. Elvis would sing, and I would get sick to my stomach.[57]

There was, of course, more to the former Belchertown State School than land, buildings, and carousels, more even than lost jobs and lost tax revenue. Most important, there were the boys, girls, men, and women who had lived there—the school's former residents. What happened to the residents living there when the school was closed?

We have seen that, following publication of the "Tragedy of Belchertown" series in 1970, official state policy shifted from institutionalization of the mentally disabled to so-called community care or community placement programs. Gradually, many hundreds of the school's residents were resettled in communities throughout western Massachusetts. By 1989, when the state announced plans to close the school for good, only 266 persons still resided there; most of them, according to the state commissioner of mental retardation, would be similarly relocated within three years. To build and renovate the forty additional homes that were needed, the state planned a $10–$12 million bond issue.[58]

The community-care rubric encompasses a variety of living arrangements and care provider options that have evolved over time. These include "supervised living" (also called staffed arrangements), in which the state or a private subcontractor purchases or rents housing on behalf of a group of disabled individuals (up to eight), operates the facility, and employs care providers to assist the residents with daily living; "supported living," in which a group of individuals buy or rent their own house or apartment, choose their own roommates, and employ their own care providers (sometimes a non-disabled roommate or neighbor who provides part-time care in exchange for free rent or a small salary); and "home care," in which the disabled individual either lives in his or her own home and employs a live-in care provider (home sharing) or lives in the home of the care provider who is a family or single person unrelated to the disabled individual (shared living or adult foster care).

Initially, most of the school's former residents moved into staffed supervised living arrangements—usually four-person community homes. There were 384 such homes in western Massachusetts as of December 1992, 46 of them operated by the Department of Mental Retardation, the rest by private (mostly nonprofit) subcontractors. A newly built house in the small town of Granby, with a separate bedroom for each resident, living room, family room, kitchen with dining area, and one and a half baths, was typical.[59] Direct care attendants (who were often former Belchertown employees, regardless of whether the home was run by subcontractors or the state) would assist residents with housekeeping, shopping, bathing, toileting, managing money, and the like. A typical home with four residents might have one, two, or three attendants working the day shift (depending on the residents' level of self-sufficiency), and one at night during sleeping hours. The least self-sufficient would have one-on-one care twenty-four hours a day. In all, some 1,050 former state school residents lived in these community homes; twenty-four of the homes had around-the-clock nursing care.[60]

Both anecdotal evidence and contemporaneous surveys suggest that most former state school residents liked their new homes.[61] The comments of Jeannette Gaboury, a resident of Belchertown for fifty-nine years until her transfer to a group home in Amherst in 1990, are typical. "I kept refusing to go," she admitted to an interviewer two years later. But "Now I am glad I did it. This is much better. . . . I have my own place and can get up in the morning when I feel like it. Sometimes even the staff asks permission before coming into my room."[62]

Some former residents opted for supported living or shared living arrangements. For example, Tom Maroney, after living in group homes for several years, moved in with a foster family in the village of Montague and began working in nearby Greenfield recycling milk jugs and laundry detergent bottles. Jonas Garson moved into an apartment with two roommates—one of them, Oscar Williams, a former mental health care worker who was studying landscape science. "It supplements my living expenses," Williams said. "I wouldn't be able to work full-time and go to school full-time. Everyone benefits. Jonas has needs I'm able to meet and I have needs the organization is able to meet."[63]

Lawrence Barnes was one of the first beneficiaries of community care. Born in 1927, he was sent to the state school while still a child and remained there well into adulthood, until his experimental release in the early 1970s to one of the first community care programs. He spent several years at halfway houses in the area, learning basic survival skills, and then moved into his own apartment in the busy college town of Northampton, where he lived for the rest of his life. He was assisted in his daily living by direct care providers. Barnes became something of a legend in Northampton, passing many hours each day walking about the town. It was said that he relished his freedom too much to stay inside. His daily routine included stops at the local Starbucks for a grande coffee (he always brought his own red mug), where he also "acted as an unofficial host, always introducing customers to one another," and (several times a day) at a homemade ice cream shop—usually, for more coffee. He would also stop at a Main Street clothing store; according to the owner, "He loved clothes [and] women. He would sit in the back of the store and tell people how pretty they looked. He tried to . . . make a sale for us." Apparently, Barnes was also very well informed about local news like car accidents and road work. As one area resident put it, talking to him was "better than reading the newspaper" because "Lawrence was always the first to have the news." Barnes died in 2005, a free man. In tribute to his friendship, several Starbucks employees fashioned a memorial of sorts—a chalkboard outside the store with two candles in front of it, Barnes's picture taped to the surface, and a hand-written message chalked on the board: "Rest in Peace. We will miss you . . . our Lawrence."[64]

Not all community placements were successful, and not everyone who was promised community placement ended up there. In 1998, advocacy groups filed a class action on behalf of mentally disabled persons living in nursing homes in Massachusetts (estimated to be 1,600 in number) including Bruce Ames, a former resident of the Belchertown school with Down syndrome.[65] Like Barnes, he had been released into community care in the 1970s—in his case, a shared living arrangement. He had a job and was able to do his own laundry and cooking. But sometime in the 1990s the family with whom Ames was living withdrew from the program. Ames, then forty-seven, was placed in a nursing home. The placement was sup-posed to be temporary—three months at most. Two years later he was still there.[66] The lawsuit alleged that nursing home residents like Ames were entitled to be moved into community settings, and that those not imme-diately capable of such a move were entitled to specialized services while awaiting community placement. The lawsuit was settled in 2000.[67] As a result, more than 1,000 class members were moved from nursing homes to community settings, at a cost of $85 million. Another 750 were sched-uled for community placements over the next seven years. A disagreement arose as to whether and what specialized services should be provided in the interim, however. The plaintiff class reopened the settlement and the court held that the state had not complied; it ordered that additional ser-vices be provided to the remaining nursing home residents. The parties then concluded a second settlement agreement in 2008 regarding the spe-cific specialized services to be provided.[68]

Disagreements also arose as to whether community living was always to be preferred to institutionalization. A small but determined group of advocates argued that community living wasn't for everyone. In 2004 they filed a lawsuit *opposing* the state's efforts to close Fernald, the last of the state schools still open, arguing that such closings actually violated Judge Tauro's order, issued in 1993 when the Ricci class actions were finally closed, regarding the state's duty to maintain a high level of care for all mentally disabled persons. A supporting affidavit on behalf of two blind brothers still living at Fernald stated that the brothers had numerous medical problems and were severely retarded, and that any change of venue could be so upsetting it would kill them.[69]

Are we witnessing a resurgence of the state school concept? No. The state schools are finished. Community care has deservedly prevailed. The argument in its favor is simple but powerful: "Like the rest of us, people with mental retardation enjoy a chance to walk along a neighborhood street, to buy their own food, clothing and sundries, to go into a restaurant for ice cream or a meal, to go to the park on Sunday afternoon. Most important, like the rest of us, they need what a family offers—stable, mutual, loving relationships with a small number of people who care about them and live with or near them."[70] Surely Lawrence Barnes would have agreed.

To be fair, though, the issue has always been less what to do with the Lawrence Barneses of the world (badly mistreated though many of them were) than with the profoundly retarded and the not-so-profoundly retarded who have severe physical disabilities or exhibit radically unacceptable social behavior (perhaps as a consequence of mental illness suffered in addition to retardation) that make integration into a community setting far more problematic. The Americans with Disabilities Act and the Social Security system (Medicaid and Medicare, in particular) have provided a legislative framework and funding for humane care of disabled persons. Supplemental state legislation has further aided these efforts. Previously unimaginable sums of money are now routinely spent on behalf of the mentally disabled—in Massachusetts alone, $716.3 million of state and federal funding in fiscal year 1990, and $1.25 billion two decades later.[71] Roland Nagle, briefly superintendent of Belchertown State School after the "Tragedy of Belchertown" exposé, lamented in a letter to the editor explaining his resignation that the "existing treasury is not sufficient to meet all of the ordinary demands placed upon it and to underwrite all of the additional personnel and space required to serve those who cannot flourish in an open competitive system without extensive special programs for their unique pattern of needs."[72] No doubt a true statement even after the expenditures authorized by the Americans with Disabilities Act, Medicaid, and Medicare—but much, much more has been spent in the years since those words were written than Nagle dared imagine.

Looking to the future, what seems certain is that, money and good intentions notwithstanding (and human nature being what it is), this oft-forgotten class of persons will someday somewhere be victims once again, their unimagined future plight the subject of another shocking exposé: "The Tragedy of ——." Next time, though, it seems safe to say, the name "Belchertown" will not figure in the title.

Lastly, there were the dead, many of them—residents of the school at the time of their deaths—buried in nameless graves in a pine forest by the intersection of routes 21 and 202, long forgotten. What of them?

Death was a not infrequent visitor to the Belchertown State School. As early as 1923, the school's first full year of operation, eleven residents died—five from tuberculosis, two from diphtheria, and one each from bronchitis, pneumonia, gastric ulcer, and nephritis.[73] We do not know what was done with their bodies. But two years later, during the summer of 1925, a small burial ground was cleared in a pine grove across the state highway—"away," as the annual report for that year put it, "from the main institution." The first person to be buried there was interred in 1926, one of seventeen residents who died at the school that year. The farm boys dug the grave; residents were told only that So-and-so had left.

The burial ground, more a potter's field than a cemetery, was land-scaped in 1938.[74] Sequentially numbered cement headstones were placed on all the graves—a practice that continued over the ensuing decades as more were buried there. One report from the early 1960s says those of the Catholic faith had prayers said at burial and a church Mass recited the following morning; otherwise, we know nothing of the burial ceremonies themselves.[75] The cemetery was closed to new burials in 1977.

It may be that care was taken in the early years to maintain the site.[76] Not so later; the graveyard became a dump strewn with trash and debris—a "mud-hole," some called it, full of flies and mosquitoes, its cement markers now broken as well as nameless.[77] This disturbed Albert Warner, a former resident of the school whom we met in chapter 3. Warner, whose mother had been mentally ill, was made a ward of the state, declared feeble-minded, and institutionalized when he was three years old. In 1922, when he was nine, he was transferred to Belchertown State School—one of the school's first admissions, possibly the very first. He lived at Belchertown for fifteen years, until 1937, when he was transferred into a work release program. He worked as a painter, resettled in nearby Amherst, and married.

Years passed, but Warner could not forget his friends and acquaintances buried at the school—like the blind man he once knew, otherwise friendless, who had "put his head on my chest."[78] Warner visited the graveyard regularly to pay his respects, but the disrepair bothered him. One day he resolved that the dead there should be properly remembered. He wrote letters, made phone calls, and lobbied friends. Ben Ricci learned of his quest and took up the cause. In 1987 the state responded, erecting a monument near the graveyard with the names of all who were buried there. It was a start, but Warner wanted more: restoration of the graveyard itself and respectful recognition of the individual gravesites. So he persisted. Finally, in 1994, the state agreed to refurbish the cemetery. The grounds were cleaned and replanted. Granite markers with names and dates were placed on each gravesite. The state also constructed a new entrance, fence, gate, and sign, and the graveyard was renamed in Warner's honor as the Warner Pine Grove Memorial Cemetery.[79] Although it had by then long been closed to burials, Warner and his wife were given permission to be buried in the cemetery. Each year, during the week before Memorial Day, a memorial service is held at the cemetery honoring the 204 former state school residents buried there. "I came here when the cemetery was bad, when it needed to be fixed," Warner said. "I knew a lot of them. It makes me feel good that they are well remembered."[80]

Albert Warner, first citizen of Belchertown State School, died January 13, 2006, survived by his wife of sixty years, Agnes, also a former state school resident.[81] He was buried in the cemetery that now bears his name, surrounded by the many deceased state school acquaintances and friends whose dignity he helped reclaim. Agnes died in April 2009, and hers became the last remains laid to rest there—together with Albert, the last of the girls and boys of Belchertown to consecrate this ground.

Notes

1. Beginnings

1. The events, which occurred on Thursday, February 17, 1916, were reported in the next week's *Sentinel* (February 25) under the headline "Belchertown Jubilant: Success Crowns Effort to Secure School for Feeble-Minded."

2. Belcher's Town (as it was called when it was incorporated in 1761) was named in honor of Jonathan Belcher, prominent local landowner and governor of Massachusetts from 1730 to 1740. Usage extinguished the possessive and the name became Belchertown. See *Along the Country Road: Belchertown Discovered* (Belchertown, Mass.: Belchertown Historical Commission, 1982). On the town's reputation for fine carriages see J. G. Holland, *History of Western Massachusetts*, 2 vols. (Springfield, Mass.: S. Bowles, 1855), 2:182; Holland noted that Belchertown "has probably produced a greater number of single wagons than any other town in the State, of whatever size." See also Doris M. Dickinson and Cliff McCarthy, *Images of America: Belchertown* (Charleston, S.C.: Arcadia, 1998); Shirley Bock, Doris Dickinson, and Dan Fitzpatrick, "Belchertown History" (2005; revision for the town's website of an earlier work of the same title by Kenneth P. Dorey, 1960), www.belchertown.org/departments/history/bhistory.htm.

3. Holland, *History*, 2:182; "The Ford Gift," *Sentinel*, August 10, 1923, quoting Lucy Thomson, paper presented at Old Home Day Celebration (1902).

4. A. F. Bardwell, "Former Carriage Industries" (paper presented at opening of the Ford Building in Belchertown, June 1924), reprinted in *Sentinel*, June 20, 1924. Belchertown's carriage industry succumbed to western competition in the 1870s; Bardwell writes: "The handmade products of the Belchertown shops could not withstand the competition of the highly organized factories of the west and the larger centers, where machine work supercedes the older methods. . . . Early in the seventies the business began to fade away. Belchertown— once the Detroit of the carriage industry, now recalls it with difficulty."

5. Charles W. Eddy, *Belchertown: Illustrated with Pen and Camera* (Ware, Mass.: C. W. Eddy, 1888), n.p.

6. Mass. Resolves, 1915, Chapter 127, adopted May 27, 1915; "Board of Trade Faces Problems," *Springfield (Mass.) Union*, March 15, 1914.

7. "Death of Daniel Dwight Hazen," *Sentinel*, May 8, 1936.

8. Something of Hazen's character can perhaps be inferred from his selection as a Ford Motor dealer. Henry Ford had strict requirements for his dealers, which he enforced rigorously. Ford wrote in his autobiography: "We were careful in the selection of our salesmen. . . . Among the requirements for an agent we laid down the following: . . . A progressive, up-to-date man keenly alive to the possibilities of business. . . . The adoption of policies which will ensure absolutely square dealing and the highest character of business ethics." Henry Ford and Samuel Crowther, *My Life and Work* (Garden City, N.Y.: Doubleday, Page, 1922), 59–60.

9. "Board of Trade Faces Problems," *Springfield Union*, March 15, 1914. Securing a reliable water supply had been a goal of the town for many years, not yet achieved. Recently, though, the Belchertown Water Company, under the direction of Trade Board treasurer Milton Baggs, had driven some wells, the flow from which was highly promising as to both quality and quantity. It was thought to be "only a matter of a short time" before the streets would be piped. Ibid.

10. Some local reports at the time said there were 890 acres. There was a significant discrepancy between the reported acreage (whether 800 or 890) and the deeds eventually acquired by the state (660 acres). The difference was attributed by the authorities, somewhat obscurely, to the "indistinctiveness of old titles." "Belchertown May Lose School for Feeble Minded," *Daily Hampshire Gazette* (Northampton, Mass.), May 18, 1917.

11. "Coming of the State School, November 27, 1922," *Cold Spring Gazette* (published as part of the Belchertown Bicentennial Celebration), 1977.

12. Hinsdale, another small rural town, was turned down at the beginning. Holyoke, though a formidable contender, did not apply until the end. Attention therefore focused on Belchertown, Conway, and Westfield. At first Conway— also a rural farming town—seemed to have the edge, but its chances faded when it could not guarantee an adequate water supply. Westfield, despite significant opposition within the town itself, lobbied hardest, and no one had any idea what the outcome would be when the state's Insanity Board met on February 17 to make its decision. Hazen, as we know, was there to press Belchertown's case, but the board saw him for a few minutes only. The bulk of the time was given over to a delegation from Holyoke, which had formally entered the bidding only the week before. Hazen was cooling his heels in the board's antechamber, hoping for more time, when the board suddenly announced its decision in favor of Belchertown. "Belchertown Site Chosen by Board," *Springfield Union*, February 18, 1916.

13. Henry H. Goddard, "The Menace of Mental Deficiency from the Standpoint of Heredity," *Boston Medical and Surgical Journal* 175 (1916): 271.

14. "New Institution to Benefit Town," newspaper clipping (possibly the *Springfield Union*) circa March 5, 1916, Belchertown State School Papers, Clapp Memorial Library, Belchertown, Mass.

15. "State Home for the Feeble Minded," *Sentinel*, October 29, 1915.

16. Mass. Resolves, 1916, Chapter 160 (approved June 2, 1916); "Text of Resolve

Concerning School for the Feeble-Minded," *Sentinel*, August 25, 1916. The $150,000 appropriation was divided into $50,000 for a 105-bed girls' dormitory, $25,000 for a 50-bed farm boys' dormitory, $20,000 each for a laundry/service building and a kitchen/storehouse, $15,000 for the water system, $5,000 for the sewer system, $5,000 for grading the railroad track, and $10,000 for repairs and renovations to the existing houses and barns.

17. "New Institution to Benefit Town."

18. "Favors Belchertown," *Sentinel*, December 10, 1915.

19 "Water at Belchertown," *Springfield (Mass.) Republican*, September 5, 1917.

20. Ibid.

21. "Drs. Kline and Wallace Address Townspeople," *Sentinel*, September 21, 1917.

22. "New Institution to Benefit Town."

23. "Urges That Belchertown School Site Be Used," *Daily Hampshire Gazette*, May 19, 1917.

24. "Superintendent's Report," *Eleventh Annual Report of the Wrentham State School for the Year Ending November 30, 1917* (Boston: Wright & Potter, State Printers, 1918), 13. The identities of these first transferees are unknown, and later reports state that their number was ten, not eleven. Did one return to Wrentham? Run away? Die? Was the original number incorrect?

25. "A Welcome at the State School," *Sentinel*, July 5, 1918. In 1918 the farm colony shipped 1,500 bushels of potatoes, 200 barrels of apples, 600 bushels of turnips, 280 bushels of shell beans, and 3 beehives to the parent institution. "Superintendent's Report," *Twelfth Annual Report of the Wrentham State School for the Year Ending November 30, 1918* (Boston: Wright & Potter, State Printers, 1919), 15–16.

26. "Welcome at the State School."

27. "The House: Representative Pierce of Greenfield Calls Feeble-Minded Project in Belchertown a Great Fraud," *Springfield Republican*, May 2, 1918; "Passes 97 to 41," *Sentinel*, May 10, 1918. See also General Acts 1918, Chap. 224 (approved May 24, 1918), and Special Acts, 1918, Chap. 186 (approved June 3, 1918), appropriating $50,000 for water supply. In 1922–23, after the waterworks were completed, the state authorized the school to begin selling excess water to the town for fire and other domestic purposes and the town voted to tie into the school's water system, thus ending a quarter century of shortages. "Water for Belchertown," *Sentinel*, July 7, 1922; "Water Supply Assured," *Sentinel*, July 27, 1923. The supply contract with the State Department of Mental Diseases was only for five years, and the department would not guarantee renewal, so beginning in 1924–25 the town developed its own pumping station and supply. "Standpipe Being Erected," *Sentinel*, March 27, 1925; "Standpipe Filled," *Sentinel*, April 24, 1925; "75th Anniversary: Highlights of the History of Belchertown Water District 1922–1997," *Sentinel*, April 10, 1997.

28. "Visit State School," *Sentinel*, February 14, 1919. The Kendall, Taylor firm, located in Billerica, Massachusetts, was established in 1890.

29. "Boys Are Working at Belchertown," *Springfield Sunday Republican*, November 19, 1922.

30. Special Acts, 1919, Chap. 211 (approved June 24, 1919).
31. "Favorably Reported," *Sentinel*, April 25, 1919; "Bids for Local Work," *Sentinel*, September 19, 1919; "Work Begins at State School," *Sentinel*, April 1, 1921. Besides providing additional funding for previously authorized construction, the $350,000 supplemental appropriation included $84,000 for a 140-bed custodial facility and $108,000 for a power station. During 1920–22, further appropriations were made for the core campus, including additional dormitories, employee housing, furniture, and equipment.
32. "Trustees' Report," *Annual Report of the Trustees of the Belchertown State School for the Year Ending November 30, 1923* (Gardner, Mass: Occupational Printing Plant, Dept. of Mental Diseases, 1924), 3; "Boys Are Working at Belchertown."
33. "State School Plant Developing," *Sentinel*, November 17,1922. Two other contemporaneous reports state that the initial group of transfers was from Waltham, not Wrentham. One puts the number at 67, not 75. "New State School Starts Activities," *Springfield Union*, November 16, 1922; "Boys Are Working at Belchertown."
34. "Superintendent's Report," *Annual Report of the Trustees of BSS for 1923*, 4; "State School Plant Developing."
35. "Boys Are Working at Belchertown." The reporting does not reveal the ages of the male and female transferees, other than the reference to "varying ages from six up" quoted in the main text. Local press stories and annual school reports always used the terms "boys," "girls," and "children" when referring to the new residents. Nevertheless, it is likely the case that some of the transferees—possibly more than a few—were adult men and women, since the main criteria for transfer was not age per se but having a connection to western Massachusetts; and the resident population of the transferring institutions included adult men and women from all over the state.
36. "State School Plant Developing."

2. "Idiots for Life"—The Language of State Care

1. Mass. Resolves, 1848, Chapter 65 (approved May 8, 1848), reprinted in *Mental Retardation in America: A Historical Reader*, ed. Steven Noll and James W. Trent Jr. (New York: New York University Press, 2004), 26. At about the same time, Hervey Wilbur, a young physician in western Massachusetts, opened a private school for the feeble-minded in Barre. James W. Trent Jr., *Inventing the Feeble Mind: A History of Mental Retardation in the United States* (Berkeley: University of California Press, 1994), 14.
2. Mass. Resolves, 1846, Chapter 117 (approved April 11, 1846). On Howe see James W. Trent, *The Manliest Man: Samuel G. Howe and the Contours of Nineteenth-Century American Reform* (Amherst: University of Massachusetts Press, 2012).
3. Samuel G. Howe, *Report Made to the Legislature of Massachusetts, upon Idiocy* (Boston: Coolidge & Wiley, 1848), 15, 23–26. The term "feeble-minded" as a synonym for "idiot" (in its broad sense) did not come into widespread use until the late nineteenth century. Steven Noll and James W. Trent Jr., "Introduction," in Noll and Trent, *Mental Retardation*, 3. It was in use at the

time Howe wrote his report, but in a more restricted sense to refer to the third, and possibly the second, of Howe's three categories of intellectually deficient persons.

4. The population of Massachusetts grew from approximately 738,000 in 1840 to 995,000 in 1850, according to the U.S. Census Bureau. Utilizing Howe's definitions and figures, this would mean that 0.1–0.2 percent of the state's population in 1848 was feeble-minded. By way of comparison, in 1991 it was estimated that approximately 0.4 percent of the population (in Massachusetts, roughly 22,000 persons) "are so severely disabled by mental retardation or related conditions that they could benefit from lifelong services." Edward Moscovitch, *Mental Retardation Programs: How Does Massachusetts Compare?* (Boston: Pioneer Institute for Public Policy Research, 1991), 13. Perhaps Howe's estimate was low. Alternatively, the different percentages might be explained by different definitions or by relatively higher mortality rates then than now for the feeble-minded when compared to the rest of the population.

5. Howe, *Report upon Idiocy*, 52–53.

6. Dorothea Dix, *Memorial to the Legislature of Massachusetts* (Boston: Printed by Munroe & Francis, 1843), 2. In early nineteenth-century America, the dependent feeble-minded were lumped together with other categories of the indigent (the insane, the sick and elderly poor, other dependent persons) for purposes of state care. "The important distinction was one of dependency, not disability. . . . The etiology of your indigence was seldom an urgent question." Philip Ferguson, "The Legacy of the Almshouse," in Noll and Trent, *Mental Retardation*, 40, 43. Almshouses (poor houses) were one of several methods by which such "paupers" were supported at public expense. Other methods included auctioning the care of particular indigent persons to the lowest bidder or contracting with a single caregiver for a fixed fee. The number of almshouses in Massachusetts grew during the second quarter of the nineteenth century from eighty-three to over two hundred, reflecting their growing importance. Ibid., 48. At the same time, reformers began to differentiate among the different classes of the indigent, seeking more specialized care.

7. R. C. Scheerenberger, *A History of Mental Retardation* (Baltimore: Paul H. Brookes, 1983), 106. Howe read Dix's speech to the state legislature, instead of Dix herself, because women were not then permitted to address that body.

8. Howe, *Report upon Idiocy*, 53–54.

9. Leo Kanner, *A History of the Care and Study of the Mentally Retarded* (Springfield, Ill.: Charles C. Thomas, 1964), 40 (quoting Howe's daughter, Laura E. Richards).

10. Martin Luther, *Colloquia Mansalia* (London: William DuGard, 1652), quoted in Scheerenberger, *History*, 32.

11. See Parnel Wickham, "Conceptions of Idiocy in Colonial Massachusetts," *Journal of Social History* 35 (Summer 2002): 935–54.

12. Howe, *Report upon Idiocy*, 9–10, 17.

13. Besides Séguin, these pioneers included Jacob Rodrigues Péreire (1715–1780), Philippe Pinel (1745–1826), Jean-Marc-Gaspard Itard (1774–1838),

and Johann Jacob Guggenbühl (1816–1863). Péreire was one of the first to teach deaf mutes how to read and speak. Observation of one of his successful pupils, a sixteen-year-old boy, so excited King Louis XV that he awarded Péreire an annual pension of 800 francs. Although Péreire himself never worked with the feeble-minded, his demonstration that the severely disabled could be taught inspired those like Howe who did. Kanner, History, 10–12. Pinel, a French physician, was for a number of years director of the Bicêtre and Salpétrière asylums in Paris. Appalled by unspeakable conditions at both facilities, he was among the first to unchain patients (one man at the Bicêtre had been bound for forty years) and to practice what came to be called moral treatment (provision of medical, psychological, and education services in a humane living environment). Although never the recipient of a kingly pension (the Committee of Public Safety, not the king, now ruled Paris), Pinel was rewarded in a manner befitting the French Revolution: a drunken athlete named Chevigne, whom Pinel had earlier released from the asylum, saved him from a public lynching. Scheerenberger, History, 45–46. Itard, another French physician, was best known for his efforts to teach the "wild boy of Aveyron," an apparently feeble-minded boy who had been living, naked and alone, in the woods of Caunes. Itard worked with the boy for five years. He judged his work a failure and eventually gave up. But the boy had learned, among other things, to identify objects and letters of the alphabet—more than anyone at the time thought possible. The French Academy of Science issued a highly laudatory commendation. Kanner, History, 12–16. Guggenbühl was one of the first to combine residential care with training of the feeble-minded. In 1836, during a walk in a Swiss village, he was "stirred by the sight of a 'dwarfed, crippled cretin of stupid appearance' mumbling the Lord's Prayer before a wayside cross. He followed the man to a nearby shack where the cripple's mother related that she had taught the prayer to her son during his childhood without too much difficulty and that since then he had gone to pray before the cross regularly every day at the same hour in any kind of weather." Guggenbühl "wondered if more might have been achieved" by a program of "consistent and intensive training," thereby stumbling upon the novel idea that perhaps the feeble-minded could be taught in a proper residential setting. The residential care facility he established at Abendberg became world-renowned. Kanner, History, 17 and 22.

14. Kanner, History, 35–36.
15. A useful, succinct explanation of physiological education, from which my summary is drawn, can be found in Trent, Inventing the Feeble Mind, 46–52.
16. George Sumner, "Letter to S. G. Howe [dated 1 February 1847]," in Trent, Inventing the Feeble Mind, 43–44. Howe quoted from Sumner's letter in his Report upon Idiocy (39–40). Séguin's record was not, however, without blemish. He was accused of mistreating children and otherwise engaging in "abominable practices." Bicêtre fired him a year after he began working there. Trent, Inventing the Feeble Mind, 40–42.
17. Howe, Report upon Idiocy, 17.

18. Trent, *Inventing the Feeble Mind*, 43. Apparently, Howe and Séguin did not get along; Séguin left after several months.

19. Walter E. Fernald State School, Agency History Record, http://archnet.asu. edu/archives/crm/Mass/built/hs.htm. Waverly, rather than Waltham, is sometimes given as the site of the school's relocation, as there was a train station of that name nearby.

20. *On the Causes of Idiocy: Being the Supplement to a Report by Dr. S. G. Howe and the Other Commissioners appointed by the Governor of Massachusetts to inquire into the condition of the idiots of the Commonwealth, dated February 26, 1848, with an Appendix* (1858; repr., New York: Arno Press, 1972), 1. The supplement, with its own introduction and appendix, was not published until ten years after the *Report upon Idiocy*.

21. Ibid., 2.

22. Ibid., 25–35; quotation on 25.

23. Ibid., 23–37, quotation on 27. It is obvious that Howe took great pains to be rigorously scientific in his approach. But the scientific method was still in its infancy. It seems not to have occurred to Howe, for example, to establish a control group and to test his correlations against the control. Also, of course, the existence of correlations does not establish cause.

24. Speech at the cornerstone-laying ceremony at Pennsylvania Training School (1857), *Fifth Annual Report of the Board of Directors of the Pennsylvania Training School for Feeble-Minded Children* (Philadelphia: Harry B. Ashmead, 1858), 43–44, quoted in Trent, *Inventing the Feeble Mind*, 30.

25. "Discussion of a Paper Presented by Dr. W. E. Fernald," *Journal of Psycho-Asthenics* 27.3 (March 1912): 105.

26. For a thoughtful and more detailed discussion of this transformation, see Trent, *Inventing the Feeble Mind*, 23–39, 53–59.

27. Ibid., 70.

28. Ibid., 78. Apparently it did not occur to anyone to ask whether the difference might be attributable to different definitions or faulty counting techniques rather than increased incidence. Also, no one seems to have noticed that Wines's rate was no greater than the 1848 rate for Massachusetts reported by Howe.

29. Ibid., 167, 168–69.

30. W. E. Fernald, "The Burden of Feeble-mindedness," *Journal of Psycho-Asthenics* 27.3 (March 1912): 87–99; quotations on 89–90, 92–93.

31. Ibid., 93–94, 98. The belief that "certain families should become extinct" was a powerful one in turn-of-the-century America, attracting high-profile academics, professionals, and politicians to its cause. Paul R. Reilly, "Involuntary Sterilization in the United States: A Surgical Solution," *Quarterly Review of Biology* 62.2 (June 1987): 153–70. As we saw in chapter 1, proponents of the eugenics movement sought to segregate the feeble-minded from the breeding population; they also favored sterilization for other deviant groups whose degeneracy was thought to be traceable to bad genes, "to preserve humanity's fitness." Elof Carlson, "Scientific Origins of Eugenics,"

www.eugenicsarchive.org/html/eugenics/essay2text.html. Eventually some thirty-three states would adopt forced sterilization laws, under which more than 60,000 Americans were involuntarily sterilized. In its most virulent, trans-Atlantic form, the eugenics movement inspired the Holocaust. Paul Lombardo, "Eugenic Sterilization Laws," www.eugenicsarchive.org/html/eugenics/essay8text.html; Reilly, "Involuntary Sterilization."

32. See David Wright, "Mongols in Our Midst," in Noll and Trent, *Mental Retardation in America*, 92–119.

33. Nothing if not intellectually honest, Howe was unable to correlate his cranial measurements with the mental capacities of his examinees, and said so: "Idiocy is sometimes caused by the smallness of the brain; indeed, the true type of the lowest class of idiots is a person whose brain is too small to perform its functions normally. The common notion, however, that this is generally the cause of idiocy is incorrect. Out of 338 cases, . . . only 99 had diminutive brains." Howe, *On the Causes of Idiocy*, 60.

34. Kanner, *History*, 117–22; Scheerenberger, *History*, 140–43.

35. Scheerenberger, *History*, 144, citing Lewis Terman, *The Measurement of Intelligence* (Cambridge, Mass.: Riverside Press, 1916).

36. Walter E. Fernald, "Mentally Defective Children in the Public Schools," *Journal of Psycho-Asthenics* 8, nos. 3–4 (December 1903–March 1904), 34–35, quoted in Scheerenberger, *History*, 157. Fernald would eventually soften his views—but not before the state school movement was in full swing.

3. The Officer and the Dentist

1. James W. Trent Jr., *Inventing the Feeble Mind: A History of Mental Retardation in the United States* (Berkeley: University of California Press, 1994), 88–94. On the architectural and design theories underpinning the cottage plan, see V. V. Anderson, *State Institutions for the Feebleminded* (New York: National Committee for Mental Hygiene, 1920), reprinted from *Mental Hygiene* 4, no. 3 (July 1920): 626–46.

2. According to the deeds of sale, the original tract consisted of 800 acres of farmland and buildings purchased on June 9, 1916, from Edgar and Ela Witt (130 acres), Avery and Maud Stacey (560 acres), Geraldine and Everett Howard (20 acres plus 15 rods), Sarah and David Jepson (60 acres), and Frederich and Mary Michel (30 acres). Two additional, much smaller plots (those of Rudd and Nannie Fairchild and Thomas and Kate Riley) were acquired by eminent domain in 1923. Apparently, though, the acreage was substantially overstated in the original deeds; the school's records for 1926 show aggregate land holdings at the time of 622 acres only—and no sales subsequent to 1916 that might account for the reduced acreage. The additional purchases were made in 1928 (the 99.1-acre town poor farm), 1929 (2.6 acres), 1930 (50.5 acres from Fred and Mabel Doerpholz) and 1938 (69 acres from the Lamson family). Additional land was also leased from time to time; for example, in 1940 the school leased 75 acres of additional pasture.

3. "State School Plant Developing," *Sentinel*, November 17, 1922; "Boys Are Working at Belchertown," *Springfield (Mass.) Sunday Republican*, November 19, 1922. Not all of the planned dormitories were built, and the resident population never reached 1,800.

4. "Boys Are Working at Belchertown."

5. "The Story of 1932," *Sentinel*, January 6, 1933; "Belchertown State School: Institution Now Cares for Total 1307 Feeble-Minded Men, Women and Children," newspaper clipping, *Holyoke Shopping News*, April 3, 1935 (possibly a special section of the *Holyoke (Mass.) Daily Transcript and Telegram*), Belchertown State School Papers, Clapp Memorial Library, Belchertown, Mass.

6. "1930 State School Program," *Sentinel*, March 21, 1930.

7. JoAnne Newman, "Former State School Resident Remembers the Good Times," *Sentinel*, February 28, 1990; Anonymous, interview by author, June 12, 2007.

8. "Belchertown State School: Institution Now Cares for Total 1307."

9. "An Afternoon at the State Farm," *Sentinel*, September 11, 1931; "The State School and Its Work," *Sentinel*, January 26, 1945.

10. Joe McCrea, telephone interview by author, November 8, 2008.

11. Afternoon at the State Farm."

12. "Produced at State School in 1940, from Annual Report," *Sentinel*, January 24, 1941.

13. A *Sentinel* reporter who visited the remodeled poor farm building in 1931 noted approvingly that it included a recreation room on the ground floor with a radio, piano, and Victrola. "Story of 1930," *Sentinel*, January 2, 1931; "Afternoon at the State Farm."

14. Anonymous, interview by author, June 12, 2007.

15. "Death of Dr. George E. McPherson," *Sentinel*, June 22, 1945.

16. "Waiting Game," *Daily Hampshire Gazette* (Northampton, Mass.), September 17, 2003.

17. "The Steeple Soliloquizes: In Which the Steeple Bids Good-bye to a Grand Citizen," *Sentinel*, June 18, 1943.

18. "Death of Dr. George E. McPherson"; Anonymous, interview by author, June 12, 2007.

19. "Refuses to Sell Town Farm," *Sentinel*, April 8, 1927.

20. Ibid; "Town Farm Article Again," *Sentinel*, February 10, 1928; "Annual Appropriations' Meeting," *Sentinel*, February 17, 1928.

21. "Annual Appropriations' Meeting."

22. "Behind the Bulfinch Front," *Springfield Sunday Union and Republican*, June 28, 1931.

23. Ibid.; the remaining 62 children presumably fell into other categories. The clinic's recommendations were not always followed. In 1928, after examining 265 candidates, the clinic recommended 40 for commitment. In the school's annual report for that year, the clinic noted that their advice "has thus far been ignored." "School Clinic Report," *Annual Report of the Trustees of the Belchertown State School for the Year Ending November 30, 1928* (Dept. of Mental Diseases, n.d.), 10–11.

24. "Belchertown State School: Institution Now Cares for Total 1307." Those admitted for thirty-day observation had to be released after that time unless the authorities took further action to extend the commitment. Custodial commitment was for an indefinite period.

25. "Tells of State School," *Sentinel*, June 28, 1929.

26. "Behind the Bulfinch Front."

27. "Superintendent's Report," *Annual Report of the Trustees of the Belchertown State School for the Year Ending November 30, 1923* (Dept. of Mental Diseases, n.d.), 5.

28. Information in this and the following paragraph taken from "Habit Training Makes Mentally Deficient Self Supporting Folk," *Springfield Sunday Union and Republican*, January 30,1927; and "Belchertown State School: Institution Now Cares for Total 1307."

29. "Belchertown State School: Institution Now Cares for Total 1307."

30. Robert Francis, "Two Days among the Feeble-Minded," MS [n.d.], Robert Francis Papers, collection 143, series 4, box 14:180, Special Collections and Archives, W. E. B. Du Bois Library, University of Massachusetts Amherst.

31. Although the reliability of the school's classifications may be questioned, the impression that, over time, there were fewer residents capable of helping care for the neediest among them is consistent with anecdotal evidence of declining quality of care.

32. "Tells of State School."

33. "Habit Training Makes Mentally Deficient Self Supporting Folk."

34. "Belchertown State School: Institution Now Cares for Total 1307."

35. "Habit Training Makes Mentally Deficient Self Supporting Folk."

36. Ibid; "Tells of State School."

37. "Tells of State School."

38. "Exhibit at State School," *Sentinel*, October 22, 1926.

39. "The State School Exhibit," *Sentinel*, October 11, 1929.

40. "Second Annual Exhibit," *Sentinel*, October 21, 1927.

41. Ibid.; "State School Exhibit," *Sentinel*, October 11, 1935.

42. "State School Exhibit," *Sentinel*, October 11, 1935.

43. "Habit Training Makes Mentally Deficient Self Supporting Folk."

44. "Christmas at the State School," *Sentinel*, December 26, 1924.

45. "Play at the State School," *Sentinel*, February 6, 1925; "Play at State School," *Sentinel*, December 24, 1926; "State School Entertainment," *Sentinel*, December 9, 1927; "Entertainment at State School," *Sentinel*, April 20, 1928; "Light Opera at State School," *Sentinel*, May 25, 1928; "Entertainment at State School," *Sentinel*, May 3, 1929.

46. Quotations in this and the next two paragraphs are from "Habit Training Makes Mentally Deficient Self Supporting Folk."

47. The racial makeup of the school's population during the McPherson era was (like that of Massachusetts) mostly white. Only 33 of 860 residents in 1928, and 29 of 1,306 in 1939, were classified as "colored." "Statistical Tables," *Annual Report of the Trustees of BSS for 1928*, 14, and "Statistical Tables," *Annual Report of the Trustees of the Belchertown State School for the Year Ending November 30,*

1939 (Gardner, Mass.: Occupational Printing Plant, Dept. of Mental Diseases, n.d.), 14. On the minstrel-show tradition and its longevity in the United States see the collection *Burnt Cork: Traditions and Legacies of Blackface Minstrelsy*, ed. Stephen Johnson (Amherst: University of Massachusetts Press, 2012).

48. "Minstrel Show at State School," *Sentinel*, March 25, 1927.

49. "Minstrel Show at State School," *Sentinel*, December 30, 1927; "State School Minstrel," *Sentinel*, April 24, 1936.

50. "Entertainment at State School," *Sentinel*, February 22, 1929.

51. "Entertainment at State School," *Sentinel*, January 6, 1928.

52. "State School Minstrel," *Sentinel*, April 30, 1948; "State School Minstrel," April 15, 1949.

53. "State School Minstrel," *Sentinel*, February 20, 1931.

54. "State School Minstrel," *Sentinel*, May 7, 1943.

55. "State School Minstrel," *Sentinel*, May 17, 1946.

56. According to the *Sentinel*, prizes were awarded. A certain Albert Stokes won three first prizes, and "the tug o' war was won by Capt. Ralph O'Brien's men." "The Fourth at the State School," *Sentinel*, July 7, 1922. Afterward, a picnic dinner was served on the lawn; then, in the afternoon, the "farm boys" defeated the teamsters 11–6 in a game of baseball.

57. "The Fourth at the State School," *Sentinel*, July 11, 1924.

58. "The Fourth at the State School," *Sentinel*, July 6, 1928; "The Fourth at the State School," *Sentinel*, July 5, 1929.

59. "Fourth at the State School," *Sentinel*, July 9, 1926; "State School Parade," *Sentinel*, July 8, 1932.

60. "The Fourth at the State School," *Sentinel*, July 8, 1938.

61. "The Fourth at the State School," *Sentinel*, July 3, 1942; "War-Time Fourth," *Sentinel*, July 2, 1943.

62. "Dr. Westwell Honored," *Sentinel*, April 30, 1948.

63. "Dental Department Report," *Annual Report of the Trustees of the Belchertown State School for the Year Ending November 30, 1933* (Gardner, Mass.: Occupational Printing Plant, Dept. of Mental Diseases, n.d.), 11.

64. "Dental Department Report," *Annual Report of the Trustees of the Belchertown State School for the Year Ending November 30, 1934* (Gardner, Mass.: Occupational Printing Plant, Dept. of Mental Diseases, n.d.), 14.

65. Joe McCrea, e-mail to Doris Dickinson, July 17, 2007.

66. "Trustees' Report," *Annual Report of the Trustees of BSS for 1933*, 3.

67. "Belchertown State School: Institution Now Cares for Total 1307."

68. Newman, "Former State School Resident Remembers," quoting a former resident from the 1920s and 1930s.

69. Joe McCrea, e-mail to Doris Dickinson, February 22, 2007.

70. Newman, "Former State School Resident Remembers."

71. Benjamin Ricci, writing about a later time in the school's history, asserts that clandestine abortions were performed and that aborted fetuses were "occasionally 'disposed of'" in the school's cemetery. Benjamin Ricci, *Crimes against Humanity: A Historical Perspective* (New York: iUniverse, 2004), 30.

72. "Trustees' Report," *Annual Report of the Trustees of the Belchertown State School for the Year Ending November 30, 1930* (Gardner, Mass.: Occupational Printing Plant, Dept. of Mental Diseases, n.d.), 3.

73. *Purgatory: 20 Minute Documentary Sample*, video recording, directed by James Whalen (Arbez Productions, 2010), available at http://vimeo.com/12632025. Ricci, again writing about a later time in the school's history, asserts that homosexual acts—"often encouraged by *voyeur* attendants"—were commonplace. He quotes "many attendants and some unlicensed physicians" as saying, "It was to be expected, after all." Ricci, *Crimes against Humanity*, 30.

74. "Habit Training Makes Mentally Deficient Self Supporting Folk"; "Tells of State School." Nothing was said of the other 40 percent. Perhaps McPherson meant to imply they were no worse off.

75. "Habit Training Makes Mentally Deficient Self Supporting Folk." The happiness theme was perennial. In 1964 the editor of *The Bell* (a parents' newsletter), reporting on a talk by the school's chief hospital supervisor at a recent meeting with parents and friends, wrote: "I am certain she alleviated many of the fears we have when our loved ones first entered at the Belchertown School. She assured us that in 98 out of 100 cases a child adapts well to his surroundings and is happier than he has been before because he is with children of his own type." *The Bell*, November 1964, Belchertown State School Friends Association Records, 1954–86, collection MS 302, box 1B, folder 5a, Special Collections and Archives, W. E. B. Du Bois Library, University of Massachusetts Amherst.

76. Quoted in "Waiting Game," *Daily Hampshire Gazette*, September 17, 2003.

77. Quoted in Newman, "Former State School Resident Remembers."

78. "Habit Training Makes Mentally Deficient Self Supporting Folk."

79. "Trustees' Report," *Annual Report of the Trustees of BSS for 1934*, 3; "Habit Training Makes Mentally Deficient Self Supporting Folk."

80. The trustees may have been emboldened to favor sterilization "in select cases" by the recent U.S. Supreme Court decision in *Buck v. Bell*, 274 U.S. 200 (1927), in which Justice Oliver Wendell Holmes, writing for a majority of the court in upholding the constitutionality of Virginia's compulsory sterilization law, famously stated, "The principle that sustains compulsory vaccination is broad enough to cover cutting the Fallopian tubes. . . . Three generations of imbeciles are enough." George McPherson, too, seems to have been favorably disposed to forced sterilization. In an address in 1929 to the American Association for the Study of the Feebleminded, of which he was then president, McPherson said it was especially important to sterilize "girls" before they were paroled or discharged. James W. Trent, "To Cut and Control: Institutional Preservation and the Sterilization of Mentally Retarded People in the United States, 1892–1947," *Journal of Historical Sociology* 6.1 (March 1993): 65, citing "Address of the President" (1929), *Proceedings and Addresses of the American Association for the Study of the Feebleminded*, vol. 34. At the association's 1930 meeting, he responded to remarks by the supervisor of another school's parole program to the effect that feeble-minded women were often just as capable of marrying, keeping house,

and raising children as were many maids, store clerks, and telephone operators by asking, incredulously, "Have you no sense of responsibility towards the girl that has been committed to you? You are not responsible for the telephone operators and the maids that have not been committed to you. Did you ever see a feeble-minded girl that was able to bring up a child properly?" (To which the supervisor replied, "Many.") "News and Notes," *Journal of Psycho-Asthenics* 43 (1938): 210, quoted in R. C. Scheerenberger, *A History of Mental Retardation* (Baltimore: Paul H. Brookes, 1983), 191. Based on these remarks, it would not be unreasonable to infer that some of the female residents of the Belchertown State School may have been sterilized involuntarily.

Unlike Virginia and thirty-two other states, however, Massachusetts never enacted legislation authorizing compulsory sterilization, and there is no evidence in the school's annual reports, or anecdotally, that sterilizations were in fact performed. Moreover, in 1938, McPherson is reported to have said that he preferred not to place women out in the community until after menopause—presumably an unnecessary precaution if the women had previously been sterilized. Scheerenberger, *History*, 196, citing "News and Notes," *Journal of Psycho-Asthenics* 43 (1938): 210. Perhaps this is indirect proof that compulsory sterilization was not a common practice at the school, at least during the 1930s.

81. A 1935 newspaper article states, "With good training in the schools and in handiwork of all sorts, about 15 per cent of the patients can eventually be put out on parole," of which "[about] 90 per cent . . . are usually successful." "Belchertown State School: Institution Now Cares for 1307." The numbers reported in the annual reports indicate a much lower parole rate, however.

82. "State School Here Nearly a Quarter-Century," *Sentinel*, April 5, 1940.

83. Gladys A. Meyer, "Twelve Years of Family Care at Belchertown State School," *American Journal of Mental Deficiency* 55 (1950–51): 414.

84. Ibid., 415.

85. Ibid., 416. The program may also have saved the state money. In 1949 the per capita cost of family care was $13 per week, including $10 boarding charge and $3 for medical care. The per capita cost of institutional care was $15.24 per week. Ibid., 417. Of course, the cost of caring for the severely handicapped, and providing education and training to those able to benefit from it, may have inflated the per capita institutional cost, thus rendering any comparison of costs rather meaningless.

86. Anonymous, interview by author, June 12, 2007.

87. Ibid. This resident, one of the lucky ones, was subsequently paroled and then discharged. He worked variously as a farm hand, golf course attendant, and postal employee—eventually marrying and learning to drive a car.

88. "The Fourth at the State School," *Sentinel*, July 10, 1942; "State School," *Sentinel*, January 1, 1943; "Dr. McPherson Retiring," *Sentinel*, June 11, 1943; "The Steeple Soliloquizes: In Which the Steeple Bids Good-bye to a Grand Citizen"; "Death of Dr. George E. McPherson." McPherson was replaced as superintendent by Dr. Henry Tadgell.

89. "Leaving in July," *Sentinel*, April 29, 1949; "Reception for Dr. Westwell," *Sentinel*, January 26, 1962. Westwell had a distinguished second career in Montana, including a term as president of the American Association on Mental Deficiency. He also served as an adviser to President John F. Kennedy's Panel on Mental Retardation under the chairmanship of Eunice Shriver, the president's sister and wife of Sargent Shriver. "Old Steeple Soliloquizes: Letter from 'Our' Dr. Westwell Finds Him Busy in Retirement," *Sentinel*, July 20, 1962.

90. "State School Here Nearly a Quarter Century," *Sentinel*, April 5, 1940.

4. Working at the State School

1. "Boys Are Working at Belchertown," *Springfield (Mass.) Sunday Republican*, November 19, 1922. This ratio of roughly one Belchertown resident for every three positions persisted throughout the school's history.

2. "Statistical Tables," *Annual Report of the Trustees of the Belchertown State School for the Year Ending November 30, 1930* (Gardner, Mass.: Occupational Printing Plant, Dept. of Mental Diseases, n.d.), 15; "Statistical Tables," *Annual Report of the Trustees of the Belchertown State School for the Year Ending November 30, 1940* (Gardner, Mass.: Occupational Printing Plant, Dept. of Mental Diseases, n.d.), 14; Shirley Dorey (chairman, Belchertown State School Reuse Committee), "State School Reuse Committee to Discuss Findings at Public Meeting" (letter to the editor), *Sentinel*, May 19, 1982; JoAnne Newman, "Belchertown State School to Phase Out in Three Years," *Sentinel*, March 14, 1989.

3. Quoted in "State School's 25th Anniversary," *Sentinel*, November 29, 1947. During the Great Depression, when jobs were otherwise scarce, George McPherson was said to have been especially solicitous toward local families with children to support, giving many of them employment at the school. "The Steeple Soliloquizes: In Which the Steeple Bids Good-Bye to a Grand Citizen," *Sentinel*, June 18, 1943.

4. Initially (in 1923), the administrators, called "resident officers," comprised the following positions: superintendent, senior (or senior assistant) physician, two assistant physicians, dentist, chief engineer, bookkeeper/treasurer, head farmer, foreman mechanic (later called maintenance foreman), chief supervisor, head dietician, head matron (later called supervising institution housekeeper), social worker (later called psychiatric social worker), and head teacher. The position of chief engineer was split into two jobs—state hospital steward and chief power plant engineer—a few years later, and a psychologist was added to the resident officer staff. *Annual Report of the Trustees of the Belchertown State School for the Year Ending November 30, 1923* (Dept. of Mental Diseases, n.d.), 2; *Annual Report of the Trustees of the Belchertown State School for the Year Ending November 30, 1927* (Dept. of Mental Diseases, n.d.), 2. Several other administrative positions were also added, including a resident pharmacist in 1944, bringing the total of resident officer positions as of 1945 to 22. "The Year at the State School," *Sentinel*, January 5, 1945.

5. Hollis Wheeler, "These Kids Aren't Babies—They're Grownups! The Socialization and Work of Attendants at a Changing Institution" (master's thesis, University of Massachusetts Amherst, 1977), 21.

6. "Waiting Game," *Daily Hampshire Gazette* (Northampton, Mass.), September 17, 2003.

7. Anonymous, interview by author, June 12, 2007. This former farm employee married a fellow employee and left the school in 1940 for a higher-paying job in private industry.

8. Robert Francis, "Two Days among the Feeble-Minded," MS [n.d.], 4, Robert Francis Papers, collection 143, series 4, box 14:180, Special Collections and Archives, W. E. B. Du Bois Library, University of Massachusetts Amherst.

9. Anonymous, interview by author, June 12, 2007.

10. Ibid.; Francis, "Two Days among the Feeble-Minded," 9.

11. Anonymous, interview by author, June 12, 2007.

12. Joe McCrea, e-mail to Doris Dickinson, July 17, 2007.

13. "Honor Roll of Those in State Service 5 Yrs. or More," *Sentinel*, May 12, 1944; "On State Service Honor Roll," *Sentinel*, May 26, 1944; and "State School Opened 22 Years Ago," *Sentinel*, November 24, 1944. Four officers—Arthur Westwell (dentist), John Cronin (head farmer), Frank Farrington (chief engineer), and Aubrey Lapolice (foreman mechanic)—had been with the school since its inception.

14. "Public Service Award to Mrs. McClean," *Sentinel*, May 4, 1967; Joe McCrea, e-mail to Doris Dickinson, July 12, 2007.

15. Wheeler, "These Kids Aren't Babies," 29, 22–23.

16. Anonymous, interview by author, June 12, 2007.

17. Ibid.

18. Joe McCrea, e-mail to Doris Dickinson, July 12, 2007. Rats, as on any farm, were a problem. McCrea noted that those who worked in the vegetable storage would tie their pant legs with string at the ankles, to keep the rats from crawling up their legs.

19. Anonymous, interview by author, June 12, 2007.

20. Steven J. Taylor, "A Working Paper on the Nature of Life and Experience of Institutionalization at Belchertown State School" (paper sponsored by Syracuse University Center on Human Policy, 1975; in author's possession), 23–24. This report, which was based on observations recorded by Taylor and a number of researchers who accompanied him on a visit to the school, was prepared for the defense team in the murder trial of Russell Daniels, a former resident (see chapter 7).

21. Francis, "Two Days among the Feeble-Minded," 6.

22. RB, letter to author, August 15, 2007.

23. Ruth Sienkiewicz-Mercer and Steven B. Kaplan, *I Raise My Eyes to Say Yes: A Memoir* (Boston: Houghton Mifflin, 1989), 49–50.

24. Wheeler, "These Kids Aren't Babies," 24–25.

25. William A. Fraenkel, "A Twenty-Four-Hour Visit to a State School for the Mentally Retarded" (February 14, 1969), 13. Fraenkel's report is reproduced as

Exhibit B of Massachusetts General Court, *Report of the Joint Special Commission on Belchertown State School and Monson State Hospital* (March 14, 1971), which will hereafter be cited as Joint Commission, 1971 *Report on BSS.*

26. Sienkiewicz-Mercer and Kaplan, *I Raise My Eyes,* 52–53.

27. James Shanks, "The Tragedy of Belchertown: State Breaks the Law Every Day," *Springfield (Mass.) Union,* March 16, 1970.

28. On the long workweeks and sparse vacations in the early years, see "State School's 25th Anniversary," *Sentinel,* November 29, 1947.

29. The following discussion of control is indebted to Taylor, "Working Paper," 18–37.

30. Wheeler, "These Kids Aren't Babies," 2.

31. Fraenkel, "Twenty-Four-Hour Visit," 4.

32. Taylor, "Working Paper," 24.

33. Ibid., 25–26. Ruth Sienkiewicz-Mercer describes what it was like to be fed:

> The attendants shoved globs of food into my mouth and expected me to swallow them in big gulps while I was flat on my back, not even propped up in a sitting position.
>
> The food itself was awful, the worst I had ever tasted. They fed me either boiled vegetables or steamed meat, ground into a tasteless pulp. Most of the time the food was so bad I couldn't tell what it was. From the outset, eating at the State School was a painful experience, and I had a terrible time of it. To make matters worse, whenever I choked while they were shoveling food down my throat, the attendants became angry. They thought I was being uncooperative.

Sienkiewicz-Mercer and Kaplan, *I Raise My Eyes,* 41.

34. Fraenkel, "Twenty-Four-Hour Visit," 8.

35. Taylor, "Working Paper," 27.

36. Sienkiewicz-Mercer and Kaplan, *I Raise My Eyes,* 47. There was more recreational time outdoors in the early years—as much as three hours per day for some residents—although, even then, outdoor activity was always done en masse. Francis, "Two Days among the Feeble-Minded," 13.

37. Francis, "Two Days among the Feeble-Minded," 15–16.

38. Shanks, "Tragedy of Belchertown: State Breaks the Law Every Day"; Anonymous, interview by author, June 12, 2007.

39. Joint Commission, 1971 *Report on BSS,* 9.

40. Taylor, "Working Paper," 32.

41. Fraenkel, "Twenty-Four-Hour Visit," 5.

42. Shanks, "Tragedy of Belchertown: State Breaks the Law Every Day."

43. Taylor, "Working Paper," 31.

44. Tranquilizing drugs were first used as an instrument of control in institutions for the mentally ill, but their use spread quickly to other venues, including state schools for the mentally retarded. According to Robert Whitaker, by 1970, "more than 50% of mentally retarded children in America were being drugged." Robert Whitaker, *Mad in America: Bad Science, Bad Medicine, and the Enduring Mistreatment of the Mentally Ill* (Cambridge, Mass.: Perseus, 2002), 205.

45. Joint Commission, 1971 *Report on BSS*, 19. The commission also found that "unnecessary and incorrect medication has been given to residents." Ibid.
46. Taylor, "Working Paper," 33–34.
47. Ibid., 34.
48. "Adult Living and Learning Unit Report," *Annual Report of the Trustees of the Belchertown State School for the Year Ending June 30, 1974* (Dept. of Mental Health, n.d.).
49. Fraenkel, "Twenty-Four Hour Visit," 11; Anonymous, interview by author, October 20, 2009.
50. Wheeler, "These Kids Aren't Babies," 56. Wheeler notes that at this time "the act of referring to residents as 'kids' [was] no longer officially allowed," but adds that "this long-standing habit dies hard in the absence of a well-integrated effort to teach attendants to perceive residents as other adult people." Ibid.
51. Taylor, "Working Paper," 16–17.
52. Ibid.
53. Fraenkel, "Twenty-Four-Hour Visit," 4.
54. Sienkiewicz-Mercer and Kaplan, *I Raise My Eyes*, 50–51.
55. Fraenkel, "Twenty-Four-Hour Visit," 5, 13.
56. Sienkiewicz-Mercer and Kaplan, *I Raise My Eyes*, 50.
57. Wheeler, "These Kids Aren't Babies," 80.
58. Ibid., 82.
59. Ibid., 80 (quoting from interview notes).
60. Quoted in David Bergengren, "Out of Sight, Out of Mind, into Decline," *Springfield Sunday Republican*, December 20, 1992 (Springfield edition). Benjamin Ricci, who sued the state school on behalf of his son in a widely publicized lawsuit discussed later in this book, was less charitable. According to Ricci, a "considerable number" of employees "were untrained and emotionally ill-prepared as well as ill-suited to serve mentally retarded persons. They liberally dispensed verbal, physical, and social abuse. Some even participated in sexual abuse. The residents at the institution learned fast—they were capable of readily conforming. Residents who had witnessed a physical beating would deny any knowledge of it—as if it never took place. Morally bankrupt, bully[ing] attendants did not need to physically punish a resident; they merely encouraged older and stronger residents—enforcers—to 'beat people up.' The law of the barren, stench-filled, concrete and terrazzo jungle prevailed." Benjamin Ricci, *Crimes against Humanity: A Historical Perspective* (New York: iUniverse, 2004), xv–xvi.
61. Sienkiewicz-Mercer and Kaplan, *I Raise My Eyes*, 53–54.
62. JoAnne Newman, "Former State School Resident Remembers the Good Times," *Sentinel*, February 28, 1990.
63. Joe McCrea, e-mail to Doris Dickinson, March 7, 2007.
64. Quotations in this and the following paragraph are from Joe McCrea, e-mail to Doris Dickinson, June 20, 2007.
65. Ibid.

66. This insight is Wheeler's ("These Kids Aren't Babies," 56).

67. Ibid., 56–57, 25.

68. Wheeler, "These Kids Aren't Babies," 57.

69. "Employees' Entertainment," *Sentinel*, December 31, 1926; "The Story of 1929," *Sentinel*, January 3, 1930.

70. "Entertainment at State School," *Sentinel*, January 6, 1928.

71. "State School Minstrel," *Sentinel*, April 1, 1932.

72. "Entertainment at State School," *Sentinel*, September 7, 1923; and "Entertainment at State School," *Sentinel*, April 20, 1928.

73. "Scout Drive Successful at State School," *Sentinel*, August 16, 1946.

74. "State School Party," *Sentinel*, November 27, 1936.

75. Charlie Caron, "Out in the Cold," *Charlie Caron* (blog), entry posted January 10, 2003, http://forum.akmhcweb.org (no longer available).

5. Family and Friends

1. Benjamin Ricci, *Crimes against Humanity: A Historical Perspective* (New York: iUniverse, 2004), 3. My narrative of Bobby's early years is based on Ricci's first chapter, "Beginning Anew after World War II."

2. Ibid., 5–6.

3. See Katherine Castles, " 'Nice, Average Americans'—Postwar Parents' Groups and the Defense of the Normal Family," in *Mental Retardation in America: A Historical Reader*, ed. Steven Noll and James Trent Jr. (New York: New York University Press, 2004), 351–71, esp. 361–65. Castles notes that the desire to give the rest of the family a normal and healthy life manifested itself in the growing number of retarded or otherwise disabled children between 1945 and 1955 who were institutionalized at a very young age, even after adjusting for population growth. Where the condition could be diagnosed at birth (such as Down syndrome), many physicians sought to separate mother and child at the hospital, before attachments developed. Ibid. The Belchertown State School was at the forefront of the movement to institutionalize children at an increasingly early age. As we saw earlier, the construction of two nurseries in 1930 and 1932 enabled it to admit children as young as two years old.

4. Ricci, *Crimes against Humanity*, 7.

5. Ibid., 9.

6. Ibid., 10.

7. In 1929 the trustees noted, "This board is constantly importuned by letters, some of which are concise and others voluminous; by the appearance at the board meetings, of parents, or relatives near and sometimes distant, and also by members of the legal fraternity—but all having the same purpose in view, namely—the release of the pupil from school." "Trustees' Report," *Annual Report of the Trustees of the Belchertown State School for the Year Ending November 30, 1929* (Dept. of Mental Diseases, n.d.), 2–3. The trustees had their own, rather cynical explanation for this: "There seems to be an element of selfishness entering into too many of these applications, as it is evident that the individuals are more desirous of gaining what the discharged pupil's work might

bring to them than in helping the one who is going from the institution." Ibid., 3. Curiously, the trustees did not seem to see that a similar incentive might be impelling them to reject the discharge request.

8. Very occasionally, something disquieting would be covered. For example, in a January 1946 article reviewing the school's prior year, the *Sentinel* reported that there were eighty-five positions vacant at the end of the year, including sixty-three in the ward service—a vacancy rate of 36 percent. Disturbing though this surely was, a reader might well have seen it as temporary, the consequence of four years of world war and a military not yet demobilized.

9. "Superintendent's Report," *Annual Report of the Trustees of the Belchertown State School for the Year Ending November 30, 1925* (Dept. of Mental Diseases, n.d.), 7. Overcrowding and inadequate facilities were recurring themes in the annual reports. For example, in their 1937 report the trustees wrote: "The problem of adequate plant facilities continues to be a serious one if the institution is to meet the need of the community. Originally planned for 2500 beds, our present legal capacity is 1250, though we recently have accommodated as many as 1316 patients. We are seriously over-crowded and these figures are indicative of the demands on the institution." "Trustees' Report," *Annual Report of the Trustees of the Belchertown State School for the Year Ending November 30, 1937* (Gardner, Mass.: Occupational Printing Plant, Dept. of Mental Diseases, n.d.), 3.

10. "State School Friends Organize," *Sentinel*, January 21, 1954.

11. On the Waltham group, see "State School Friends Organize." On the broader movement see, for example, Castles, " 'Nice, Average Americans' "; Kathleen Jones, "Education for Children with Mental Retardation: Parent Activism, Public Policy, and Family Ideology in the 1950s," in Noll and Trent, *Mental Retardation in America*, 322–50. The impetus for parental activism in the early 1950s may have been the conscientious objectors of World War II, many of who were assigned to be attendants in mental hospitals and schools for the feeble-minded throughout the United States. These conscientious objectors were appalled by what they saw. They sought to arouse public concern by writing reports and taking photographs for circulation to interested legislators and journalists. This led, after the war, to the publication of a number of books and magazine articles exposing conditions at the institutions. Joel Freedman, *On Both Sides of the Gate* (New York: Vantage Press, 1980), 3. Other impelling factors probably included exclusion of low-IQ children from public schools, the paucity of community services geared to disabled persons, long waiting lists for admission to state schools, and parental dissatisfaction with conditions at those schools. See Robert Segal, "The National Association for Retarded Citizens," www.thearc.org/page.aspx?pid=2342. Whatever the impetus, the National Association of Parents and Friends of Mentally Retarded Children (later the National Association for Retarded Citizens; now The Arc of the United States) was established in 1950. By 1955 the group had 29,000 members, with 412 local units that were providing, among other things, classes for the "trainable" or "educable" retarded, counseling and

guidance for parents, parent education classes, institutional services (such as equipment), and information and referral services. Ibid. Interestingly, parents also began organizing in other countries at about the same time. Leopold Lippman, "The Public," in *Changing Patterns in Residential Services for the Mentally Retarded*, ed. Robert B. Kugel, rev. ed. (Washington, D.C.: President's Committee on Mental Retardation, 1976), 98.

12. Ricci, *Crimes against Humanity*, 17.

13. *The Bell*, June 1957. Copies of all issues of *The Bell* cited in this chapter can be found in Belchertown State School Friends Association Records, 1954–86, collection MS 302, box 1B, folder 5a, Special Collections and Archives, W. E. B. Du Bois Library, University of Massachusetts Amherst.

14. "State School Friends Meeting," *Sentinel*, September 17, 1954.

15. "Recounts Year of Activity," *Sentinel*, May 13, 1955; *The Bell*, September 1957 and June 1958.

16. *The Bell*, September 1955.

17. Ibid.

18. In its first year, the group raised $1,550 from such activities. "Recounts Year of Activity," *Sentinel*, May 13, 1955.

19. It should be noted that the parents and staff did in fact benefit as well. For example, the Friends occasionally provided scholarships for individual staff members to attend courses, and parents learned from guest speakers about special trust and estate-planning techniques for families with mentally retarded children. *The Bell*, April 1958 and November 1959.

20. *The Bell*, June 1957; "Completing Three Years," *Sentinel*, July 6, 1957.

21. Parents' ambivalence about whether to engage with their children at the state school was not limited to dormitory parties. A former employee who worked mostly with younger children remembers parents having to be called and reminded that their sons and daughters had outgrown their clothing and needed new outfits. Anonymous, interview by author, October 20, 2009. Did such indifference reflect a loss of parental love? Or were these fathers and mothers merely practicing lessons learned when they were told they must "choose" between a disabled offspring and the rest of their family? It is perhaps instructive that this same former employee also remembered that mothers, but not fathers, were usually responsive to such phone calls.

22. "Friends Association Meeting," *Sentinel*, September 16, 1955.

23. "Friends Association Projects," *Sentinel*, March 22, 1957.

24. "Friends Association Meeting," *Sentinel*, May 17, 1957.

25. "Friends Association Meeting," *Sentinel*, January 24, 1958.

26. "The Steeple Soliloquizes: No 'Scrap Heap' Here," *Sentinel*, August 6, 1948.

27. "State School News," *Sentinel*, August 1, 1958. Barbara Valliere, who headed the school's newly established volunteer service department and also acted as information officer, reported in 1959 that a total of 270 news articles were published about the school during fiscal year 1958/59 in the *Belchertown Sentinel, Holyoke Daily Transcript, Springfield Daily News, Springfield Union,* and *Boston Herald.* "Report of the Volunteer Services Department," *Annual Report of*

the Trustees of the Belchertown State School for the Year Ending June 30, 1959 (Dept. of Mental Health, n.d.), 29.

28. Ibid.; "State School News," *Sentinel*, August 8, 1958.

29. *The Bell*, March 1969. The relationship between parents and attending staff—the employees responsible for the day-to-day care of the residents—was among the most difficult to improve. The association's first president, Robert Robbins, focused on the issue in his report to the membership at the end of his two-year term. He wrote, "I do not think we have done as much as we might have to improve the relationship between the school and the parents. Particularly those who are with our children most of the time, the matrons and attendants." "Friends Association Meeting," *Sentinel*, May 18, 1956.

30. "At the State School," *Sentinel*, December 16, 1927.

31. "Guests of Amherst Theatre," *Sentinel*, December 6, 1929.

32. See, e.g., "Entertainment at State School," *Sentinel*, January 6, 1928; "The Story of 1929," *Sentinel*, January 3, 1930.

33. "The Year at the State School," *Sentinel*, January 4, 1946.

34. "An Afternoon of Enjoyment," *Sentinel*, October 17, 1947; "Coleman Day," *Sentinel*, October 17, 1952; "Here Some Forty Years," *Sentinel*, October 16, 1964. It ended badly. In 1964, after twenty consecutive years of attending the fair, the school's residents were denied this treat; the school said there was a shortage of help and that therefore it could not participate. The following year, however, Coleman's concessions were shut down by the town's board of selectmen—allegedly because he refused to give rides any longer to the state school residents. The *Sentinel*, which investigated the matter, concluded that the explanation was more complicated. Although Coleman had, indeed, refused to give free rides, his refusal was tied to a larger issue: his complaint that the town was not giving him enough set-up and paid operating time, and therefore he did not have sufficient time or funds to continue the free program. "The Pot Boils Again," *Sentinel*, October 15, 1965. A *Sentinel* columnist, William Squires Jr., writing the following week, summed it up in a word: "inflation." The "days of free rides," he said, "are over." He called for a private group to step in and provide funding. "From the Middle Chair," *Sentinel*, October 22, 1965.

35. "Volunteer Awards," *Sentinel*, May 25, 1962; "Give Talk at St. Hyacinth," *Sentinel*, March 5, 1965.

36. "Birthday Box Organization," *Sentinel*, August 2, 1957; "Birthday Box Needs Stamps," *Sentinel*, July 28, 1961. The Birthday Bus project was the brainchild of Barbara Valliere, the school's director of volunteers. It was common at the time for grocery store chains around the country to offer their retail customers "trading stamps" with each purchase. The customer would paste the stamps into books that could be traded for merchandise like toasters and ovens (so many books for such-and-such item)—the 1960s equivalent of today's credit card points. Valliere persuaded the Top Value Stamp Company to set up collection centers at Stop & Shop stores in Springfield, Northampton, and Holyoke. Top Value and a local bank donated radio spots advertising the project and

encouraging customers to donate their stamps. It took several years (thousands of people donated stamps in twenty-one states), but on February 18, 1963, the Birthday Box group took delivery of the new bus (valued at $11,300) in a festive ceremony at the front of the administration building. The official drive had actually ended several months earlier, but delivery was delayed because, at the last minute, Top Value raised the quota by three hundred books to cover "extras" on the bus, and more time was needed to collect the additional stamps. "Project Birthday Bus," *Sentinel*, August 11, 1961; "Report on September Issue of Newsletter 'Limelighter,'" *Sentinel*, October 12, 1962; "A Dream Comes True," *Sentinel*, February 21, 1963; *The Bell*, March 1963.

37. "Fairyland Dedicated," *Sentinel*, April 17, 1959; "State School News," *Sentinel*, May 15, 1959.

38. "State School News," *Sentinel*, February 4, 1962.

39. "State School News," *Sentinel*, January 16, 1959.

40. "State School News," *Sentinel*, May 19, 1961.

41. "State School News," *Sentinel*, March 20, 1964.

42. "Year at the State School," *Sentinel*, January 22, 1965.

43. Ibid.

44. Valliere's responsibilities shifted in later years from volunteer supervision to rehabilitation. In the 1970s, in her later capacity as assistant superintendent for adult services, she played a leading role in teaching school residents how to register and vote, following the Massachusetts Supreme Judicial Court's ruling in 1975 (see *Boyd v. Board of Registrars of Voters of Belchertown*, 368 Mass. 631 (1975)) that state school residents not adjudicated incompetent and not placed under guardianship were entitled to vote. See Barbara Armstrong, "The Mentally Disabled and the Right to Vote," *Journal of Hospital and Community Psychiatry* 27 (1976): 578–79.

45. The Friends had an eye for supporting talent. In 1959 they paid Valliere's way to attend a course at Boston University. *The Bell*, November 1959. They were also careful to show appreciation for the volunteer work of others. For example, in June 1963 a group of members attended the recognition party given by the school's volunteer services office to honor the many other volunteers who were now donating their time to the school. "It was an inspiration," wrote the editor of *The Bell*, "to see the number of boys and girls from the area colleges, office workers, church groups, social clubs, Westover Wives Club members, and individuals who gave their time—in many cases 100 to 150 hours—to bring pleasure and assistance to our children."

46. *The Bell*, September 1957.

47. See, e.g., *The Bell*, November 1954. Following the first convention in Boston, the main speaker counseled the attendees about publicity campaigns and fund-raising.

48. "Completing Three Years," *Sentinel*, July 6, 1957. The other host was the Hampden Country ARC.

49. "Friends Association Meeting," *Sentinel*, May 17, 1957. The subject of his talk was "personal relations." Among other things, he encouraged the members

to "personally see . . . your legislators to make sure they are informed on current legislation."

50. *The Bell*, March 1956.
51. *The Bell*, April 1957. The Committee on Public Welfare was a committee of the Massachusetts House of Representatives.
52. *The Bell*, June 1957.
53. "Friends Association Projects," *Sentinel*, March 22, 1957. A hearing on the issue in Boston the previous year had attracted six hundred spectators—a turnout which, according to the *Sentinel*, "made considerable of an impression on the solons."

6. The Tragedy of Belchertown

1. James Shanks, "The Tragedy of Belchertown," *Springfield (Mass.) Sunday Republican*, March 15, 1970 (the *Republican* was the *Union*'s Sunday edition at this time). Building K had inspired a different rhetoric when it opened in 1922. The *Sentinel* called it "really alluring. . . . One of more normal propensities might find suggestions to greater health and happiness. The pictures in the large and sunny day room are inescapable voices calling one to noble living; the play yard, entered from this room, beckons one to a wonderful view of the Holyoke range and gorgeous sunsets, while the sleeping rooms with their immaculate cleanliness and wealth of sun and fresh air leave nothing to be desired to bring refreshing sleep." "State School Plant Developing," November 17, 1922.
2. James Shanks, "The Tragedy of Belchertown: State Breaks the Law Every Day," *Springfield (Mass.) Union*, March 16, 1970.
3. Ibid.
4. Ibid.
5. Shanks, "The Tragedy of Belchertown" (March 15).
6. Massachusetts General Court, *Report of the Special Commission Established to Make an Investigation and Study Relative to Training Facilities Available for Retarded Children*, House no. 3601 (Boston: Wright & Potter, 1964), 23–24.
7. American Association of Mental Deficiency, *Final Report for Belchertown State School* (May 1968), 12. The AAMD report is reproduced as Exhibit A of the General Court of Massachusetts, *Report of the Joint Special Commission on Belchertown State School and Monson State Hospital* (March 24, 1971), which will hereafter be cited as Joint Commission, *1971 Report on BSS*. Another visitor in 1968 was Burton Blatt, the assistant commissioner, director of the Department of Mental Retardation, and a professor and former chairman of the Special Education Department at Boston University. In 1970 Blatt published a book about conditions at the state schools in Massachusetts. His descriptions of his 1968 visit to Belchertown are as horrific as those of Shanks. Burton Blatt, *Exodus from Pandemonium: Human Abuse and a Reformation of Public Policy* (Boston: Allyn and Bacon, 1970); see also Blatt and Fred Kaplan, *Christmas in Purgatory: A Photographic Essay on Mental Retardation* (Boston: Allyn and

Bacon, 1966), and for Blatt's biography see http://archives.syr.edu/collections /faculty/blatt/bio.html.

8. William A. Fraenkel, "A Twenty-Four Hour Visit to a State School for the Mentally Retarded," (February 14, 1969), 2, 5, 6–8, 11, 13–14. Fraenkel's report is reproduced as Exhibit B of Joint Commission, 1971 Report on BSS. We do not know whether Fraenkel, in his role as assistant commissioner, gave the school's superintendent, Lawrence Bowser, a copy of his visit report, but, as we'll see, he sent a memo to Bowser suggesting a number of changes, and another to M. Phillip Wakstein, the regional administrator for the state's Department of Mental Health, asking him to monitor progress; he also made a second visit to the school about a month later. Letter from W. Fraenkel to Superintendent Bowser dated February 14, 1969, reproduced as Exhibit C of Joint Commission, 1971 Report on BSS; memo from W. Fraenkel to M. P. Wakstein dated March 13, 1969, and letter from W. Fraenkel to M. P. Wakstein dated May 14, 1969, reproduced as Exhibits C and D of Joint Commission, 1971 Report on BSS. It was Wakstein, apparently in the discharge of his monitoring duties, who arranged the 1970 visit to the school by James Shanks and others that culminated in the Springfield Union's "Tragedy of Belchertown" series. The visitors included, besides Shanks and Wakstein himself, the executive director of Hampden County Association for Retarded Children, and a state legislator.

9. James Shanks, "The Tragedy of Belchertown: Legislators Bear Much of the Blame," Springfield Union, March 17, 1970.

10. Ibid. The prior horrors of infirmary life have been chillingly recounted by Ruth Sienkiewicz-Mercer in her memoir (written with Steven B. Kaplan), I Raise My Eyes to Say Yes (Boston: Houghton Mifflin, 1989). After being admitted to Belchertown State School in 1962 at the age of twelve, she was assigned to the infirmary and spent the first three years of her life there "flat on my back, day in and day out," with "nothing to do" (see note 33 in chapter 4 for her account of being fed by attendants). There was no wheelchair, no physical therapy, no purposeful human contact. Her weight fell to thirty pounds; her limbs atrophied. "The present was too repulsive," she writes. "I retreated into my own private world of memory and imagination . . . mark[ing] the passage of time by feedings and diaper changes" (56–57). Sienkiewicz-Mercer's memoir, though, tends to corroborate Shanks's report that conditions in the infirmary had begun to improve somewhat by 1970. In the fall of 1965, a group of new attendants arrived on her ward. They were, by her account, attentive and considerate (102–10). She was started on a modest regime of physical therapy, and was allowed to wear clothes for the first time (114–18, 123). Beginning in 1968, also for the first time, she was taken outside for walks several times a week (144). In 1969 she started school, attending regular classes for nonverbal residents (148–51).

11. Lewis Blackmer, the original editor and publisher of the Sentinel since its founding in 1915, had retired in 1965. Peter Dearness, his replacement, cut back coverage of the state school shortly after taking over. So there was already a five-year lull in local reporting about the school when the Shanks

exposé was published in the *Springfield Union*. In that sense, the *Sentinel*'s non-coverage of the exposé was business as usual.

12. "From the Middle Chair," *Sentinel*, April 17, 1970. The only other stories about the state school published by the *Sentinel* during the next twelve months concerned the construction of a sheltered workshop on the school grounds (April 17, 1970), a Friends' Association card party (May 1, 1970), and a proposal for transporting residents around the grounds by train (December 4, 1970).

13. "An Objective Review of Belchertown State School," reproduced as Exhibit I of Joint Commission, 1971 *Report on BSS*. The report included an attachment, "Innovative Programs at Belchertown State School," which described various existing programs for the care and training of residents.

14. Letter, Fraenkel to Bowser, March 24, 1970, reproduced as Exhibit G of Joint Commission, 1971 *Report on BSS*.

15. *Annual Report of the Trustees of the Belchertown State School for the Year Ending June 30, 1970* (Dept. of Mental Health, n.d.), 4a–4b.

16. The members were senators Philip Quinn, John Conte, Joseph Ward, and John Barrus; representatives Alexander Lolas, Frederic Schlosstein Jr., Steve Chmura, James Grimaldi, John Olver, Louis Morini, and Paul Corriveau; and citizens Benjamin Ricci and Doris S. Fraser. Beryl Cohen was counsel, Ruth Nelson executive secretary, and James Frieden research assistant. The second citizen appointee, Doris S. Fraser, was a PhD candidate at the Heller School for Social Policy and Management at Brandeis University and a researcher at Heller's Institute for Child, Youth and Family Policy.

17. Joint Commission, 1971 *Report on BSS*, 5, 13, 43–44.

18. Fraenkel, who himself had been appalled by what he saw during his one-day stay at the school in 1969, may well have been feigning sympathy in order to gain Bowser's confidence—the better to prod Bowser to make reforms quickly. As we've seen, his letter included several suggestions—fourteen in all—for fast change, some of which were substantial.

19. Joint Commission, 1971 *Report on BSS*, 45–46, 48.

20. Ibid., 10n19.

21. His letter of resignation, published by the *Sentinel*, was a game attempt to save face, claiming it had been his intent from the outset (when he was appointed superintendent in 1960) to retire from state service after ten years, and that he was now merely fulfilling that intention. He praised the "highly competent, dedicated, and greatly supportive" staff he had assembled to assist "all my endeavors to improve Belchertown and to reduce the severe overcrowding" that had existed for some years. He hoped his successor would not find himself handicapped, as he had been, by "a hypocritical and negative climate from outside sources" that "often compounded the difficulties in administering the inner institution with its many problems," and that "at times has saddened our entire staff." "Bowser Resigns from B.S.S.," *Sentinel*, April 8, 1971.

22. "Editorial—'Tragedy of Belchertown'—What Was It?" *Sentinel*, April 8, 1971.

23. Joint Commission, 1971 *Report on BSS*, 36–37, 6, 4. Other appropriated funds went unused and were allowed to lapse. Ibid., 21.

24. The population reduction that Bowser achieved (from 1,560 to 1,236 residents) happened between 1966 and 1970 and was a result of several separate initiatives including community placements, transfers to other institutions, and a freeze on new admissions. Since Bowser had also presided over the earlier increase in resident population between 1960 and 1966 (1,428 to 1,560), the net reduction for the decade was somewhat less than the isolated reduction figures from 1966 to 1970 would suggest. The nonspecialized residential dormitory that Bowser was responsible for constructing was Building G, which opened in 1968. (Two specialized residential facilities had been constructed during the tenure of the prior superintendent, Henry Tadgell: the infirmary, which opened in 1952, and Tadgell Nursery, which opened in 1960.) Bowser also added staff, significantly improving the staff-to-resident ratio from 1:3 in 1960 to 1:2 in 1970. As discussed elsewhere in this chapter, new, caring attendants hired for the infirmary were able to get some of that area's bedridden residents up and about and taught many of the men in the back wards of Building K to feed themselves. Finally, Bowser presided over a significant expansion of the school's volunteer program. Between 1968 and 1970, the number of volunteer hours (already on the rise) increased further, from 9,000 hours per year to more than 13,000. In addition, new volunteer programs were developed. For example, the ambitious Boltwood Program was established in early 1970. Its goal was to train up to 1,000 area college students to teach the school's more able residents skills sufficient for them to transfer to community homes, and otherwise to help provide a "contented and useful life in the institution for those [residents] unable to reach the level of community living." "A New Concept—the Boltwood Program at BSS," *Sentinel*, February 13, 1970.

25. The new volunteer programs included, besides the ambitious Boltwood Program described in the previous note, smaller but no less interesting initiatives such as "I Care," a program that required each volunteer (there were sixty-four) to donate two hours of time per week and to be assigned one-on-one to a specific resident. "The 'I Care' Program First Annual Report," *Annual Report of the Trustees of the Belchertown State School for the Year Ending June 30, 1971* (Dept. of Mental Health, n.d.), 44–45. The new halfway house in Springfield, though not a volunteer project, was interesting in its own right. It was managed by a local married couple, whose job it was to teach the men transferred there how to cook, handle money, manage interpersonal relationships, and the like. "Report of the Social Service Department," ibid., 40.

26. Letter from Fraenkel to Bowser, February 14, 1969, reproduced as Exhibit C of Joint Commission, 1971 *Report on BSS.*

27. Shanks even quotes a state legislator, Alan Sisitsky of Springfield (one of those who toured Belchertown with him) as blaming the legislature: "Since we (the Legislature) appropriate the funds and possess the authority to correct the situation at Belchertown, we are in a sense ultimately responsible for the conditions that exist." Shanks, "Tragedy of Belchertown: State Breaks the Law."

28. "Commissioner Speaks on B.S.S. Problems," *Sentinel*, April 15, 1971.

29. The older institutions, he conceded, were still overcrowded and handicapped by serious staff shortages and deteriorated physical plants, despite recent "gains" including population reduction of more than 4,000 in four years, decentralization and unitization, and outreach programs into the community. Belchertown, in particular, "lagged in these historic developments" although "positive changes" were taking place there too.

30. The plan called for closure of the infamous Buildings A and K by the end of the year, adoption of unitization, immediate reassessment of each resident, further transfers out of the school or to more appropriate wards within the school, hiring of fifty new attendants for the back wards, repair of buildings, grounds beautification, and development of a new student volunteer program.

31. "Thoughts on State School System," *Sentinel*, June 3, 1971.

32. Ibid.

33. Fraenkel's interim appointment took effect April 1, 1971, one day after Bowser's resignation. The trustees' annual report for 1970/71 did not acknowledge that Bowser had resigned, reporting instead that he was "on vacation" and that in his absence Fraenkel had been assigned as "senior officer in charge of the institution." "Superintendent's Report," *Annual Report of the Trustees of BSS for 1971*, 22.

34. "BSS Interim Superintendent Gives Progress Report," *Sentinel*, July 15, 1971.

35. Fraenkel described other ambitious reform activities that he said were under way at the school, including the conversion of two former employee cottages into rehabilitation homes for semi-independent men and women, the conversion of Building D into a forty-eight-unit "roomette type residence" for young women who were being prepared for eventual independent living, and the overhaul of school visitation hours to allow parents and relatives visitation rights twenty-four hours a day, seven days a week, year round.

36. Building A was now closed down (as promised), the reassessment of all residents in Buildings A and K was completed, five former employee cottages had been transformed into service facilities (two for intensive care, two for rehabilitation, one for speech and hearing training), fifty children had received complete dental treatment from a team of specialists from Boston University, and fifteen children had undergone orthopedic surgery at the Hospital and School for Crippled Children in Canton, Mass. "B.S.S. News," *Sentinel*, September 10, 1971.

37. "DMH Administration Blamed for Conditions at Belchertown School," *Sentinel*, October 1, 1971.

38. "State School Controversy Continues," *Sentinel*, October 1, 1971.

39. All quotations in this paragraph are from Benjamin Ricci, *Crimes against Humanity: A Historical Perspective* (New York: iUniverse, 2004), 220–22.

40. One of the Friends' projects was called Adopt-A-Building. Members were assigned to each of the school's residential buildings and charged with monitoring how well the needs of its residents were being met. Other members

monitored specific areas of concern, such as cleanliness of buildings, sufficiency of supplies and equipment, and availability of direct care staff. Ricci's charge, which Fraenkel denied, was that Fraenkel pressured those involved in this monitoring to stop doing so.

41. Ricci, *Crimes against Humanity*, 223.

42. Ricci was the recipient of a Fulbright Research Scholar Award to do research at the Institute for Work Physiology in Oslo, Norway.

43. Ricci, *Crimes against Humanity*, 21–28. To be sure, the history of caring for mentally disabled persons in Scandinavia is not without blemish. For example, sterilization laws in Sweden that led to the involuntary and coercive sterilization of thousands of mentally disabled Swedes were not repealed until 1976. See Stephanie Hyatt, "A Shared History of Shame: Sweden's Four-Decade Policy of Forced Sterilization and the Eugenics Movement in the United States," *Indiana International and Comparative Law Review* 8 (1998): 475–503.

44. Ricci, *Crimes against Humanity*, 221–22.

45. *The Bell*, March 1972, Belchertown State School Friends Association Records, 1954–86, collection MS 302, box 1B, folder 5a, Special Collections and Archives, W. E. B. Du Bois Library, University of Massachusetts Amherst.

46. "Next friend" is a legal term used to describe someone who acts on behalf of a person lacking the legal capacity to act for himself or herself.

7. Endings

1. See *Wyatt v. Stickney*, 344 F. Supp. 387 (M.D. Ala. 1972).

2. All quotations in this and following four paragraphs are from Benjamin Ricci, *Crimes against Humanity: A Historical Perspective* (New York: iUniverse, 2004), 94–100.

3. The full text of the complaint is reprinted in Ricci, *Crimes against Humanity*, 56–87.

4. *The Bell*, March 1972. Copies of all issues of *The Bell* cited in this chapter can be found in Belchertown State School Friends Association Records, 1954–86, collection MS 302, box 1B, folder 5a, Special Collections and Archives, W. E. B. Du Bois Library, University of Massachusetts Amherst.

5. "Physical Therapy Department Report," *Annual Report of the Trustees of the Belchertown State School for the Year Ending June 30, 1972* (Dept. of Mental Health, n.d.), 37.

6. *Annual Report of the Trustees of BSS for 1972*, 53–55 (education and training), 65–69 (occupational therapy), 77 (volunteer service).

7. The physical grouping of dormitory buildings, size of resident population per unit, and the need to prepare some residents for their anticipated transfer into community homes were also taken into account. The seven reorganized units were:

> The Children's Unit, located in Tadgell Nursery and Nursery buildings 1 and 2.
>
> The Medical Unit, located in the infirmary, for residents fourteen

years and older who were severely physically handicapped or non-ambulatory, or who otherwise suffered from chronic medical problems that required full-time nursing care.

The Vocational Rehab Unit, located in four former employee cottages, for residents who worked in the school or community and who were older than twenty-one years of age. This unit was supposed to emphasize independence and community living skills, vocational habilitation and training, sex education, and placement in community residences and employment.

The Adolescent Training Unit, located in Building D and one of the former employee cottages, for residents between twelve and twenty-four years of age who possessed self-help skills and at least moderate socialization skills.

The Adolescent Living and Learning Unit, located in Building G, for residents between twelve and twenty-four years of age who were "extremely dependent" in terms of self-care and lacked socialization skills.

The Adult Training Unit, located in Buildings E, F, and M, for residents twenty-five and older who possessed self-help skills and at least moderate socialization skills. The goal in this unit was to train residents sufficiently to enable them to move to the Vocational Rehab Unit or community placement.

The Adult Living and Learning Unit, located in Buildings B, C, and K, for residents twenty-five and older who were extremely dependent in terms of self-care and lacked socialization skills.

"Report of Unit Coordinator," *Annual Report of the Trustees of the Belchertown State School for the Year Ending June 30, 1973* (Dept. Mental Health, n.d.), 37–40.

8. "Letter to the Editor: B.S.S. Superintendent Cites Inadequate Treasury," *Sentinel*, June 29, 1972.

9. Nagle also had harsh things to say about Ricci and his colleagues. He described what he called their "enraged demands" as "self-righteous" and "irrational."

10. "Budget Recommendations for B.S.S. Called 'Mean Trick,'" *Sentinel*, March 30, 1972.

11. Ibid. Ricci also called the college student programs at the school "invaluable." "The youth at the school have taught us a lesson—they've gotten involved and instead of encouraging them—we pull the rug out by not funding them." Volunteer hours dropped in fiscal year 1973 by 25 percent, or 5,000 hours. Apparently, the reduced budget allocation did make a difference: fewer supervisors meant fewer student volunteers.

12. The investigation was commissioned by the governor only after the Department of Mental Health and the school's trustees, respectively, had issued "investigative" reports of their own, exonerating the state and its employees from blame. In the case of Linda Buchanan, both faulted the girl's parents for not speaking up when the search was cancelled.

13. Massachusetts Executive Office of Human Services, *Report of Investigation of Deaths at Belchertown State School* (Boston: Massachusetts Executive Office of Human Services, 1973). The authors of the report were Peter Goldmark and Richard McLaughlin.

14. Ricci, *Crimes against Humanity*, 209.

15. The scandal involving the candidate, Arnold Cortazzo, and Ricci's investigative efforts uncovering it are described in Ricci, *Crimes against Humanity*, 228–31. See also "Retardation Head Warns Cortazzo," *Sarasota Herald-Tribune*, May 12, 1972. Briefly, a number of mentally retarded teenage boys living at the Florida facility were allegedly abused by attendants there: forced to masturbate in public, hold feces-soiled underwear to their noses, and eat bars of soap. When Miami newspapers exposed the scandal, Cortazzo was placed on annual leave and transferred to a different job. The scandal notwithstanding, Greenblatt's choice of Cortazzo as his preferred candidate for the Belchertown position was not as absurd as Ricci's account might lead one to believe. Cortazzo had been sufficiently well regarded nationally in 1971 to be retained by the President's Committee on Mental Retardation to investigate and evaluate activity centers in the United States for retarded adults. His study, *Activity Centers for Retarded Adults*, was published by the Department of Health Education and Welfare in 1972.

16. Ricci, *Crimes against Humanity*, 237.

17. "B.S.S. Head Appointed," *Sentinel*, November 22, 1972; "State School Boss Resigns Post Here," *Sentinel*, November 27, 1985; Ricci, *Crimes against Humanity*, 237. Prior to his tenure at St. John's, Jones had been a school psychologist and assistant superintendent of schools in British Columbia, as well as a frequent consultant to schools elsewhere, including Michigan and New York. He had also authored several "resource manuals" for educators working with mentally retarded and learning disabled children.

18. Don Aucoin, "Tauro Ending an Era of Change," *Boston Globe*, May 25, 1993; "Massachusetts Gaining in Its Care for the Retarded," *New York Times*, January 4, 1987.

19. Ricci, *Crimes against Humanity*, 177.

20. Quoted in Esther Scott, "Judge Tauro and the Care of the Retarded in Massachusetts" (unpublished case study, C15-87-739.0, Kennedy School of Government, Harvard University, 1987), 4.

21. The legacy of *Ricci v. Greenblatt* has been profound. It inspired a number of similar class action lawsuits elsewhere in New England, including Connecticut (*Conn. ARC v. Thorne*, 1978 [Mansfield Training School]), Maine (*Wuori v. Zitnay*, 1975 [Pineland Training Center]), New Hampshire (*Garrity v. Gallen*, 1978 [Laconia State School]), Rhode Island (*Iasimone v. Garralry*, 1977 [Ladd Center]), Vermont (*In re Brace*, 1978 [Brandon Training School])—and beyond. Indeed, the use of class action lawsuits like *Ricci v. Greenblatt* "to safeguard the rights of retarded citizens and to obtain improved or new types of services for them" has been described as "perhaps the most dramatic advance in advocacy in the 1970s." Phillip Ross and Brian M. McCann, "Major Trends in Mental

Retardation," *International Journal of Mental Health* 6.1 (1977): 11. For an over-view of the principal class action lawsuits in the United States on behalf of institutionalized, mentally disabled individuals, see Mary F. Hayden, "Class Action, Civil Rights Litigation for Institutionalized Persons with Mental Retardation and Other Development Disabilities: A Review," *Mental and Physical Disability Law Reporter* 21 (1997): 411–24.

22. Fernald State School: *McEvoy v. Goldmark*, Civil Action No. 74-2768-T (D. Mass. 1975); Wrentham State School: *M.A.R.C. v. Dukakis*, Civil Action No. 75-5023-T (D. Mass. 1975); Dever State School: *M.A.R.C. v. Dukakis*, Civil Action No. 75-5210-T (D. Mass. 1975); Monson State Hospital: *Gauthier v. Benson*, Civil Action No. 75-3910-T (D. Mass. 1975).

23. The legislature did not always appropriate these funds without a fight, though. In one famous incident, after the state legislature failed to act on the gover-nor's supplemental budget request of $35 million for further improvements at the state schools, the chairman of the House Ways and Means Committee locked himself in his office to avoid being served with a subpoena from Judge Tauro. (Even though he couldn't force the legislature to appropriate, Tauro could issue subpoenas and ask questions.) Eventually, the chairman accepted the subpoena and the funds were appropriated. See Scott, "Judge Tauro and the Care of the Retarded," 7–9.

24. Ibid., 5. One study notes, "At the Belchertown State School, the federal fund-ing stream under the amendments to Title XIX of the Social Security Act opened up entirely new possibilities for reform. By enrolling in the Federal Medicaid Assistance Program of Title XIX, the state of Massachusetts received federal reimbursement for the 'Active Treatment' it provided at Belchertown. With the new funds, the School hired new staff to provide active treat-ment. Because the funding came with explicit mandates to improve stan-dards and accountability, the new staff directed their efforts toward meet-ing those mandates." Laura Stein, "Understanding Mental Retardation in America through the Closing of the Belchertown State School" (bachelor's thesis, Amherst College, 2008), 66. "From 1977 to 1988, total spending on Mental Retardation/Development Disabilities increased [in Massachusetts] from $105 million in 1977 to $606 million in 1968. Similarly, the daily cost per resident of Massachusetts institutions went from $39 in 1977 to $274 in 1988." Ibid., 67, citing David L. Braddock, *The State of the States in Developmental Disabilities* (Baltimore: Paul H. Brookes, 1990), 231–32.

25. "Report of Adult Living and Learning Unit Director," *Annual Report of the Trustees of BSS for 1973*, 56, 58.

26. "Report of Adult Living and Learning Unit Director," *Annual Report of the Trustees of the Belchertown State School for the Year Ending June 30, 1974* (Dept. of Mental Health, n.d.), 37.

27. Ibid., 37–38.

28. Ruth Sienkiewicz-Mercer and Steven B. Kaplan, *I Raise My Eyes to Say Yes: A Memoir* (Boston: Houghton Mifflin, 1989), 152–53.

29. Ibid., 153. Sienkiewicz-Mercer's progress was painstaking and slow, but

there was progress. For example, the word board went through several itera-
tions, with each version gradually improving the workability of the device.
Fifteen years later, she would be outfitted with a computerized communications device with state-of-the-art software that she operated with a head
switch to select words and phrases on a screen. Ibid., 154–56.

30. Ibid., 165.

31. Ibid., 165–67.

32. "B'Town State School: 25 Years of 'Notes,'" *Sentinel*, June 19, 1985. Not every
    reform was applauded. For example, the $2.6 million renovation of the physi-
    cal plant that the court ordered in 1976 was said to have been done "with great
    haste" and without design or programmatic input of any sort. Hollis Wheeler,
    "These Kids Aren't Babies—They're Grownups! The Socialization and Work
    of Attendants at a Changing Institution" (master's thesis, University of
    Massachusetts Amherst, 1977), 2–3.

33. Letter dated March 7, 1973, printed in *The Bell*, April 1973.

34. *The Bell*, April 1973. Daniels's conviction was later set aside by the Supreme
    Judicial Court of Massachusetts, which ordered a new trial. The court held
    that evidence should have been presented as to whether Daniels was more
    suggestible and subject to intimidation than a person of normal intelligence
    and thus may not have fully understood that he was entitled to a lawyer and
    had the right to remain silent. Daniels was never retried; instead, the charges
    against him were dismissed in exchange for his return to Belchertown State
    School. *Commonwealth v. Daniels*, 366 Mass. 601 (1975). Daniels's appeal was
    financed by the Friends Association; see *The Bell*, March–April 1975.

35. For an excellent analysis of the community living movement as it affected
    Belchertown State School, see Michael Kendrick, "Leadership, Ideology and
    the Community Living Movement" (PhD diss., University of Massachusetts
    Amherst, 2000). My discussion of the community living movement in
    Massachusetts draws heavily on Kendrick.

36. With the Community and Family Living Amendment to Title XIX, families
    were able to waive their rights to get Title XIX services in an institution and
    instead opt to get those services in the community. Stein, "Understanding
    Mental Retardation," 69. As Stein observes, "One cannot underestimate the
    significance of this change in funding for the community movement. . . . As
    community options developed, parents could actually see the merits of com-
    munity life which many had first questioned" (67, 69).

37. Robert Lane, "Celebration in Support of Community Living," *Sentinel*,
    November 22, 1983.

38. Ibid. Ricci continued to argue that large institutions would always be neces-
    sary for some, and that therefore institutional reform should remain a pri-
    ority. But his audience was dwindling. At another town-common rally for
    community living the following year, Dybwad dared to criticize Ricci publicly.
    "Ricci feels there are always people at BSS who'll need to be there . . . I and
    countless others disagree," he said. In response to Ricci's argument that the
    state's Department of Mental Health was incompetent to run a community

program, Dybwad replied, "My answer to that is Rhode Island, Maine and New Hampshire [do it]. . . . Why can't we do it ?" "Gathering on Common Draws," *Sentinel*, October 24, 1984.

39. Bengt Nirje, "The Normalization Principle," in *Changing Patterns in Residential Services for the Mentally Retarded*, ed. Robert B. Kugel, rev. ed. (Washington, D.C.: President's Committee on Mental Retardation, 1976), 231–40, quotations on 231–32.

40. Wheeler, "These Kids Aren't Babies," 3. Nirje also insisted that mentally retarded people are "basically as 'normal' as you and I, though coping with a handicap. A person is a person first, the handicap is secondary. A child is a child first, secondarily blind or mentally retarded; an adult is first of all a man or woman in a social situation—an engineer, worker, sportsman—and only secondarily or thirdly paraplegic, deaf, retarded, etc." Nirje, "Normalization Principle," 232.

41. Kendrick, "Leadership, Ideology and Community Living," 104.

42. Earl Butterfield, "Some Basic Changes in Residential Facilities," in Kugel, *Changing Patterns in Residential Services*, 15–34.

43. Kendrick, "Leadership, Ideology and Community Living," 153.

44. Kendrick attributes the triumph of the community living movement at the Belchertown school to the "build up of extensive ties with the broader community through service providers, families, use of community resources, and other points of contact" and gives special emphasis to the "wide variety of student volunteers and interns from colleges and universities in the surrounding communities" who had been invited into the school. Ibid., 61. This is not to say there wasn't local opposition to locating group homes in the surrounding communities. See, e.g., Elsie Osterman, "Critics of Palmer Group-Home Plan to Grill State," *Springfield (Mass.) Republican*, December 1, 1990; Kendrick, "Leadership, Ideology and Community Living," 67–69. According to Kendrick, "The broader community . . . selectively expressed its resistance to community placement particularly in the case of larger and more visible community residential programs. This resistance might be thought of as the 'fear of property value decline' factor often called 'NIMBY.' On occasion, this was coupled with genuine concerns about the appropriate conduct of particular individuals with mental retardation while in community settings." The former was addressed by limiting the number of people in any one location to four. The latter was addressed by negotiating with neighborhood residents to ascertain their concerns, provide reassurance or install safeguards where possible and, sometimes, resettle the intended transferees elsewhere. Still, on the whole, local resistance in western Massachusetts was relatively mild.

45. Shirley Dorey (chairman, Belchertown State School Reuse Committee), "State School Reuse Committee to Discuss Findings at Public Meeting" (letter to the editor), *Sentinel*, May 19, 1982.

46. Jack Flynn, "Belchertown School's Fate to Be Revealed Today," *Springfield (Mass.) Union*, March 7, 1989 (Springfield edition); Jack Flynn, "State School's Closing

Impacts WMass," *Springfield Union*, March 8, 1989 (Springfield edition); JoAnne Newman, "Belchertown State School to Phase Out in Three Years," *Sentinel*, March 14, 1989. Despite the verbal reassurances about future job opportunities in the community living system or at other state institutions, the employees of Belchertown State School were thrown into a state of high anxiety by the announcement of the school's impending closure. A series of meetings with state officials failed to allay their concerns. When the school began to announce layoffs, the head of one of the three employees' unions called the phase-down plan a "farce" and accused the school's administration of bargaining in bad faith. JoAnne Newman, "State School Employees Air Concerns over Their Job Futures," *Sentinel*, January 17, 1990; JoAnne Newman, "State School Commission Hears Responses to Labor Questions," *Sentinel*, February 14, 1990; "State School Phase Down Hits Home," *Sentinel*, April 25, 1990.

47. Flynn, "State School's Closing." McCarthy, who admitted the closing could save the state up to $10 million a year, insisted it was not motivated by budgetary concerns.

48. David Bergengren, "With an Emotional Goodbye, the State School Era Comes to an End," *Springfield Union*, December 18, 1992 (Metro East edition).

49. David Bergengren, "Crowd Cheers End of State School," *Springfield Republican*, January 1, 1993 (Metro East edition).

50. "Remarks of Philip Campbell, Commissioner, Department of Mental Retardation" (Belchertown State School, December 31, 1992), Belchertown State School Papers, Clapp Memorial Library, Belchertown, Mass.

51. "Remarks of Ruth Sienkiewicz-Mercer" (Belchertown State School, December 31, 1992), ibid.

8. Ghosts and Graveyards

1. "Haunted Places in Massachusetts," *The Shadowlands*, http://theshadowlands. net/places/massachusetts.htm.

2. The committee presented its first report in 1982. "State School Reuse Public Meeting May 27," *Sentinel*, May 26, 1982.

3. "BSS Development Committee Holds First Meeting, Reviews Proposals," *Sentinel*, July 23, 1992.

4. Suzanne McLaughlin, "Prison Said Likely to Replace State School," *Springfield (Mass.) Republican*, September 26, 1989; David Bergengren, "State Letter Gives Outline for Prison," *Springfield Republican*, March 24, 1992; "State Letter of Intent to Selectmen," dated June 8, 1992, *Sentinel*, June 18, 1992; David Bergengren, "Forum Considers Belchertown Prison," *Springfield Republican*, June 14, 1992; Tom Sweet, "Pros and Cons of All Proposals for BSS Reuse Compared," *Sentinel*, June 18, 1971; David Bergengren, "Prison Rejected by Belchertown," *Springfield Republican*, June 23, 1992.

5. "Formation of EDIC and IDFA for the Town of Belchertown," *Sentinel*, October 29, 1992; A. Joseph DeNucci, Auditor of the Commonwealth, letter to Belchertown board of selectmen,, April 7, 2009, 5, www.mass.gov/sao/ Audit%20Reports/2009/2008146830.pdf.

6. See the New England Small Farm Institute website, www.smallfarm.org/main /our_farm/.

7. David Bergengren, "Belchertown Quest for Space Resisted," *Springfield (Mass.) Union-News*, October 2, 1990 (Metro East edition); Suzanne Bay, "Town Officials Ask Legislators for Help on F," *Sentinel*, April 24, 1991; Jane Kaufman, "Town Weighs Issue of Buying, Renting," *Springfield Union-News*, June 2, 1993 (Metro East edition); Jane Kaufman, "Former State School Leases Tadgell Hall," *Springfield Union-News*, July 30, 1993 (Metro East edition); Jane Kaufman, "State Sells Ex-school Site for $1," *Springfield Union-News*, March 17, 1998 (Metro East edition). In 1990, Ben Ricci, unhappy that state school buildings were being used for unrelated purposes, said the town should stop "encroaching" on state school facilities "until the entire facility is declared surplus by the state Department of Mental Retardation." "Belchertown Quest for Space Resisted."

8. Mass. Acts, 1996, Chapter 353 (approved August 9, 1996); Jennifer Picard, "School Land Deal Complete," *Springfield Republican*, April 23, 2002 (Metro East edition); DeNucci, Auditor's letter, 6. The act authorizing the sale required that the purchase price be for the full and fair market value of the property. Parcels B, D, and E were appraised at $1,920,000. The fire-sale price was justified on the basis that the site (in particular, Parcel B) contained environmental hazards and asbestos that had to be removed, and buildings that had to be demolished, before the property could be developed; the estimated cost of the cleanup—more than $3 million—exceeded the appraised value. The state retained the right to approve future sales and development of the land, and BEDIC was required to turn over to the state net proceeds from future sales, meaning net profits, if any, after cleanup and demolition.

9. The developer bought Parcel E for $125,001. He built a combination bank/ office building on a half-acre portion of the property and installed water lines, sewer lines, and a sewer pumping station. He then subdivided the property into two parcels (approximately 36 acres and 7 acres, respectively) and sold them to other developers for $3,048,200. The larger parcel was further subdivided, sold off, and developed into several retail establishments. The smaller parcel was used to build a new courthouse for the county—the East Hampshire District Court. Jennifer Picard, "School Land Deal Complete," *Springfield Republican*, April 23, 2002 (Metro East edition); Jennifer Picard, "State School Office Park Site Planned," *Springfield Republican*, June 7, 2002 (Metro East edition); DeNucci, Auditor's letter, 14. See also Jennifer Picard, "Mototown Plan Dropped," *Springfield Republican*, March 18, 2004 (Metro East edition).

10. BEDIC sold off one small, 2.5-acre section of Parcel D. Debbi Strauss, "Selectmen Present United Front," *Sentinel*, March 28, 2002; "Belchertown Economic and Industrial Development Corporation," www.belchertown. org/towninfo/Web%20BEL%20ECON%20%20DEV%20AND%20INDL%20 CORP.htm; DeNucci, Auditor's letter, 7.

11. "First Business Locates at Former BSS," *Daily Hampshire Gazette* (Northampton, Mass.), May 1, 2004; DeNucci, Auditor's letter, 7.

12. Dan Fitzpatrick, "A Study in Frustration—State School Reuse" (six-part

series), *Sentinel*, March 13, March 20, March 27, April 3, April 10, and April 17, 2003; Debbi Strauss, "Development Plans Progressing on Former State School Land," *Sentinel*, July 22, 2004.

13. Jennifer Picard, "Property Owner Envisions Tourist Mecca," *Springfield Republican*, January 30, 2005 (Springfield edition); George O'Brian, "Determined State of Mind: Group Pursues New Uses for the Abandoned Belchertown State School," *BusinessWest Online*, May 16, 2005, www.businesswest.com (no longer available).

14. The spring, which still exists, is located on property owned by the University of Massachusetts and used as a horticultural research center. Doris M. Dickinson and Cliff McCarthy, *Images of America: Belchertown* (Charleston, S.C.: Arcadia, 1998), 9.

15. Jennifer Picard, "Plans Discussed for Resort, Spa," *Springfield Republican*, August 5, 2005 (Metro East edition).

16. Hunter Interests, Inc., "Master Plan and Development Strategy for the Belchertown State School Property" (prepared for Belchertown Economic Development and Industrial Corporation, September 15, 2005; copy in author's possession), 10.

17. Stephen Hill, "State School Resort Plan Has Skeptics," *Daily Hampshire Gazette*, August 30, 2005.

18. Joan Axelrod-Contrada, "Resort Spa May Replace Closed State Institution," *Boston Globe*, February 11, 2006.

19. Jennifer Picard, "Old State School Developer Picked," *Springfield Republican*, March 3, 2006.

20. BEDIC press release, May 24, 2006; copy in author's possession.

21. BEDIC press release, March 2, 2006; copy in author's possession.

22. Quoted in Stephen Hill, "Belchertown Picks Developer for Resort and Spa," *Daily Hampshire Gazette*, March 3, 2006.

23. In retrospect, this was perhaps an ill-fated choice of name. "Quabbin" alluded to the Quabbin Reservoir, a 39-square-mile body of water several miles east of Belchertown that was created in the 1930s by flooding the former towns of Dana, Enfield, Greenwich, and Prescott. See Thomas Conuel, *Quabbin: the Accidental Wilderness*, rev. ed. (Amherst: University of Massachusetts Press, 1990); Elizabeth Peirce, *The Lost Towns of the Quabbin Valley* (Portsmouth, N.H.: Arcadia, 2003).

24. BEDIC press release, May 24, 2006.

25. Debbi Strauss, "Paper Signing Makes Resort Spa Plans a Reality," *Sentinel*, June 1, 2006.

26. BEDIC press release, May 24, 2006.

27. Debbi Strauss, "Selectmen 'In the Dark,' " *Sentinel*, June 21, 2007.

28. Stephen Hill, "A Deal Undone: Bad Check Halts State School Plan in Belchertown," *Daily Hampshire Gazette*, October 26, 2006; George O'Brien, "Back to the Drawing Board," *BusinessWest Online*, November 12, 2007, http://businesswest.com/2007/11/back-to-the-drawing-board.

29. O'Brien, "Back to the Drawing Board."

30. Ibid.; Debbi Strauss, "Little Lady with the Big Idea," *Sentinel*, December 27, 2007.

31. Although as of 2011 disagreements persist as to whether the concept of a resort or wellness spa really makes sense for Belchertown and the former state school site, there is consensus that the property needs cleaning up. According to a *Sentinel* editorial published shortly after the Bridgeland contract was terminated, soil tests at the property showed "asbestos, arsenic, lead paint and PCBs left behind when electric poles were removed," and "the state would never allow any development on that property until it is cleaned." The *Sentinel* reported that cleanup estimates ranged from $14 million to $30 million." "Clean It and They Will Come . . . ," *Sentinel*, November 22, 2007.

     Since the collapse of the Quabbin Resort project, several other feasibility studies and project proposals have been put forward including, most recently, a plan to build an assisted living facility. See, e.g., Sustainable Community Design Studio, University of Massachusetts, *Belchertown State School: Sustainable Community Design* (Amherst: The Departments of Architecture, Landscape Architecture and Regional Planning, 2008), available at www.umass.edu/larp/Student%20Work/BSS%20Final%20Report.pdf; Fuss & O'Neill, *Site Development Feasibility Assessment: Belchertown State School, Priority Development Site* (2009), available at www.belchertown.org; Patrick Johnson, "Weston Solutions Offers to Develop Former Belchertown State School Site Providing Town Finances New Roads and Other Improvements," *Springfield Republican*, January 22, 2011; John Appleton, "Town Meeting on Belchertown State School Property Canceled Due to Missing Information," *Springfield Republican*, September 28, 2011.

32. "The Year at the State School," *Sentinel*, January 16, 1948; Bob Jackson, "Old Steeple Soliloquizes," *Sentinel*, October 8, 1948. Benjamin Ricci writes that the carousel was given to the school by "a greater-Springfield dentist" (*Crimes against Humanity*, 16), but I have not found any evidence to support this. Newspaper articles in the early 1990s, when the carousel was put up for auction, say that Dr. Arthur Westwell (the school's longtime dentist) bought the carousel. Again, however, I haven't found evidence to support this. Contemporaneous reports, though, did attribute the *idea* for acquiring the carousel to Westwell. "Dr. Tadgell [at the dedication ceremony] gave a brief history of the project, which he said originated in the 'gray matter of Dr. Westwell.'" "The Dedication," *Sentinel*, October 22, 1948.

33. Two other dates besides 1922 have been cited for the origin of the carousel: 1909 and 1912. For 1909, see O'Brien, "Determined State of Mind"; "Catch the Brass Ring," *Sentinel*, December 10, 1992. For 1912, see "Carousel Horses Go for Bargain Prices," Associated Press, October 17, 1993 (Sunday, AM cycle). For 1922, see Ricci, *Crimes against Humanity*, 310. Symmetry more than source has caused me to favor the 1922 date: Belchertown State School opened that year.

34. "Bushnell Park, Points of Interest: The Carousel," www.bushnellpark.org/Content/The_Carousel.asp; American Folk Art Museum, "Gilded Lions and Jeweled Horses—The Synagogue to the Carousel, Carousels, Solomon Stein

and Harry Goldstein," http://gildedlions.org (no longer available). See also Murray Zimiles, *Gilded Lions and Jeweled Horses: The Synagogue to the Carousel—Jewish Carving Traditions* (Hanover, N.H.: University Press of New England, 2007), 31–32, 140–41, 143, 146–47, 150.

35. "The Dedication," *Sentinel*, October 22, 1948.

36. "State School Merry-Go-Round," *Sentinel*, July 30, 1948; "Merry-Go-Round," *Sentinel*, September 17, 1948. See also "Merry-Go-Round Dedication," *Sentinel*, June 21, 1963 ("All agree that [in 1947] there was every intention of housing the merry-go-round, that plans were made for a building . . . and that efforts were made to get a requisition for the expense from Boston, but funds never came through for the project, and so it languished").

37. *The Bell*, November 1961; Ricci, *Crimes against Humanity*, 16–17. Copies of all issues of *The Bell* cited in this chapter can be found in Belchertown State School Friends Association Records, 1954–86, collection MS 302, box 1B, folder 5a, Special Collections and Archives, W. E. B. Du Bois Library, University of Massachusetts Amherst.

38. *Bell*, November 1961; Ricci, *Crimes against Humanity*, 17.

39. "Merry-Go-Round Dedication"; Ricci, *Crimes against Humanity*, 17–18; *The Bell*, June 1965.

40. "State School News," *Sentinel*, September 20, 1963.

41. Ricci, *Crimes against Humanity*, 18.

42. Ibid.

43. Richard Hurley, "Court Proceedings Won't Delay 'Horse' Auction," *Sentinel*, December 12, 1984; Carol Murphy, "Old Belchertown Carousel Nearing Auctioneer's Block," *Springfield Republican*, February 17, 1990 (Metro East edition). The same article reported that two Springfield men were convicted of the theft. In exchange for suspended sentences, they testified that the crime was masterminded by a local attorney, who hoped to sell the two horses for $30,000.

44. Jack Flynn, "Carousel Sale Wins Approval," *Springfield Republican*, January 15, 1992 (Springfield edition).

45. Ricci began lobbying for the sale in 1984, but it was not approved by the legislature and signed by the governor until 1992. Ibid.

46. "Save the Carousel," *Sentinel*, January 28, 1993.

47. David Bergengren, "Doris Stockton—Belchertown Fights to Keep Carousel," *Springfield Republican*, November 2, 1992 (Metro East edition); David Bergengren, "Carousel Auction Set in Belchertown," *Springfield Republican*, February 10, 1993 (Metro East edition).

48. Paul Bouchard, "Carousel Viewing Delayed," *Springfield Republican*, April 24, 1993 (Metro East edition), 13; Ricci, *Crimes against Humanity*, 19.

49. John Christoffersen, "Rare Carousel Sold to Mysterious Bidder," *Springfield Republican*, April 25, 1993 (Springfield edition); "Cries and Whispers," *Springfield Republican*, May 2, 1993 (Springfield edition); Ricci, *Crimes against Humanity*, 19.

50. David Bergengren, "Mich.-based Park Acquires Carousel," *Springfield Republican*,

April 27, 1993 (Metro East edition); David Bergengren, "Seattle Business-man to Sell Antique Carousel in Pieces," *Springfield Republican*, May 5, 1993 (Metro East edition). Moodenbaugh chided the state of Massachusetts for not having sold the horses individually itself, claiming they would have made more money. The act authorizing the sale specified that the carousel had to be sold whole.

51. "Carousel Horses Go for Bargain Prices."
52. Bergengren, "Seattle Businessman to Sell"; Cosmo Macero Jr., "Carousel Nets Less Than Hoped," *Springfield Republican*, October 19, 1993 (Metro East edition).
53. Ibid.
54. Ricci, *Crimes against Humanity*, 19; Fred Contrada, "Carousel Horses Pay Dividends to Trust," *Springfield Republican*, October 6, 1995 (Metro East edition).
55. Judy Walker, "Writer's Block, Memories of B.S.S.," *Sentinel*, October 30, 1991.
56. Quoted in "Carousel Horses Go for Bargain Prices."
57. Ruth Sienkiewicz-Mercer and Steven B. Kaplan, *I Raise My Eyes to Say Yes: A Memoir* (Boston: Houghton Mifflin, 1989), 177–78.
58. Renee Loth, "Administration to Unveil 3-Year Plan to Close Belchertown State School," *Boston Globe*, March 7, 1989. A few of the school's last residents—presumably among the most profoundly retarded—would, according to the commissioner, be transferred to other state institutions.
59. David Bergengren, "Former Patients Gratefully Go 'Home,'" *Springfield Republican*, December 20, 1992 (Springfield edition). These homes, particularly the ones that were large (for eight residents) and newly constructed, were sometimes criticized for looking too much on the inside like well-designed institutions (with wide corridors and special doors and floors to accommodate wheelchairs and the like) rather than homes. See Edward Moscovitch, *Mental Retardation Programs: How Does Massachusetts Compare?* (Boston: Pioneer Institute for Public Policy Research, 1991), 69.
60. Don Labrecque, personal communication, July 2, 2008; Bergengren, "Former Patients." For a more detailed description of a group home, see Laura Stein, "Understanding Mental Retardation in America through the Closing of the Belchertown State School" (bachelor's thesis, Amherst College, 2008), 79–80.
61. For anecdotal evidence, see, e.g., Trudy Tynan, "At 70, Finally a Home," *Sentinel*, July 6, 1992. For contemporaneous surveys, see Valerie J. Bradley, Celia S. Feinstein, James A. Lemanowicz and Mary Ann Allard, "Results of the Survey of Current and Former Belchertown Residents and Their Families" (submitted to Massachusetts Dept. of Mental Retardation by the Belchertown Follow-Project, December 1992), available at www.hsri.org/files/uploads/publications/378_Results_of_the_Survey_of_Current_and_Former_Belchertown_Residents_and_Their_Families.pdf; David Bergengren, "State Patients Give DMR High Marks," *Springfield Republican*, January 5, 1993 (Metro East edition); David Bergengren, "State School Alumni Like New Homes," *Springfield Republican*, January 21, 1993 (Metro East edition). Some advocates and union

leaders discounted the surveys, contending that the quality of care had not really improved. Benjamin Ricci, though he did not dispute their general conclusion, called the surveys "window dressing" and said they should be banned. Ibid. Perhaps he was not really convinced, or possibly he feared they would bring complacency.

62. Tynan, "At 70, Finally a New Home."

63. Brian Melley, "Program Offers Independence for Mentally Disabled Adults," *Springfield Republican*, December 4, 1994 (Chicopee/Holyoke edition). See also John O'Connell, "State Helps Handicapped People Live Alone," *Springfield Republican*, March 21, 1996 (Springfield edition).

64. Ryan Davis, "A Man Who Left His Mark," *Daily Hampshire Gazette*, December 2, 2005.

65. *Rolland v. Cellucci*, Civil Action No. 3:98-CV-30208 (D. Mass. 1998).

66. "Massachusetts Accused of Dumping the Disabled," Associated Press (New York), January 13, 1999, www.fortunecity.com/victorian/goya/336/wb199b.txt; "Pact Helps Handicapped into Housing," *Springfield Union*, October 22, 1999.

67. *Rolland v. Cellucci*, 191 F.R.D. 3 (D. Mass. 2000).

68. *Rolland v. Patrick*, 2008 WL 2470003 (D. Mass. 2008). There are a number of good summaries of the lawsuit and the two settlements, including Stephanie Barry, "Fighting for Their Rights," *Springfield Union*, October 31, 1999; Phyllis Hanlon, "Rolland v. Cellucci: State to Settle 10-Year-Old Complaint," *New England Psychologist*, June 2008, www.nepsy.com/leading /0806_ne_rolland. html; Disability Law Center, "Massachusetts Settles Community Placement Lawsuit, Again," www.dlc-ma.org/CLRD/DCB/index.htm#Massachusetts_ settles _community_placement_lawsuit,_again.

69. Jay Lindsay, "Judge Asked to Oversee Care of Mentally Retarded," *Springfield Republican*, July 15, 2004; *Ricci v. Okin*, 499 F. Supp. 2d 89 (D. Mass. 2007), *rev'd and remanded*, *Ricci v. Patrick*, 544 F. 3d 8 (1st Cir. 2008), *cert. denied*, 129 S. Ct. 1907 (2009).

70. Moscovitch, *Mental Retardation Programs*, 15.

71. Ibid., 29; www.malegislature.gov/Budget/PriorBudget/2009.

72. "Letter to the Editor—B.S.S. Superintendent Cites Inadequate Treasury," *Sentinel*, June 29, 1972.

73. "Superintendent's Report," *Annual Report of the Trustees of the Belchertown State School for the Year Ending November 30, 1923* (Dept. of Mental Diseases, n.d.), 4–5.

74. "The State School," *Sentinel*, January 6, 1939.

75. "St. Francis Church Notes," *Sentinel*, July 19, 1963.

76. For example, the *Sentinel*'s report on "The Year at the State School" for 1947 states that, in May, "the graves at the B.S.S. Pine Grove cemetery were appropriately decorated by a group of boys and girls on Memorial Day." *Sentinel*, January 9, 1948.

77. Doug Hanchett, "Former Resident of State School Honors Friends," *Springfield Republican*, May 24, 1997.

78. Lee Hammel, "Names Replace Grave Numbers," *Worcester (Mass.) Telegram & Gazette*, September 23, 1999.
79. Cosmo Macero Jr., "Belchertown Rite Honors Old Friends," *Springfield Republican*, September 24, 1994; Doug Hanchett, "1-Man Crusade Creates Facelift for Cemetery," *Springfield Republican*, May 24, 1997.
80. Susan E. Bosman, "Belchertown Cemetery Repairs Honor the Buried," *Springfield Republican*, May 28, 1995.
81. Lori Stabile, "Restorer of State School Cemetery Dies," *Springfield Republican*, January 17, 2006 (Hampshire/Franklin edition).

Index

Abbott, John, 111
abortions, 42, 155n71
Abrams, Arnold, 95–96, 98
Adams, Christopher, 111
admissions, 30–34; and age, 31, 32–33; by custodial commitment, 31, 32, 71–72, 152n2; freeze on, 110, 122, 170n24; by transfer, 30–31
Adult Living and Learning Unit, 107, 116–17, 173n7
Allen, Roswell, 1, 2
Almeidi, Lisa, 126
almshouses, 11, 20, 149n6; parallels to, of state-funded schools, 9, 17, 18
American Association of Mental Deficiency (AAMD), 86, 91
Americans with Disabilities Act, 141
Ames, Bruce, 140
Amherst College, 3, 5, 27, 47
Anderson, Dana, 137
appropriations. See federal funding; legislative appropriations
Arc of Massachusetts, 82. See also Massachusetts Association for Retarded Children
attendants, 49, 52–56, 57–59, 62–64, 66–67; backgrounds of, 49; in back wards (Buildings A and K), 85, 97, 101; duties of, 52–53, 56, 85; inadequate number of, 53, 55–56, 89; turnover among, 51
Atwood, Harrison H., 7
Aubin, Rena, 111

back wards: changes in, 98, 99, 101–2, 107, 117, 170n24; confinement to, as form of punishment, 58, 59, 85; poor conditions in, 54, 84–87, 97, 101; proposals for, 90, 94, 96, 98, 171n30; in "Tragedy of Belchertown" series, 84–86, 87, 88, 101. See also Building A; Building K
Baggs, Milton, 2, 146n9
Barnes, Lawrence, 139–40, 141
Barry, Richard, 134
baseball, 28, 43, 155n56
Belchertown, Mass., 1–2, 3, 29–30, 77–79, 125, 145n2; Board of Trade of, 2, 4–5, 7, 48, 129; carriage industry in, 1–2, 145nn2,4; and founding of the school, 2–7; many residents of, as school employees, 8, 9, 48, 125, 158n3; population of, 48; and plans for reuse after school's closing, 128–34, 179n7; rallies in, for community placement, 122, 176–77n38; water supply of, 3, 146n9, 147n7. See also Belchertown Sentinel; town-school relations
Belchertown Community Garden, 129
Belchertown Economic Development and Industrial Corporation (BEDIC), 129, 130, 132–34, 179n8
Belchertown Fair, 79, 165n34
Belchertown Sentinel, 73, 77–78, 81, 108, 165n34, 167n1, 168–69n11; on founding of school, 1, 5, 8–9;

Belchertown Sentinel (continued)
    response of, to criticisms of school,
       88–89, 92–93, 96, 168–69n11; after
       school's closing, 133, 181n31; on
       school's public events, 35–36, 38,
       39, 47, 67, 77–78, 135, 137; on
       town-school relations, 46–47, 78; on
       volunteering, 81, 109–10
Belchertown State School Friends
    Association, 74–80, 81–83, 100, 102,
       107, 165n29; Benjamin Ricci and, 74,
       83, 102, 104–5, 107, 120; and class
       action lawsuit, 104–5; founding
       of, 74; projects undertaken by, for
       the school, 74–75, 76–77, 79, 135,
       164n19, 171–72n40, 176n34; and
       school's increased transparency,
       77–79. See also *Bell, The*
Bell, The, 74, 76, 82–83, 119–21, 156n75,
       166n45
Binet, Alfred, 20–21. See also Stanford-
       Binet Test
Birthday Box, 80. See also Birthday Bus
       project
Birthday Bus project, 80, 165–66n36
Blatt, Burton, 167n7
Bleinberger, Ernest, 130–32
boarding out (family care program),
       44–45
Board of Insanity, 4, 5, 6
Board of Trade, 2, 4–5, 7, 48, 129
Boltwood Program, 170n24
Bowser, Lawrence, 93–94; changes
       introduced by, 93–94, 170n24; res-
       ignation of, 92, 96, 169n21, 171n33;
       and William Fraenkel, 90, 92, 94,
       168n8, 169n18
"boys" (term), xiv, 6, 27, 33, 61, 148n35.
       See also rhetoric of childhood
Bridgeland Development LLC, 132–34
Buchanan, Linda, 111, 173n12
Building A, 85–87, 89; closing of, 96,
       99, 101–2, 171n36
Building C, 24, 81, 173n7
Building D, 24, 171n35, 173n7
Building E, 24, 129, 173n7
Building F, 24, 76, 111, 129, 173n7

Building G, 24, 97, 102, 111, 113,
       170n24, 173n7
Building K, 24, 89, 96, 97, 167n1,
       171nn30,36; improvements in, 97,
       170n24; poor conditions in, 84–85,
       113
Building L, 24, 79, 81, 97
Building M, 24, 33, 53, 173n7
burial, 9, 46, 142, 143
Busquet, Michelle, 118

Campbell, Levin, 110
Caron, Charles, 68
carousel, 9, 46, 134–35, 137,
       181nn32,33; sale of, 135–37, 183n50
carriage industry, 1–2, 145nn2,4
cemetery, xiv, 142–43, 184n76; naming
       of, after Albert Warner, xiv, 143. See
       also burial
Central Vermont Railroad, 3
class action lawsuit. See *Ricci v. Greenblatt*
closing of school, 125, 178nn46,47; cer-
       emony for, 126–27; and community
       placement, 125, 138–40, 177n44; and
       sale of carousel, 135–37, 183n50;
       and town's search for new uses of
       site, 128–34
clothing, 26, 51, 61
coffee breaks, 65–66
Cohen, Beryl, 104, 105–6, 113, 169n16
Coleman, Richard J., 79, 165n34
college and university students: as
       interns, 97, 99, 109–10, 118, 125;
       as volunteers, 125, 170n24, 173n11;
       work-study, 109–10
Commission on Mental Diseases, 6, 7;
       replacement of Board of Insanity by, 6
commitment. See custodial commitment
Committee in Support of Community
       Living, 122
community placement, 108–9, 120–21,
       122, 138–41, 177n44; Benjamin Ricci
       and, 119–22, 176–77n38, 184n61;
       and closing of school, 125, 138–40,
       177n44
Comprehensive Mental Health and
       Retardation Services Act of 1966, 123

consent decree (1973), 114–15, 116, 117–18
control, methods of, 56–61
Conway, Mass., 4, 146n12
"cottage plan," 23
cranial measurements, 20, 152n33
custodial commitment, 31, 32, 71–72, 154n24

Daniels, Russell, 121–22, 176n34
Dansereau, Theresa, 126
Dearness, Peter, 92–93, 168n11
deaths, 9, 41, 46, 111, 142
deinstitutionalization, 113, 120–21, 122. See also community placement
DeLisa, Andrew, 126
dental care, 40–41
Department of Mental Health, 45, 94–96, 112, 173n12; and community placement, 123; criticisms of, 91–92, 95, 98, 120; and 1973 consent decree, 114–15. See also Greenblatt, Milton
Department of Mental Retardation, 48, 125, 126, 138. See also Division of Mental Retardation
Dever State School (Taunton, Mass.), 115
direct care staff, 48–49, 51–52, 55–56; in community placement, 126, 138–39. See also attendants
discharge of residents, 44, 73, 162–63n7
diseases, 16, 41, 46, 142
Division of Mental Retardation, 112. See also Department of Mental Retardation
Dix, Dorothea, 11, 12, 149n7
dormitories, 8, 23–24, 27, 172–73n7; and family visits, 72. See also back wards; dormitory parties; individual buildings
dormitory parties, 74–75, 76
drugs, tranquilizing, 56, 60, 160n44
Dumas, Al, 82
Dybwad, Gunnar, 122, 176–77n38

employee cottages, 23, 24, 48–49, 171n36
employees, 48–52, 87–88, 92, 98, 161n60; acts of kindness by, 63–67, 118; assistance to, from some residents, 52; in back wards, 85, 97, 101; long tenure of many, 50–51; many Belchertown residents as, 8, 9, 48, 125, 158nn1,3; morale of, 67–68; number of, 8, 48; personal safety of, 61–63; and school's impending closure, 178n46. See also direct-care staff; employee cottages; staff-to-resident ratio
enrollment, 8, 9, 32–33
escapes, 32, 43, 45–46; punishment for, 46, 59
Esquirol, Jean Étienne, 13–14
eugenics, 4, 151–52n31
exhibits, 35–36, 47, 73, 78

Fairchild, R. E., 6
family care program (boarding out), 44–45
family visits, 72, 73
"farm boys," 27–28, 46, 52, 53, 142, 155n56
farm (at the school), 8, 27–28, 35, 49, 52, 159n18. See also "farm boys"; farm colony
farm colony, 6–7, 24, 27, 29, 38, 147n25
federal courts, 95, 110. See also Tauro, Joseph L.
federal funds, 115–16, 141, 175n24
"feeble-minded" (term), xiii–xiv, 4, 31, 148–49n3
Fernald, Walter E., 15, 19–20, 22, 124, 152n36
Fernald State School. See Walter E. Fernald State School
food: production of, by school's farm, 27, 35. See also meals
Ford, Francis J. W., 110
Ford, Henry, 3, 146n8
Foth, Ann, 126
Fourth of July festivities, 29, 38–40, 46, 47, 73, 155n56

Fraenkel, William, 56, 112; as interim
    superintendent (1971), 96–97,
    98–100, 101–2, 107, 116, 171n35,
    172n40; observations of back wards
    by, 54, 58, 59, 60, 62, 86–87, 91, 106,
    168n8; reforms urged by, 89–90, 94,
    169n18
Francis, Robert, 33, 53, 58–59
Friends Association. See Belchertown
    State School Friends Association
Friends of the Belchertown Carousel, 136
Fuller, E. A., 2
Fuller, Tom, 131
funding. See federal funds; legislative
    appropriations

Gaboury, Jeannette, 139
Garson, Jonas, 139
gender segregation, 26, 32, 34, 42
"girls" (term), xiv, 61, 148n35. See also
    rhetoric of childhood
Goddard, Henry, 4, 21
Gold, Frank, 30
Goldstein, Harry, 134. See also carousel
Governor's Commission for Retarded
    Children, 82
graduates, 17–18, 19, 43–44
graveyard. See burial; cemetery
Greenblatt, Milton, 102, 111–12, 174n15;
    as lead defendant in class action law-
    suit, 103; response of, to Joint Special
    Commission report, 95, 96, 98
Greenwood, Fred P., 7

haircuts, 61, 86
halfway house, 94, 120, 139, 170n25
Hanrahan, Thomas, 40
happiness, 42–43, 45, 126–27, 137,
    156n75
Hawes, Mr. and Mrs. John, 6–7
Hazen, Clara Dwight, 2
Hazen, Daniel Dwight, 1, 2–3, 4–5, 7,
    79, 146nn8,12
Hazen, Daniel L., 2, 3
health of residents, 40–41. See also
    diseases
Holmes, Oliver Wendell, 156n80

Holyoke, Mass., 4, 51, 67, 80. See also
    Mount Saint Vincent orphanage
homosexual behavior, 42, 156n73
Howe, Julia Ward, 12
Howe, Samuel Gridley, 10–13, 14–18;
    campaign of, for state-funded
    schools, 11–12, 15, 95; and Dorothea
    Dix, 11, 12, 149n7; and Édouard
    Séguin, 13, 14–15, 150n16, 151n18;
    ironic legacy of, 22, 124; and phre-
    nology, 20, 152n33; school founded
    by, 10, 15 (see also Walter E. Fernald
    State School); views of, on feeble-
    mindedness, 10–11, 12–13, 15–17,
    124, 149n4, 151n23
Hunter, Don, 132
Hunter Interests, Inc., 130–32

"idiot" (term), 10, 21, 31
"imbecile" (term), 10, 21, 31
immigrants, 17, 19
industrial buildings, 26
infirmary, 24, 79, 113; improved condi-
    tions in, 88, 168n10; residential
    population of, 24, 53–54, 172–73n7;
    Ruth Sienkiewicz-Mercer in, 54–55,
    58, 61–62, 63–64, 66, 126–27,
    160n33, 168n100; volunteers and, 81
injuries, 41
International Congress on Mental
    Retardation, 112
Itard, Jean-Marc-Gaspard, 149–50n13

Jacobsen, Christine, 131
Jepson, David, 3, 152n2
Joint Special Commission on
    Belchertown State School and
    Monson Hospital, 91–92, 169n16;
    Benjamin Ricci and, 91, 101, 102,
    169n16; creation of, 91; criticisms
    of Department of Mental Health by,
    91–92, 102
Jones, William E., 113, 116, 174n17
Julian, Anthony, 110

Kasparyan, Aran, 111, 112
Kendall, Taylor & Co., 7

Konopka, Barbara, 125
Kump, Richard, 133–34

LaBroad, Mickey, 49
Lampson Brook Farmstead, 129
laundry building, 24–26
lawsuits, 115, 140–41, 174n21. See also
    Ricci v. Greenblatt
legislative appropriations, 93, 110, 141,
    148n31; for founding of school, 2, 5,
    6, 7, 147nn16,27, 148n31; and 1973
    consent decree, 114, 115; for other
    state schools, 10, 15; supplement-
    ing of, by federal funds, 115–16, 141,
    175n24
Legislative Committee on Public
    Institutions, 7, 8

Mann, Horace, 12
Maroney, Tom, 139
Marshall, Mary, 126
Massachusetts Association for Retarded
    Children (MARC), 82–83, 119–21, 123
Massachusetts Medical Society, 18,
    19–20
Massachusetts School for Idiotic and
    Feeble-Minded Youth. See Walter E.
    Fernald State School
Massachusetts School for the Feeble-
    Minded. See Walter E. Fernald State
    School
McCarthy, Mary, 48, 125, 178n47
McCrea, Joe, 49–50, 52, 64–66, 159n18
McDermott, Paul, 132, 133
McLean, Laura, 51
McPherson, George E., 8, 28–29, 38,
    41–43, 45, 73; background of, 28;
    death of, 46; characterization of resi-
    dent population by, 31, 32, 33–34;
    on school's educational function,
    34–35, 44, 156n74; and town-school
    relations, 30; views of, on steriliza-
    tion, 156–57n80
meals, 26, 49, 57–58, 85, 89, 160n33
media coverage, 43, 73, 77–79. See also
    Belchertown Sentinel; Springfield Union
Medicaid, 115–16, 141, 175n24

Medicare, 141
mental age, 31, 32, 33–34, 37
merry-go-round. See carousel
Meyer, Gladys, 44–45
Minnie, Andrew, 67
minstrel shows, 38, 67, 73, 78
Monson State Hospital, 38, 91, 115
Moodenbaugh, Michael, 136, 183n50
"morons" (term), 21, 31, 33
Mount Saint Vincent orphanage
    (Holyoke, Mass.), 38, 40

Nagle, Roland, 106, 107–10, 173n9;
    appointment of, 102, 107; and parent
    activists, 102, 106, 107, 116, 173n9;
    resignation of, 108, 111, 141; support
    of, for deinstitutionalization, 108–9
New England Small Farm Institute
    (NESFI), 129
New Jersey Training School, 4, 21
"next friend" (term), 172n46
Nichols, Wilbur, 2
Nirje, Bengt, 122, 124, 177n40
"normalization," 122–23, 124. See also
    community placement
Northampton State Hospital, 38
Norton, David, 136
nurseries, 24, 31, 77, 88, 129, 162n3. See
    also Tadgell Nursery
nursing homes, 140

occupational therapy, 107
O'Conner, M. J., 8
O'Malley, Terence Patrick, 113–14
outpatient clinic, 31

parents, 72–74, 75–76, 83, 164n21,
    165n29; activism by, 163n11 (see also
    Belchertown State School Friends
    Association); and deinstitutionaliza-
    tion, 120–21; and family visits, 72,
    73. See also Ricci, Benjamin
parole, 32, 44, 45, 157n81
Péreire, Jacob Rodrigues, 149–50n13
Perkins Institution (Boston, Mass.),
    10, 13
personal safety, 61–63

phrenology, 20, 152n33
physical disabilities, 17, 24, 33–34,
    53–54
physiological education, 14
Pierce, Frederick, 7
Pinel, Philippe, 149–50n13
Pioneer Valley Transit Authority, 130
Pittsfield, Mass., 31
poor farm, 27, 29–30, 46
public events, 47, 73, 125. See also
    exhibits; Fourth of July festivities;
    theatrical presentations
punishment, 42, 58–59, 85; for escap-
    ing, 46, 59

Quinn, Philip, 91

rats, 159n18
reading skills, 34
Real, Manual, 110
resident population: age profile of, 9,
    32–33; disabilities of, 30–32, 33–34,
    40–41, 53–56, 61–62; gender break-
    down of, 32; methods of control
    of, 56–61; racial composition of,
    154n47; size of, 8, 9, 32–33
rhetoric of childhood, 56, 60–61, 66
Ricci, Benjamin, 69–72, 143, 173n11,
    174n15; and appointment of super-
    intendents, 102, 107, 111–13, 174n15;
    and Belchertown State School Friends
    Association, 74, 83, 102, 104–5, 107,
    120; and class action lawsuit, 103,
    104–6, 113–14; and closing of school,
    125, 126; and community place-
    ment, 119–22, 176–77n38, 184n61;
    and disposal of school property, 135,
    179n7, 182n45; and Joint Special
    Commission, 91, 101, 102, 169n16;
    and Roland Nagel, 107, 109, 110,
    173n9; and Scandinavian models,
    100–101; on the school's history,
    155n71, 156n73, 161n60; and William
    Fraenkel, 99–100, 101–2, 116, 172n40
Ricci, Robert Simpson (Bobby), 69–72,
    103, 122
Ricci, Virginia, 69–72

Ricci v. Greenblatt, 102–7, 112, 113–14,
    141; Benjamin Ricci and, 103, 104–6,
    113–14; consent decree resulting
    from, 114–15, 116, 117–18; influence
    of, 115, 174n21
Robbins, Robert, 165n29
Rosazzi, Irving, 131

Sargent, Francis, 110, 114
segregation by gender, 26, 32, 34, 42
Séguin, Édouard, 13–15, 18, 150n16
sexual activity, 41–42, 156n73
Shanks, James, 84. See also "Tragedy of
    Belchertown" series
Sienkiewicz-Mercer, Ruth, 137; on
    community placement, 126–27; and
    improved conditions, 66, 118–19,
    175–76n29, 168n10; on life in infir-
    mary, 54–55, 58, 61–62, 63–64, 66,
    126–27, 160n33, 168n10
Simon, Théodore, 20–21
"simpleton" (term), 10–11
Sisitsky, Alan, 170n27
solitary confinement, 59
special commission. See Joint Special
    Commission on Belchertown State
    School and Monson State Hospital
"special needs" children, 31–32
Springfield Union, 84. See also "Tragedy of
    Belchertown" series
staff-to-resident ratio, 55, 117, 119,
    170n24
Stanford-Binet Test, 21–22, 31
Staples, Eileen, 43
State Board of Insanity, 6
Stein, Solomon, 134. See also carousel
sterilization laws, 42, 44, 151n31,
    152n31, 156–57n80, 172n43
Stockton, Doris, 136
students. See college and university
    students
Sumner, Charles, 12, 14
Sumner, George, 14–15
superintendents. See Bowser, Lawrence;
    Fraenkel, William; Jones, William
    E.; McPherson, George E.; Nagle,
    Roland; Tadgell, Henry

Tadgell, Henry, 48, 135, 157n88, 170n24, 181n32; and Friends Association, 74, 77

Tadgell Nursery, 24, 88, 118–19, 129

Taras, Elizabeth, 130, 134

Tauro, Joseph L., 110, 113–14, 115, 116, 141, 175n23

Terman, Lewis, 21

Terry, William A., 132, 133

theatrical productions, 29, 37–38, 67

Tighe, James, 5–6

Title XIX of Social Security Act, 115–16, 141, 175n24, 176n36

town-school relations, 7, 9, 29–30, 46–47, 77–79, 125; *Belchertown Sentinel* on, 46–47, 78; and family care program, 44–45; and former poor farm, 27, 29–30, 46; Friends Association and, 81; and school's public events, 38, 46, 47, 125

"Tragedy of Belchertown" series (*Springfield Union*, 1970), 84–86, 94–95, 168n8; and assignment of blame, 87–88, 94–95, 170n27; on back wards (Buildings A and K), 84–86, 87, 88, 101; praise in, for some aspects of school, 87–88, 91; responses to, 88–91, 92–93, 95–96 (*see also* Joint Special Commission on Belchertown State School and Monson State Hospital)

tranquilizing drugs, 56, 60, 160n44

transparency, 77–79, 99, 102, 116

trustees, 41, 117, 173n12; policies of, on discharge of residents, 44, 73–74, 162–63n7; resignation of most, in 1971, 92; and *Springfield Union* exposé, 90–91; views of, on sterilization, 42, 44, 156n80

tunnels, 8, 26, 42

"unitization," 90, 102, 107, 118

U.S. Constitution, 106–7

Valliere, Barbara, 80, 81, 164n27, 165n36, 166nn44,45

vocational training, 18, 34–35

volunteering, 79–81, 93–94, 107, 170nn24,25; Friends Association and, 80–81, 166n45; by students, 125, 170n24, 173n11

Wakstein, M. Phillip, 85–86, 91, 92, 94, 168n8

Walker, Judy, 137

Walter E. Fernald State School (Waltham, Mass.), 74, 93; lawsuits over, 115, 140–41; in nineteenth century, 15, 151n19; transfers from, 8, 30, 148n33

Waltham, Mass., state school in. See Walter E. Fernald State School

Warner, Agnes, 143

Warner, Albert, 9, 43, 64, 142–43

Warner Pine Grove Memorial Cemetery, xiv, 143, 184n76

water supply: of Belchertown, 3, 146n9, 147n27; for the school, 3, 5–6, 7, 147n27

Watkins, H. M., 8

Westfield, Mass., 4, 146n12

Westwell, Arthur, 28, 29, 36–40, 43, 46; dental care by, 40–41; later career of, 46, 158n9; and school's carousel, 46, 181n32; theatrical productions organized by, 37–38, 67

wheelchairs, 8, 88, 107

Wheeler, Hollis, 49, 54, 56, 62–63, 67, 161n50

Williams, Oscar, 139

Wines, Frederick, 19, 151n28

Wolfensberger, Wolf, 120, 122

Woman's Home Companion, 78

work-study students, 109–10

World War II, 38, 39, 163n11

Wrentham State School, 115; transfers from, 6, 8, 27, 30, 148n33

ROBERT HORNICK, a graduate of Amherst College and Harvard Law School, is an independent scholar and international lawyer. He is an authority on Indonesian law, a subject about which he has written extensively, including the first introduction to Indonesian law in English. After retiring from private practice in 2006, he became an adjunct professor at the University of Arizona law school, where he teaches courses on international investment law and international arbitration. He also chairs the Committee to Support Chinese Lawyers, a group based in New York that supports lawyers in China who are being persecuted because of the clients and causes they represent. Hornick has lived in India, Indonesia, and Singapore. He is married and has one son, and he now resides in Tucson, Arizona, and New York City. His interest in the Belchertown State School dates from the 1960s, when he was a volunteer at the school.